$51 K

Carnations and Pinks for Garden and Greenhouse

Carnations and Pinks
for
Garden and Greenhouse

THEIR TRUE HISTORY AND COMPLETE CULTIVATION

---

by

John Galbally

with

Eileen Galbally

Timber Press
Portland, Oregon

Copyright © 1997 by Eileen Galbally
All rights reserved.

Published in 1997 by Timber Press, Inc.

ISBN 0-88192-382-6

Printed in Hong Kong

Timber Press, Inc.
The Haseltine Building
133 S.W. Second Avenue, Suite 450
Portland, Oregon 97204, U.S.A.

Library of Congress Cataloging-in-Publication Data

Galbally, John.
Carnations and pinks for garden and greenhouse : their true history and
complete cultivation / by John Galbally with Eileen Galbally.
p.   cm.
Includes bibliographical references (p.   ) and index.
ISBN 0-88192-382-6
1. Carnations. 2. Pinks. I. Galbally, Eileen. II. Title.
SB413.C3G29   1996
635.9′33152—dc20   96-38612
CIP

To the memory of our dear friend Audrey Robinson,
historian to the British National Carnation Society,
who died tragically in August 1993 after a road accident.

Contents

Contents

List of Color Plates

(plates follow page 160)

Acknowledgments

We wish to thank the following people for information so willingly given: Dr. Giacomo Nobbio and Dr. Agostino Baratta of San Remo, Italy; Ruud Baarse of Kooij and Zonen, Aalsmeer, the Netherlands; Dr. Leonard Carrier of California, United States; Dr. Keith Hammett of New Zealand; Gary Eichhorn of Spokane, Washington, United States; English Woodlands, Petworth; the former Glasshouse Crops Research Institute (work now transferred to the Horticultural Research Institute, Warwickshire); Rollo Pyper at the Lewes office of the Ministry of Agriculture, Fisheries and Food; Royal Horticultural Society Entomologist Andrew Halstead; RHS Senior Plant Pathologist Pippa Greenwood; RHS Senior Scientist Audrey Brooks; RHS Wisley Librarian Barbara Collecott; Dr. Alan Leslie, International *Dianthus* Registrar; and Past Honorary Secretary of the British National Carnation Society, Phyllis Dimond.

In particular we thank our daughters Helena Hitchcock and Maureen Fifield; Helena for all the assistance she so willingly gave for the ultimate betterment of our manuscript, and Maureen for so capably tending our plants during our sometimes months-long absences, and without whose help we should not have had our own plants to write about.

Acknowledgments

And finally thanks to Josh Leventhal and Neal Maillet of Timber Press for their valuable help and guidance in the publication of our book.

Foreword

Many are the books and articles devoted to carnations and pinks, the two major groups of the genus *Dianthus* that have captured the hearts and imagination of gardeners for centuries and are greatly valued for their diversity of flower shape and color and particularly for the delicious fragrance of many cultivars.

Few authors, however, can claim the deep personal knowledge of the subject as the late John Galbally, who lived and breathed carnations and pinks for over 50 years and, shortly before his death, completed this book, his third on this most popular group of plants.

It was fortunate for the horticultural world that John decided to leave his work as an aircraft designer in 1955 to devote himself, with his wife Eileen, to growing and hybridizing carnations, his first love, and pinks commercially instead of maintaining his interest only as a hobby. He became an outstanding breeder of new cultivars and a very successful exhibitor, giving freely of his accumulated knowledge through articles in many gardening journals as well as in the year book of the British National Carnation Society, which he served in a number of capacities, including that of President for the 1990 term. His interests in carnations and pinks were shared fully by Eileen, whose own perseverance and knowledge has enabled her to contribute greatly to this excellent book and to ensure that it was published so that John's expertise was not left as a manuscript but was made available for the benefit of all lovers of the genus.

I first met the Galballys on the Trials Field when I was Director of the Royal Horticultural Society's Gardens at Wisley, and I was greatly impressed by their knowledge of and enthusiasm for the Trials of border carnations and pinks. As members of the RHS Joint Border Carnation and Pinks Committee with the BNCS, the Galballys were much involved in judging and advising on the cultivation of the Trials, no easy task on the infertile Wisley sand. The somewhat obtrusive staking of border carnations used was, I seem to recall, a matter on which, rightly, they felt strongly, the "ironmongery" used not being conducive to indicating the carnations' garden potential! Their input as contributors to the Trials has been very considerable, and it says much for the Galbally breeding program that twenty-two of their cultivars have received the RHS Award of Garden Merit, the highest award available for garden plants.

Carnations and Pinks for Garden and Greenhouse is an authoritative and thoroughly practical book that distills very successfully over 50 years of cultivating these delightful plants, which give so much pleasure to so many gardeners. Apart from the very detailed coverage of cultivation techniques based on long experience, there is an extensive listing of cultivars accurately described—many of which have been grown in the Galballys' own garden—that will be of great help in selecting the most suitable plants to grow for particular purposes in the garden. And in order to link present-day cultivars to those of the past, John Galbally has provided a fascinating history of carnations and pinks, old and new, with particular emphasis on their breeding and exhibition.

I am delighted to have been asked to write a foreword for this stimulating and very practical book and to recommend it to anyone, however little or great their knowledge, who wishes to learn more about this ever-popular and very beautiful genus.

Christopher D. Brickell
West Sussex, England

Introduction

Books in the nature of a botanical treatise are plentiful, so are books of reference or those which deal with horticulture as a whole. But those which describe one genus, or part of a genus, and present the special matter in a readable form, are few and far between.

The purpose of any book should be not only to inform but also to delight and entertain.

The above quotations, the first from the foreword to Will Ingwersen's *The Dianthus* (HarperCollins Publishers Ltd., 1949; reprinted with permission) and the second from the preface to the *Royal Horticultural Society Encyclopedia of Plants and Flowers* written by its editor-in-chief Christopher Brickell, then Director General of the Royal Horticultural Society, inspired us to try to produce an easily read and truly authoritative book on the growing of carnations and pinks. There is now a definite need for such a book; so much has changed recently with new breeders, new cultivars, and new methods of cultivation. Professional breeders have introduced many new, interesting cultivars; amateur enthusiasts too have found success and their new cultivars have been introduced by plant specialists. Demand for garden pinks has increased greatly since the advent of garden centers. Great interest in the various species is also wide-spread—the true natural species and the named cultivars bred from them, which are grown in troughs, rock gardens, alpine greenhouses, and garden borders. Many carnation societies are set up in various parts of England and Scotland, and their shows all include classes for novice growers. Experienced exhibitors are usually delighted to chat with newcomers and give them advice. Winning one's first prize card isn't that difficult really, and showing is a good way of making friends. In the United States, the American Dianthus Society was established in 1991 and publishes a quarterly journal called *The Gilliflower Times*.

Type Classification

Pinks and carnations are the common or garden names for plants bred from various species of the genus *Dianthus*, which botanically belongs to the family Caryophyllaceae (Greek, meaning "clove leafed"). The generic name *Dianthus* is derived from two short Greek words joined together and means "divine flower"; the flowers were said to have been dedicated to Zeus, the most powerful of all the gods. Hundreds of species exist within the genus *Dianthus*, all different, each having its own specific or special name. So every plant has two names, the second, specific name denoting some special feature to distinguish it from other species in the genus. For example, *Dianthus alpinus* denotes a species of *Dianthus* that flourishes in alpine regions, a mountain plant. *Dianthus fragrans* is a species with sweetly scented flowers.

Some species have been used extensively by breeders for centuries and have been developed beyond recognition. A prime example is *Dianthus caryophyllus*, a single five-petalled flower, from which the beautiful border carnation has been produced over the past five centuries. Many garden plants have been developed by systematic breeding, so that some species embrace hundreds of different plants. These plants are given names by their breeders or introducers to distinguish them from all others, and the individual plants are called cultivars, which means cultivated varieties. The garden pinks 'Paddington' and 'Inchmery' are examples of cultivar names seen in nursery catalogues under the heading "Garden Pinks," where the title *Dianthus* and the specific name are generally not used.

Carnations and pinks are perennial plants that have a single woody basal stem when mature. Their leaves are swordlike on some types and straplike on others, and they vary from about 3 to 12 millimeters (0.125 to 0.5 inches) wide. Leaf tips curl attractively; very curly leaves are taken as a sign of a plant's well-being. The leaves are glaucous, gray-green on some plants and blue-green on others and are coated with a waxy bloom. Stalks vary from about 2 to 6 mm (0.08 to 0.25 in) in thickness and have swollen nodes from which leaves grow in pairs, one on either side of the stem. Alternate pairs of leaves grow out at right angles to each other. Flowers are usually terminal on a main stem, followed by a succession of flowers on secondary branching stems. The calyx is cylindrical and five-toothed, with an epicalyx of one to three pairs of overlapping bracteoles enclosing the base. Flowers are bi-sexual (hermaphrodite) with ten stamens and two or sometimes three styles. Petals are colored in shades of purple, red, pink, yellow, or white, many with attractive markings of another color.

Of the several kinds of carnations, the three most popular are an-nual carnations, border carnations, and perpetual-flowering carnations. Annual carnations—which include the Marguerite, Chabaud, and Grenadin strains, among others—are descended from *Dianthus chinen-sis*, Indian pink, crossed with the perennial border carnation. Annual carnations are grown extensively in the United States and are mostly raised from seed. When well grown, annual carnations are very florif-erous. Their sideshoots all turn into flowering shoots in the same sea-son, and the plants tend to literally flower themselves to death. They grow 30 to 60 centimeters (12 to 24 in) tall, and although the flowers are showy in the garden they do not have the quality of the named border carnations. The flowers are a little smaller than those of border carnations and they are more crowded with petals, which are serrated and thereby resemble perpetual-flowering carnations. Some plants do survive a mild winter, but most gardeners who grow the annual car-nations prefer to clear them out after flowering and start afresh with a new sowing each year. They can also be grown in pots in a green-house to flower during the winter at a temperature of 13°C (55°F).

Border carnations, of which many named cultivars have been de-veloped, are completely hardy in Great Britain and grow well in parts of North America. In Alberta, Canada (zone 3), it was recorded that plants "came scatheless through a spring frost of three weeks' duration with the temperature registering 30°F below zero [−35°C] for five days"—a temperature of course unknown in Great Britain. They also grow well in New Zealand, where carnation societies similar to the British National Carnation Society (BNCS) have been established. These carnations make beautiful cut flowers for the home, and a few clove-scented blooms can fill a room with their delightful perfume. Almost every summer flower show has its classes for carnations; in fact, these have been exhibitors' flowers for centuries. Border carnations are truly perennial and can be left to increase in size for three or four years. The height of border carnations varies between 38 and 60 cm (15 to 24 in) in the open garden and about 15 cm (6 in) taller when grown in pots under glass. Their sideshoots cluster together around the base of the plant, usually about ten to fifteen in number. Young outdoor-grown plants send up between one and five stems that can produce up to six flowers each, and plants in their second and third years can produce a hundred blooms or more. The flowers are beautifully formed with smooth-edged petals, are circular in outline, and vary from 6 to 8.5 cm (2.5 to 3.5 in) in diameter when well grown in the garden. Some greenhouse-grown plants, disbudded for exhibition, have flowers up to 10 cm (4 in) in diameter. Plants generally are propagated by layers or cuttings.

Perpetual-flowering carnations originated around 1850 and were bred to produce flowers for commercial markets. They owe their origins mainly to *Dianthus chinensis* and *D. caryophyllus*, and possibly to *D. arboreus*, the Greek pink, which would account for the extra height in the older cultivars. Not truly hardy, they are grown as greenhouse perennials, massed in concrete beds in very large greenhouses, and are reproduced from cuttings. Amateurs grow their perpetual-flowering carnations in pots in a cool greenhouse and have found the newer exhibition type better than the older commercial cut-flower kind for their purpose, as the newer ones are shorter and somewhat hardier. Only just-sufficient winter heat is required to keep the plants from freezing. They will, however, continue flowering all winter if the temperature is kept no lower than 7°C (45°F).

Perpetual-flowering carnations do not have clusters of sideshoots at their base like border carnations, so they need to be stopped—that is, have the tips of their main shoots broken off—to induce them to produce the sideshoots required to turn them into bushy plants. Their internodal lengths are greater than those of all other kinds, which makes them grow taller. In their first flush the flowers of most modern cultivars reach a height of about 75 cm (30 in) from the top of the pot, and the second flush about 1.2 meters (4 ft). Flowers are mostly 7.5 cm (3 in) across but can be grown to 10 cm (4 in) in diameter with skillful cultivation. It is not possible to state reliably the number of blooms one plant will produce; so much depends on the cultivar, the quality of the greenhouse and its situation, and the grower's skill in cultivation. However, on a very broad average a pot-grown plant should produce 25 blooms or more over a two-year period, after which time most enthusiasts discard their old plants and start again with new young ones. With care it is possible to have both young and second-year plants growing in the greenhouse at the same time to ensure an even succession of blooms. Perpetual-flowering carnations take up more time and require rather more assistance than border carnations, but then they do provide flowers at times when the border carnations are resting. 'William Sim' and similar-type commercial perpetual-flowering carnation cultivars grow very tall and so are not really suitable for the majority of small amateur-type greenhouses.

Although they continue to be popular with greenhouse hobbyists in Britain, perpetual-flowering carnations generally are not widely grown by amateurs in North America. Nonetheless, when most Americans picture a carnation they are apt to think of the perpetual-flowering type, which is still favored by commercial growers and florist shops.

Spray carnations are a development of the perpetual-flowering carnation in which the objective is to produce a spray of blooms on the stem instead of the normal single-specimen bloom. This is done by removing the crown bud and retaining all others on the stem. The flowers are smaller, of course—about the size of those of modern garden pinks—and the flower stems are daintier than those of the standard perpetual-flowering carnation. They are available in a wide range of colors and color combinations and are not difficult to grow well.

Malmaison carnations were very fashionable around the end of the nineteenth century and were grown in great numbers in the country homes of the wealthy, as well as by nurserymen. They went out of fashion by the end of the Second World War and were thought to have been lost to cultivation. Some continued to be grown in a few private collections, however, and plants are once again available from carnation specialists. Malmaison carnations are generally considered to be more a collector's item, and they are described here in their own chapter.

Garden pinks have evolved over the centuries from the hybridization of various *Dianthus* species, including *Dianthus plumarius*, *D. chinensis*, and *D. caesius* (nowadays known as *D. gratianopolitanus*). Garden pinks are like miniature carnations, and they require the same kind of cultivation. Pinks' heights vary from the very dwarf rock garden cultivars, which grow only a few inches tall and make ideal subjects for growing in troughs or pots on a patio, to the cut-flower type, which grows to a height of 45 cm (18 in); however, most garden pinks grow between 25 and 38 cm (10 and 15 in) tall. Pinks are of more compact growth habit than border carnations—some could even be described as hummocks. They come in two main types: the old-fashioned, which flower profusely for a week or two in early summer, and the more modern kind, which have two or three flushes of bloom between early summer and mid-autumn. Pinks will flower well for two to three years, after which time they deteriorate and should be replaced by new young plants. This presents no problem, however, because pinks are very easily propagated by taking cuttings, preferably from young vigorous plants.

Some *Dianthus* species have never had a popular name like pinks or carnations but remain just dianthus. They are referred to by their generic and specific names, as in *Dianthus deltoides*, a wild plant with pink flowers; a white form of this species is named *Dianthus deltoides* 'Albus' and a cultivar with bright scarlet flowers is named *Dianthus deltoides* 'Flashing Light'. *Dianthus* species are widely grown in rock gardens, as well as in clay pots and pans in alpine houses, which allow the plants abundant ventilation. Although often called alpines, not all of them originated in the high Alps; some came from the foothills. Plants of this group vary considerably in shape and size, although all are delightful and at their best are seen sprawling over rocks or growing between flagstones. Some miniature cultivars grow as hummocks or cushions that become smothered by flowers on tiny stems. A great many true species and cultivars are available both as plants and seeds. Most are hardy perennials, although a few are grown as hardy biennials, like sweet william *(Dianthus barbatus)*.

Dianthus barbatus is one of the most popular of all cottage garden plants. It differs from most other dianthus in that it has comparatively broad leaves that are not glaucous, or blue-gray, but bright green. Sweet william comes in a wide variety of colors and forms, with single and double flowers, and height ranges from 12 to 60 cm (5 to 24 in). Dense clusters of flowers with bearded throats (hence *barbatus*, which is Latin for "bearded") sprout from the tops of very stout stems.

Raisers and Breeders

Before continuing, I should like to draw the reader's attention to expressions found in some of the quotations that follow in the subsequent chapters. The terms "raiser," "raised from seed," and "raised in my garden" in these quotations are also used throughout the *International Dianthus Register*, produced and published by the Royal Horticultural Society. The Register lists the names of 3000 raisers and gives the date of raising, wherever known, at the end of each of the 27,000 descriptions. The use of the word raiser for someone who grows a new plant from seed is understood throughout Britain, but since some readers of this book may be unfamiliar with the term, alternative words have been substituted in many instances, such as bred, produced, etc. However, in some chapters, and especially those listing the cultivars, the terms "raisers" and "date of raising" have been retained, as being the most appropriate.

Chapter 1

Dianthus Species

It is not certain when the first species of *Dianthus* were discovered; European references to the plants date from the sixteenth century. More than 300 species of *Dianthus* have been recorded, but the majority of these are of botanical interest only. The following are the most popular and more readily available, as both plants and seeds, for garden or rockery or for growing in troughs or even old sinks, and are also useful for hybridization purposes. Some are long flowering and will continue to add color to a rockery when the main spring show is over. Although mostly hardy perennials, some are grown as half-hardy biennials, like *Dianthus barbatus*, sweet william. The flowers of *Dianthus* species are simple, bearing five petals, usually with serrated edges, and in some species very deeply cut. The flowers may be of one clear color only, or they may have a central eye or zone of a different color.

In the United States, due to the vast size of the continent and huge temperature ranges, plants are designated with a zone rating, based on the U.S. Department of Agriculture's hardiness zones. The description of each species gives both the coldest zone in which the plant is hardy and, when available, the warmest zone in which it will grow. For example, zones 3–8 are given for *Dianthus gratianopolitanus*, meaning that the plant will grow in both zones 3 and 8 plus all the zones in between. Zone numbers are given following the name of each species. A hardiness zone chart is given in Appendix III.

It is not possible to guarantee that any particular type of plant will survive in all gardens of a given zone, however. A study of numerous publications, catalogues, etc., reveals inconsistencies in plant hardiness zones given for the same plant. As an example, three different sources state that *Dianthus alpinus* may be grown in zones 2–8, 3–8, and 4–9. Some gardens may have protected or exposed areas that could be equivalent to a whole zone above or below the zone in other areas of that same garden. It would seem, therefore, that only trial and error would provide the true answer, and a keen *Dianthus* lover will experiment in the hope of being able to grow particular favorites.

Most *Dianthus* survive long periods of drought extremely well. If at all possible, they should be given a good long drink of water in such conditions, but if this is not available, it is surprising how plants that have been looking very poor will revive after rainfall. Prolonged wet conditions probably cause more losses among *Dianthus* than any amount of dryness, although in extreme cold conditions it is the blanket of snow that gives them the protection they need throughout winter months. In the coldest areas a sudden severe drop in temperature before the expected snowfall will probably result in losses. Polyethylene (polythene) tunnels could be the answer. In Britain, which is generally damp in winter, it is recommended that a free circulation of air is essential at all times, and mulching or straw protection is not advised. Some American publications on the subject have suggested that the latter material might be laid among rows of half-hardy perennial types during winter months. The important thing to remember is to keep any such material well away from the stem, which can otherwise suffer from crown-rot.

Descriptions of the Species

Dianthus alpinus (zone 3–9), from the Austrian Alps, was introduced in England in 1759, and it is one of the first of the species to bloom. The flowers, which are large for an alpine species, are clear pink with crimson spots and a central zone or eye. Although the stems are but 5 to 7.5 cm (2 to 3 in) long, the flowers completely cover the dark green foliage in mid-summer. Extensive breeding has resulted in numerous cultivated varieties, or cultivars, some of which are listed as rock garden pinks. 'Joan's Blood', which has deep red flowers with a darker center, carried on 5-cm (2-in) stems, is a popular example.

Dianthus arenarius (zone 3–8), from northern and eastern Europe mountain regions, was introduced to England in 1804. Plants have a woody base, dividing into many close branches, with a rather densely tufted habit, forming cushions 7.5 to 10 cm (3 to 4 in) high. The flowers, about 2.5 cm (1 in) across, have five very deeply fringed, sweetly perfumed white petals with a greenish tinge at their center. These grow on erect stems 10 to 23 cm (4 to 9 in) tall and bloom throughout the summer. A hardy rock garden alpine plant, it thrives in sandy soil and is sometimes referred to as the sand pink. A popular selected form is called 'Snow Flurries'.

Dianthus arvernensis (zone 4), from the Auvergne mountains of France, is a compact cushion plant with sweetly scented rose-pink flowers on stiff 15-cm (6-in) stems. A very easy plant to grow, it is extremely floriferous. The cultivar 'Camla' is considered to be an improvement on the true species; its flowers are of a deeper color and the plant itself is even more compact.

Dianthus barbatus (zone 3–9), the original sweet william, is one of the oldest species to have been grown in Britain, first recorded in 1573. John Gerard, in his *Herball* of 1597, referred to it as a common flower in gardens, with many different varieties, having both single and double flowers. It is thought to have originated from southern and eastern Europe, on the lower mountain meadows, and was taken to North America by early colonists. Its cluster-headed flowers are light red, spotted white. Broad green leaves, not glaucous, emerge on stems varying from 22 to 75 cm (9 to 30 in) in height. A large color range of modern hybrids is available. Sweet william is a short-lived perennial, usually grown as a biennial.

Dianthus caryophyllus (zone 5–8), also known as the wild carnation or clove pink, is a native of Europe, where it thrives on rocks and ruined walls. Its exact origins are not known, but it was probably introduced to England by trading merchants. Its foliage is strong, glaucous blue-gray; its large single five-petalled flowers are white through pink to purple in color; and the plant attains a height of 30 to 60 cm (12 to

24 in). *Dianthus caryophyllus* is the ancestor of the true border carnation, to which much of this book is devoted, and is found in the ancestry of the perpetual-flowering forms as well.

Dianthus chinensis (zone 7–10), commonly known as the Indian pink and also as the rainbow pink, is a biennial or short-lived perennial from the hills and mountains of eastern Asia. It was introduced to Britain nearly three hundred years ago and introduced to North America with the colonists. Its small single flowers are rosy red with a purple eye and sweetly scented. It has greenish foliage, and height varies from 15 to 70 cm (6 to 28 in). It has been used extensively in hybridization, notably in the development of the annual Chabaud strain and Marguerite carnations.

Dianthus deltoides (Plate 1) (zone 3–10), known as the maiden pink because each stem carries only one flower, inhabits Europe and Asia and is also indigenous to Britain, where it was recorded in 1581. It makes a vigorous plant, 15 cm (6 in) tall, and is free-flowering, often well into autumn, with very small bright pink blooms and deeper colored markings in the center. The plants are variable in color, with bright red, white, and pink forms. *Dianthus deltoides* 'Albus' is a dwarf white form only 10 cm (4 in) tall. The named cultivar 'Brilliant', also dwarf, has very bright pink flowers. 'Major Sterne' has bronze foliage and carmine flowers; 'Flashing Light' has scarlet flowers and dark foliage. 'Microchip' (Plate 2), red, and 'Zing Rose', vibrant rose-red, are both very popular flower forms in the United States. The species self-seeds freely and is good for areas needing a groundcover.

Dianthus erinaceus (zone 4–9) is a unique dwarf alpine plant from the mountains of the Middle East. It forms prickly, spiny cushions 5 to 10 cm (2 to 4 in) high and bears tiny solitary, but occasionally paired, fringed rose-red flowers on 1.25-cm (0.5-in) stems. It prefers a hot, dry situation.

Dianthus freynii (zone 6) is similar to and sometimes considered to be a form of *D. microlepis*. This neat-growing plant has narrow gray-green leaves, forming tufts like 10-cm (4-in) high pincushions that spread slowly to 15 cm (6 in) in diameter, and is covered with pale pink, almost stemless flowers. It should be grown in a gritty compost with plenty of lime. A variation of this species has pure white flowers. It is a native of Hungary and Bosnia and was introduced to England in 1892.

Dianthus gratianopolitanus (Plate 3) (zone 3–8), introduced in 1792, used to be called *D. caesius* and before that *D. glaucus*. I was happier with the two previous names, which mean glaucous, referring to the gray-green, sometimes blue-green, foliage. I believe *gratianopolitanus* means "from Grenoble." No other genus suffers such a specific epithet, not even *Juglans*, the walnut tree, also from Grenoble. *Dianthus gratianopolitanus* is a splendid plant, however, and many garden pink cultivars have been bred from it. Originally called the mountain pink, it is now usually called the Cheddar pink after the district where it has been naturalized and grows wild on limestone rocks. Its single flowers are large, light rose-pink, and sweetly scented, and the plant does well in rock gardens and garden borders, where it grows 10 to 15 cm (4 to 6 in) tall. A double-flowered form is called *D. gratianopolitanus* 'Flore Pleno', meaning "petals in plenty." The cultivars 'Tiny Rubies', 'Dottie' (also known as 'Pretty Dottie'), and 'Spotty' (sometimes called 'Spottii') are popular in the United States. 'Spotty' is rose-red and edged and spotted silver. It was hybridized by Fleming Brothers in Nebraska. 'Bath's Pink', with a mass of small fringed pink flowers with maroon centers, is considered to be particularly good for hot and humid areas of the United States.

Dianthus haematocalyx (zone 8), from Mount Parnassus in Greece, is a very compact plant with bright purple flowers on 15- to 22-cm (6- to 9-in) stems. The reverse of the petals is colored yellow and the swollen calyces are blood-red. The plants have a neat cushion habit and not only flourish in the rock garden but do equally well grown in pots in an alpine greenhouse.

Dianthus knappii (zone 3–8), from Hungary, is said by some to be the only yellow species and is said to grow only 22 cm (9 in) tall. I have grown it from seeds collected in Canada and found it grows to twice that height. It is also said to be short-lived, but I have seen large clumps of it in front gardens in Victoria, British Columbia, that must have been four to five years old. Yet the climate there is very similar to that of the south coast of England. The small, clear yellow flowers are borne in clusters at the top of each long stalk. Seedling plants come true to type; it grows easily from seeds but does not propagate easily from cuttings. There is a selected form called 'Yellow Harmony'.

A few years ago at a northern England carnation show, a few

young pot-grown pink plants labelled 'Crock of Gold' were on sale. I cautiously bought one plant, remembering the words of John Rea of the seventeenth century concerning vendors of carnation plants: "most of these mercenary fellows about London are very deceitful and whosoever trusts them is sure to be deceived." It so happened the plant grew well and produced flowers of a deep yellow color, tending towards an apricot shade. It also reproduced easily from cuttings. I don't know whether the plant I bought had been propagated vegetatively (from cuttings) or grown from seed.

Dianthus microlepis (Plate 4) (zone 5), a native of the mountains of Bulgaria, has a very neat miniature, cushion-type growth and silvery gray to green leaves. The flowers are small, single, and solitary, of a light rose color, on stems not more than 5 cm (2 in) high. It blooms profusely from late spring to early summer. It is ideal for the rock garden or trough, or in a gritty soil in full sun, and may be increased by cuttings in the spring or from seed.

Dianthus myrtinervius (zone 7), a smaller species than *D. deltoides*, is found in the alpine meadows of Macedonia. The mats of prostrate stems are covered by tiny 5- to 7.5-cm (2- to 3-in) high bright pink flowers in mid-summer. A starvation diet will prevent the plant from growing too straggly and thus losing its compact habit.

Dianthus neglectus (Plate 5) (zone 4), or *D. pavonius*, from the Swiss and Italian Alps, was introduced to England in 1869. It has large flowers whose colors range from palest pink through red to bright crimson. The underside of the petals is buff colored and the foliage is glaucous. The flowers, which bloom throughout the summer, have 10-cm (4-in) stems.

Dianthus nitidus (zone 6), from the mountains of Macedonia, has tufts of bright green leaves. Its sturdy 25- to 35-cm (10- to 15-in) stems carry 2.5-cm (1-in) wide rich rose-pink flowers, which open from black buds.

Dianthus plumarius (zone 3–9), which came from southern Russia, is the ancestor of a great many cultivars of garden pinks. It was introduced in 1629 but is said to have been grown in English gardens long before then. It is a sturdy plant, 30 to 38 cm (12 to 15 in) tall, has a sweet fragrance, and flowers all summer. The abundantly produced flowers are large, and the deeply fringed petals are a pale lilac-pink color.

Dianthus squarrosus (zone 6), another species from southern Russia, was introduced to England in 1817. It has a low-spreading habit, spiny gray-green foliage, and sweetly scented white deeply fringed flowers. The flowers are produced rather sparsely in mid-summer on 15- to 30-cm (6- to 12-in) stems. It prefers sunshine and a well-drained soil and is most suitable for planting in wall crevices or among paving stones.

Dianthus superbus (zone 3–8), the fringed pink, is described in John Gerard's *Catalogue of Plants* (1596) as the Spotted Sweet John, while John Parkinson's *Herbal* (1629) calls it the Feathered Pinke of Austria. It grows to a height of 45 cm (18 in) and is very floriferous. The large fragrant lilac-colored blooms have finely laciniated petals and the color is variable, ranging from deep to pale lilac to white, and further decorated with a pale green center. The flowering period extends from late summer to late autumn. A hybrid plant, *D. superbus* var. *garnerianus*, which is sometimes called 'Gardneri', is said to be an improvement on the species, with its deeply cut flowers 7 cm (3 in) in diameter. It was hybridized around 1844 by the gardener to a Mrs. Garnier and is likely a cross of *D. superbus* with *D. chinensis* (Indian pink), or perhaps with *D. barbatus*. *Dianthus superbus* var. *chinensis* originated in or about 1898 from seeds collected by a missionary in China; its narrow, deeply fringed petals are colored mauve and flushed with rose and it has been said to flower in the open garden till the middle of winter. Although originally a European plant, *D. superbus* has three varieties from Japan: *Dianthus superbus* var. *speciosus* has large flowers in varying shades of pink; *D. superbus* var. *monticola* blooms throughout the summer with very short flower stalks; and *D. superbus* var. *amoenus* is of even shorter height. The modern Rainbow Loveliness strain, hybridized by Montagu Allwood, has a range of colors from white, crimson, pink, lilac to purple, is heavily perfumed, continues blooming throughout the summer, and is deservedly popular.

Dianthus sylvestris (zone 5), sometimes named *D. inodorus*, has large pink flowers with bluish spots at the base of the petals and blue-lilac anthers. It is an alpine plant from southern Europe. Grown in full sun it flowers on 15-cm (6-in) stems all summer long. It is very floriferous and can be increased by division in spring or by sowing seeds.

Cultivation of the Species

Where grown in the rock garden, or as edging plants in the border, most *Dianthus* species prefer the sunniest position available, and a well-drained soil is essential. On heavy soils it is advisable to raise the bed by 10 to 15 cm (4 to 6 in) above the surrounding soil level. Bonemeal should be worked into the top few inches of soil at 85 grams per square meter (about 3 ounces per square yard) shortly before planting, which may be at any time during autumn or spring. It is important to plant firmly and to avoid burying the foliage.

Lime should be applied only if the pH is lower than 6.5 (see section on Acidity and Alkalinity in Chapter 8), and it may be carefully scattered around the plants, to be washed down by subsequent rain or by watering in a dry spell, shortly after planting. A dressing of grit, granite, or limestone chippings in late autumn will help prevent winter dampness around the plants, which could otherwise cause root-rot.

The smaller, tight cushion-type species may also be grown in pots or troughs outdoors, or in an alpine cold house. A gritty compost is best and may consist of equal parts of good loam, peat, and sharp sand or grit, with the addition of 35 g (1 oz) carbonate of lime per bushel of compost. To keep the plants neat and compact, a near-starvation diet is best, similar to that in their native habitat.

Although perennial, many of the species are short-lived and may need replacing after two to four years. It is therefore advisable to have young plantlets of one's favorites in readiness.

Propagation can be by division—that is, the pulling apart of established plants, with a portion of root still attached—but preferably by the taking of cuttings of non-flowering shoots, in mid-summer just after flowering, from which the bottom pair or two of leaves are removed and which is then cut cleanly with a sharp knife or razor blade just below the lowest joint. Alternatively, with some of the stronger species, pipings can be taken by pulling out the tip of the shoot gently with one hand while holding the base of the stem in the other hand. These do not require cutting, but they are inserted directly into the rooting medium, which may be of sharp sand, or a mixture of sand and peat. Further information on rooting cuttings is given in Chapters 8 and 9.

Species may also be propagated from seed, sown early in the year in John Innes seed compost (see Chapter 10), or in a homemade compost consisting of equal parts sieved or finely crumbled fibrous loam, granulated peat, fine sand, and grit. Sow in pots or shallow pans, and cover to their own depth with a grittier compost. Placed in gentle heat, most seeds should germinate within three weeks, but some alpine seeds take much longer. When the first true leaves appear, the seedlings may be handled gently by the leaf and carefully potted on into small pots or boxes of gritty soil. When large enough they may be either repotted or planted out where required.

Seedlings do not always come true to name, however, and it is quite possible that many plants sold as species are in fact not truly genuine. The *Dianthus* family is so amoral, crossing with one another so readily, that natural hybrids are numerous. This could account for why descriptions of species often vary in many modern catalogues.

Chapter 2

History of Carnations

Border Carnations

Dianthus caryophyllus, said to have been so named because its fragrance resembles that of the culinary clove *Caryophyllus aromaticus* (more commonly known as *Eugenia aromatica*), is the ancestor of all carnations. Found originally in the Pyrenees mountains in Europe, it is a wild plant with five-petalled flowers of magenta-pink. It is believed that the perfection of border carnations has been achieved solely by the selection of seedlings over hundreds of years, and that no other species has been invólved in its evolution. Romantically inclined writers claim that carnations were used by the early Romans to flavor their wines and that monks or soldiers introduced the plant into England at the time of the Norman Conquest in the latter part of the eleventh century. Some claim Chaucer's verses as proof that carnations grew here in the fourteenth century, but a hundred years ago all "good authorities" concurred that Chaucer's "clove gilofre" was not the clove carnation but the flower bud of *Eugenia aromatica*, the clove we put into our apple pies.

That carnations were definitely grown in England in the fifteenth century was thought to have been proved by the fact that a portrait of

King Edward IV (who reigned 1461–1483) shows him holding a red carnation. James Douglas, the most famous of all breeders of hardy border carnations, wrote in or about 1910 that the portrait was sold at Christie's in 1855, catalogued as "an undoubted and rare portrait of Edward IV in a gold dress, and crimson cloak edged with fur, a chain of jewels round his neck; he wears a black cap, and holds a red Carnation in his hand"—Douglas followed in his own words in parentheses—"(it was stated to be a rose in error). The picture was bought by the Duke of Newcastle for 150 guineas" (Cook et al. 1910).

It has come to my knowledge that an expert on early portraits considers that the flower in the portrait was probably a rose, not a carnation, because portrait painters in England at that time were not very good. He also states that an original portrait of 1463 is most unlikely to be in existence at all, and that it is almost certainly one of the many copies, or copies of copies, produced in a fashionable series of the Kings of England for noble homes.

A gentleman who has reproductions of a number of portraits of Edward IV says that these show either the king holding no flower or holding a recognizable rose, and that up to now all the outstanding series have proved to be considerably later than their supposed dates. This gentleman, Dr. John H. Harvey, consultant architect to Winchester College, Hampshire, is the author of a fascinating and most scholarly article on the early history of the carnation, entitled "Gilliflower and Carnation," which appeared in the Spring 1978 edition of *Garden History* (Vol. VI, No. 1), the journal of the Garden History Society, edited by Dr. Christopher Thacker. The final paragraph in the work begins, "Leaving what is doubtful we must conclude with certainties. The garden forms of Carnations were known both in Turkey and the Middle East, and also in western Europe by 1500 but not a great deal earlier." The very last sentence states, "The supposed evidence of continuity from the association of the 'clove-gilofre' to put in ale, and the sixteenth-century use of flowers of the clove-pink as 'sops-in-wine', is rendered completely nonsensical." Let us hope Dr. Harvey's words of wisdom will dissuade all future writers from using those oft-repeated references to Pliny, the ancient Romans, the Normans, sops-in-wine, and Chaucer's clove-gilofre "to putte in ale, whether it be moyste or stale."

Turner, in his *Herbal* published in 1550, wrote that carnations are made sweet with the labors and wit of man, and not by nature. John Gerard, in his *Herball* published in 1597, stated that every climate and country brought forth new sorts. He called it the great double carnation and described very fine flowers of an excellent sweet smell and pleasant carnation color from which it took its name. He was the first to mention a yellow carnation, which he said he received from Nicholas Lete, a merchant friend in London who brought it from Poland. Early in the seventeenth century John Parkinson described those with large flowers as carnations, those with smaller flowers as gilliflowers, and those with apricot and yellow flowers as orange tawnies. Most of the cultivars then in cultivation came from Germany, Holland, Flanders, and other parts of the Netherlands, and plants, priced at 12 pence (in early-seventeenth-century currency) a layer, were imported in thousands. Later in the century, around 1665, John Rea described striped, flaked, marbled, and powdered cultivars, and in 1676 he listed 360 cultivars. In 1683 Samuel Gilbert mentioned a cultivar named 'Fair Helena', described as "only edged with purple," the first named picotee carnation.

By the eighteenth century carnations were classified as bizarres, flakes, piquettes, and painted ladies. The painted ladies had petals that were brightly colored on the upper surface and pure white on the underside. 'Mr. Bradshaw his Dainty Lady' was pale red and 'Ye Gallant's Fayre Ladye' was red-purple, and both were pure white underneath. Their clove-scented flowers were popular for a long time, but, having less-well-formed and smaller flowers, they were not considered to be of the same class as the bizarres, flakes, and piquettes. These latter forms were called florists' flowers, florists being breeders and connoisseurs. The florists held that carnations should have smooth-edged petals, although most had serrated petals. Piquettes, now called picotees, had undesirable spots and stripes on the petals as well as the required margin of contrasting color around the edge of every petal, and so were not up to the standards demanded later. The picotee, according to the writer C. Oscar Moreton (1955), was named after the French botanist Picot, but the *Oxford English Dictionary* states that picot is a thread edging to lace and that picotee is derived from the French picoté (pricked), which seems more likely.

In representations of these flowers from the nineteenth and early twentieth century, paintings and drawings tended to gloss over imperfections in flower form and color. Many of the paintings from that period, therefore, are not reliable sources for the true appearance of the flowers. William Robinson, the famous garden writer and designer of Gravetye Manor, Sussex, wrote in the 1890s that "all flowers should be drawn as they are" and artists should not be told to keep to the florists' ideal as to what the flower should be. He stated that plates of flowers of many kinds, all drawn with the compass, were quite worthless as a record. Beautiful flowers should be committed to the artist's care without comment, "and so abolish for ever the ridiculous painted lies which abound in the pictorial gardening literature of the past." I have a coffee-table book written in the 1950s that contains an illustration, specially painted for that book, depicting carnations of Robinson's time. This beautiful work of art is the result, as the book says, of the artist having "redrawn a colored drawing of carnations made about a hundred years ago by the Rev. C. Oscar Moreton's great-uncle at one of the Birmingham shows." My immediate reaction to the painting was that it would have been enough to make William Robinson turn in his grave. I have an old book containing a photograph of an exhibition box of 24 carnations exhibited by the leading exhibitor of the day at the National Carnation Show in 1902. These were real carnations, and the difference is very obvious.

SHOWS AND EXHIBITIONS

Early in the nineteenth century, carnation shows occupied the florists of the day. Flowers were dressed for exhibition and shown with paper collars pressed flat against them, and their calyces inserted into circular holes in shallow green boxes that would hold 6, 12, or 24 blooms. The pointed tips of the calyx were rolled back, thereby enlarging the flower, and ivory tweezers were used to rearrange the petals, layer by layer, to form a perfect circle, removing small malformed petals in the process. The flower stems were inserted into short tubes of water inside the box. Exhibitors used rather potent manures to obtain larger blooms, which caused many cultivars to fall by the wayside. Thomas Hogg, a schoolmaster from Paddington Green, London, wrote a book on carnations in 1820, *Treatise on the Carnation, etc.*, in which he referred to a compost that had as much manure as loam, top-dressed with "sugar-bakers' scum, soap-boilers' waste, night soil, the dung of pigeons and poultry in general, blood, soot, lime, gypsum, etc. etc." One shudders at the "etc. etc." Hogg also related that Christopher Nunn of Enfield, a barber and wigmaker, was so expert at dressing carnations that he had as much business dressing carnations as dressing wigs, his services being so eagerly sought by the exhibitors. Even more surprising is the fact that Hogg names nearly 400 flakes and bizarres and over 100 white-ground picotees.

A hundred years ago, that "old florist" J. J. Keen of Sway, Hampshire, advised beginners to under-dress their blooms, because over-dressing caused them to not last. He also advised, "Never attempt to dress a half-open flower—it is impossible." Keen believed that the beautiful markings of the carnation and the beauty of the flower were not seen till it was dressed. But, of course, he was concerned with the flakes and bizarres of his day and not with the present-day selfs and fancies. That other great florist, Benjamin Simonite of Sheffield, wrote in the National Carnation and Picotee Society's *Carnation Manual* of 1892, "The success of the exhibitor largely depends upon the care and thought bestowed on dressing and staging his flowers." He argued that carnations often lay several petals over one another so that only the uppermost petals could display their markings, and that judges do not have time to hunt for hidden beauties. He considered the skillful dresser had eye, judgement, forethought, patience, taste, and delicacy of touch. Two pairs of tweezers were employed, steel ones for turning back the points of the calyx and pulling out defective petals, and ivory ones for dressing. Defective petals were those in the center of the flower that were deformed, curled, narrow, or incorrectly colored and all self-colored petals and those without a pure white ground color. Flaked petals, those with flakes of one contrasting color on the pure white ground, had to be removed from bizarre carnations, and bizarre petals, those with flakes of two distinct contrasting colors on the pure white ground, had to be removed from the flaked carnations. Failure to remove all such nonconforming petals would result in disqualification.

Two cards were used in dressing: a white one about 10 cm (4 in) in diameter with a hole in the center large enough to allow the calyx to pass through without touching, and a smaller card with central slits arranged in the form of a star, which opened out to grip the calyx when the flower stem was passed through—this card supported the larger card above it. The lobes of the calyx sepals were turned back with the steel tweezers, which allowed the petals to move easily from side to side. Using the ivory tweezers (then obtainable from James Douglas at two shillings per pair), the outside, or guard, petals were arranged upon the larger card and drawn gently outwards to increase the size of the flower. The overlaps of the guard petals were then covered by the second tier of petals, and the third tier of petals similarly covered the second tier. Where the contrasting flakes of color dominated one side of the flower, some petals were transposed so as to distribute the mass of color evenly. Finally the top three or four petals were arranged to lie over the center of the flower. As Benjamin Simonite wrote in 1892, these last few petals would "seem to have gently and gracefully laid themselves in natural repose in the position left for them." Regarding staging, it was advised that the back flowers on the left should be the largest and best, with the smallest flowers placed towards the front of the exhibit. The reasoning behind that was that in reading, the eye concentrates more on the beginning of the page on the left than on the right, also the eye concentrates more on the next line, which again begins on the left.

James Douglas the second, son of the first James, wrote in 1946 that the border carnations of his day needed no assistance from tweezers to "improve" them. "I am quite ready to admit," he wrote, "that the border carnation of fifty years ago needed an application of the dresser's art, for I understand that many of the cultivars then available were very much on the small side" (Douglas 1946). He concluded, "The undressed flower, shown with foliage as grown, reigns supreme on the show table of today, and commonsense and sound judgement have triumphed."

By the middle of the nineteenth century the bizarres and flakes had been greatly improved and very strict standards of excellence were laid down for the guidance of exhibitors and judges. With bizarres every petal had to be ornamented with radial flakes of two distinct contrasting colors, whereas the flakes were required to have one or more flakes of one contrasting color on every petal. The pure white ground color was not allowed to be marred by spot or stain and the contrasting flakes of scarlet, crimson, rose, or purple were to be clear and bright and not run into the pure white ground. The flowers were required to be no less than 6 cm (2.5 in) in diameter and perfectly circular in outline, the petals had to be rose-leaved (smooth-edged), overlapping, and without gaps between them. These conditions were extremely demanding, and illustrations in periodicals of the day represented ideal carnations rather than the real thing and were severely criticized at the time. By this time the picotees had been greatly improved and were classified into light-edged and heavy-edged, according to the width of the red-, pink-, or purple-colored margin. For exhibition the ground color was required to be of purest white; thus the three show types, bizarre, flake, and picotee, were all of pure white ground color. Yellow-ground picotees became popular but never quite attained the quality of the white-ground picotees; their margin of color usually ran down into the yellow ground.

Some famous old cultivars were 'Admiral Curzon', a scarlet bizarre with flakes of scarlet and maroon; 'John S. Hedderley', a crimson bizarre with flakes of crimson and purple; and 'Sarah Payne', pink bizarre with flakes of pink and purple. The scarlet bizarre was esteemed the highest, the crimson bizarre second best, and the pink bizarre the least favored. The flakes were not regarded as highly as the bizarres; among the best were purple flake 'Charles Henwood', scarlet flake 'John Wormald', and rose flake 'Mrs. Rowan'. The white-ground picotee 'Ganymede', heavily edged red, and the yellow-ground 'Togo', with crimson-maroon edging, both were grown at the beginning of the twentieth century and still exhibited seventy years later, but they are no longer seen. The equally old yellow-ground picotees 'Margaret Lennox' and 'Santa Claus' are still popular with exhibitors today. The very fine yellow picotee 'Childe Harold', bred by Martin Ridley Smith, had the deepest yellow ground color, but this cultivar seems to have passed out of cultivation.

The National Society for the Exhibition of Carnations and Picotees was founded in 1850 and, on 4 August 1851, held its first show at Charles Turner's Royal Nurseries at Slough. Carnation shows became very popular, and some well-known florists of the time included James Douglas, Samuel Barlow of Manchester, Thomas Bower of Bradford,

E. S. Dodwell of Derby, the Rev. Charles Fellowes, the Rev. F. D. Horner, R. Lord of Todmorden, N. Norman of Woolwich, Ben Simonite of Sheffield, Martin Ridley Smith of Hayes, Richard Smith of Witney, and Charles Turner of Slough. Although the new Society was founded in the south, almost all the shows were held in the north of England and were well supported by blooms from southern growers. After a successful decade or so, interest seems to have died down for a decade, followed by a revival show in 1876, which James Douglas and E. S. Dodwell attended. The Society's original name must have been changed at some time because Douglas and Dodwell planned such a show for the south of England and in December 1876 consent was given for the formation of the National Carnation and Picotee Society, Southern Section. This Section held its first show at Westminster on 18 and 19 July 1877. About four years later Dodwell set up the Carnation and Picotee Union, which held its shows at Oxford, attended by a union of northern and southern growers. The original northern National Carnation and Picotee Society failed to put on a show for so many years that its Southern Section eventually became the National Carnation and Picotee Society. When the northerners did eventually put on a show in 1937 they too called themselves the National Carnation and Picotee Society, much to the annoyance of the newer parent society, which then regarded the Northern Section merely as an affiliated society. The southern-based National Carnation and Picotee Society divorced itself completely from the founding societies by stating its year of inception to be 1877.

Towards the end of the nineteenth century carnations were still shown dressed in boxes and judged on perfection of petal, purity of white ground, and regularity of contrasting markings. Carnation breeders were criticized as catering solely to exhibitors, with stem, calyx, and garden-worthiness not considered. So carnations eventually became debilitated and fell into decline. James Douglas and Martin Ridley Smith went together to Holland, France, and Germany, and in particular to the Ernest Benary nursery at Erfurt, Germany, to procure a few good cultivars for breeding. From these, both men bred many very fine new cultivars, subsequently introduced by James Douglas, one of the most successful being the yellow self 'Daffodil', which Martin Smith bred from Benary's 'Germania'. The flakes and bizarres gradually disappeared, until by the end of the First World War most nurseries had lost or discarded them altogether. Many years ago at a committee meeting I asked James Fairlie, that supreme grower and exhibitor of picotees, a question about flakes and bizarres. He said they became difficult to grow well, and with judges being so strict regarding placement of contrasting colors one had to grow many plants to obtain a few flowers, so eventually exhibitors lost interest in them altogether.

The new carnations were the self-colored and fancy types we know today, with most of them suitable for growing in the open garden. They were classified as selfs, white-ground fancies, yellow-ground fancies, other fancies, white-ground picotees, yellow-ground picotees, and cloves. The "other fancies" retained the old flaked markings, but not the white ground color; they were mostly of heliotrope-gray or pink ground color. The National Carnation and Picotee Society completely changed the style of exhibiting; boxes and collar cards were swept away and the flowers were staged in vases with dianthus foliage to set them off. Stem and calyx became almost as important as the flower itself; in fact, one burst calyx invoked disqualification for the whole exhibit. This led to many previously good show cultivars being discarded on account of a faulty calyx, and similarly most weak-necked cultivars faded from the show bench scene. Outdoor-grown trials, planted out in spring, were instituted, but since the mid-twentieth century these have been grown at the Royal Horticultural Society's garden at Wisley, Surrey, the plants set out in an open field in the autumn to stand the winter, and judged when in bloom the following summer.

The National Carnation and Picotee Society *Year Book* of 1923 shows that there were only about eighty paying members and three affiliated societies. Edmund Charrington was President, and famous florists of the time included R. H. Bath, James Douglas the second, James Fairlie, James Gibson, F. W. Goodfellow, C. H. Herbert, J. J. Keen, L. A. Lowe, G. D. Murray, and Elizabeth Shiffner. Leading cultivars of the day were the selfs 'Bookham Rose', 'Elaine', 'Gordon Douglas', and 'Joan Wardale'; the yellow-ground fancies 'Linkman', 'Pasquin', and 'Skirmisher'; the white-ground fancies 'Daisy Walker', 'Mrs. G. D. Murray', and 'Mrs. Hauksbee'; and the yellow-ground picotees 'Eclipse', 'Mrs. J. J. Keen', and 'Togo'. At that time there were no classes for white-ground picotees, although these were acknowledged to be superior to the yellow-ground type. By about 1930 white-ground picotees reappeared in the schedule and 'Fair Maiden', 'Ganymede', and 'Silas Osbaldiston' were shown.

Edmund Charrington continued as President of the Society for 27 years until his death in 1944, when Reuben Thain succeeded him but died after only a year in office. Walter Ferris became the new President in 1946, and three years later in 1949 the National Carnation and Picotee Society and the British Carnation Society, which concerned itself with perpetual-flowering carnations, amalgamated to become the British National Carnation Society. Up to the time of the amalgamation the patrons of the National Carnation and Picotee Society included the Hon. David Bowes-Lyon, R. Olaf Hambro, and Señor Martinez de Hoz and the patronesses were the Lady Daresbury, Lady Hudson, Mrs. Martin R. Smith, and Lady Stewart-Sandeman.

Some other border carnation notabilities of the time included Gordon Douglas (son of the second James Douglas), Charles Fielder, Ruby Goodfellow, George Hayward, and Horace Lakeman, as well as many amateur exhibitors. Some leading cultivars of that time were 'Alice Forbes Improved', 'Eva Humphries', 'Harmony', 'Leslie Rennison', and 'Royal Mail'. Equally successful were 'Belle of Bookham', 'Bookham Hero', 'Catherine Glover', 'Edenside White', 'Lieut. Douglas', and 'Merlin Clove', all bred by the second James Douglas. Comparing these cultivars, which I knew and grew, with photographs of cultivars from before the First World War, I consider the productions of the second James Douglas superior. On two or three occasions my wife Eileen and I were privileged to look over the numbered but unnamed seedlings at Great Bookham, Surrey, in the company of James Douglas and his son Gordon.

Perpetual-Flowering Carnations

The remontant carnation was the forerunner of the perpetual-flowering carnation, and the first of the type was known as the Mayonnais or de Mahon carnation, cultivated at Ollioulles in France in the middle of the eighteenth century. The original perpetual-flowering carnation is believed to have been raised by M. Dalmais of Lyons a hundred years later, a cross between the carnation de Mahon and a Flemish carnation. The perpetual-flowering carnation is also believed to have been derived from the same source as the annual Marguerite carnations, a cross between the Indian pink *Dianthus chinensis* and the perennial border carnation *D. caryophyllus*. Another belief is that the Grenadin strain carnation played some part in its breeding. Some other species may have contributed to the great height and the branching growth habit of the perpetual-flowering form, possibly *D. arboreus*, which also could account for its having been called the tree carnation.

In 1852 a New York florist, a Frenchman named Charles Marc, obtained seed of this type from France and raised several seedlings of remontant carnations. In 1856 the firm of Dailledouze, Gard, and Zeller of Long Island, New York, obtained seeds from Lyons and plants including 'La Pureté', bred by Alphonse Alégatière. Also in America a Frenchman named Donati bred the first good yellow-ground perpetual-flowering carnation, which he named 'Victor Emmanuel', and followed this with the first really good yellow cultivar, which he named 'Astoria'. About the same time Alphonse Alégatière selected and recrossed the remontant type with Tige de Fer (iron stem) carnations and produced 'Madame Alégatière', and a few years later introduced 'A. Alégatière' (First Class Certificate, 1877), a scarlet self, which he described as a tree carnation. By 1866 this cultivar was grown in Great Britain in quantity for the Covent Garden market. Alégatière is also credited with having been the first person to increase stocks of perpetual-flowering carnations by cuttings rather than by layering.

Towards the close of the nineteenth century several American florists introduced new cultivars that caused a great stir: 'Lady Bountiful', pure white, and 'Laddie', pink self, from Fred Dorner; 'Silver Spray', white, and 'Tidal Wave', deep pink, both in 1887, and 'Daybreak', flesh pink, in 1891, from W. P. Simmons; 'Mrs. Theo. Roosevelt' and 'Mrs. C. W. Ward', deep pink, from C. Ward. Mr. Ward, whose book *The American Carnation* was published in 1903, was Treasurer of the American Carnation Society, which held its first meeting in Philadelphia on 15 October 1891. Edwin Lonsdale was elected President, William Swayne Vice-President, and C. J. Pennock Secretary.

In 1900 the Scotsman Peter Fisher of Massachusetts caused a tremendous sensation when he sold the stock of his 1895 cerise-pink cultivar 'Mrs. Thos. W. Lawson' to "Copper King" Thomas W. Lawson for a reputed $30,000. To follow this, Fisher's blush-pink 'Enchantress' set the Covent Garden market alight in 1905. Peter Fisher, born in Dowally, Perthshire, Scotland, and naturalized in the United States in 1893, started as an apprentice gardener at the age of 15 years. He was nicknamed "Honest Peter" because of his principle to give value for money. It is said that when about to sow the seed that eventually became 'Mrs. Thos. W. Lawson', Fisher realized it was 1 April (April Fool's Day), so he postponed sowing until the following day. Fisher set up several nurseries in Massachusetts and grew and sold carnations for more than thirty years. He died in 1943 at the age of 86 years.

Two British cultivars, the scarlet self 'Winter Cheer' produced by James Veitch of Chelsea, and the pink self 'Miss Joliffe', bred by Masters, were used by American breeders to produce some of their most famous cultivars. Another cultivar to storm the English markets was 'Britannia', a scarlet self bred in 1904 by Alfred Smith of Enfield, Middlesex, nicknamed "Britannia Smith." This resulted from a cross between the American cultivar 'Mrs. Thos. W. Lawson' and the British carnation 'Winter Cheer'. I once met Smith's grandson at a horticultural research station and he recounted how his grandfather was obliged to keep fierce guard dogs in order to put a stop to mysterious losses of valuable plants from his greenhouses. Writing in about 1935, Montagu Allwood paid tribute to Smith, saying the "blood" of 'Britannia' is in nearly every present-day perpetual-flowering carnation.

The Winter-flowering Carnation Society was founded in December 1905 and held its first show at the Royal Horticultural Society hall in London the following year. The Society's foolish title was eventually changed to the Perpetual-flowering Carnation Society and finally to the British Carnation Society. In 1928 Lord Lambourne, a vice-president of the Society, invited Her Royal Highness Princess Mary to visit the summer show, staged jointly by the British Carnation Society and the National Carnation and Picotee Society. Consequent upon this visit she consented to become Patroness of the British Carnation Society. Well-known growers of the period included Montagu and George Allwood of Haywards Heath, Sussex; H. Burnett of

Guernsey; A. F. Dutton of Iver, Bucks; Carl and Eric Engelmann of Saffron Walden; C. J. Horwood of Basingstoke; Stuart Low of Enfield; Keith Luxford of Sawbridgeworth; Leslie Mason of Hampton; W. H. Page of Hampton; Charles Turner of Slough; and J. Veitch of Chelsea. Page and Dutton pioneered experiments in growing carnations in raised beds and lofty greenhouses.

Popular cultivars of the period included 'Ashington Pink', 'Betty Lou', 'Chief Kokomo', 'George Allwood', 'King Cardinal', 'Maytime', 'Peter Fisher', 'Purity', 'Robert Allwood', 'Spectrum', and 'Topsy'. Some of these were becoming old and difficult to grow well, but this situation was saved by the arrival in Britain from America in 1947 of the new scarlet self 'William Sim'. Its breeder, William Sim, was a Scotsman who emigrated to America in 1887 when 18 years old and became a naturalized citizen five years later. His first cultivar was introduced in 1925, and his scarlet self, originally named 'Farida' in 1938, was renamed 'William Sim' after his death in 1940. The plant was vigorous in growth, extremely healthy, free-flowering, and truly perpetual-flowering, and therefore the answer to the market-grower's prayer. 'William Sim' threw hundreds of sports in every known carnation color except crimson and is considered by many to be the finest perpetual-flowering carnation ever produced. Scarlet selfs have often made carnation history, starting with 'A. Alégatière' and followed by 'Winter Cheer', 'Britannia', 'King Cardinal', and then 'William Sim'.

By 1937 Captain Mullard, an electrical engineer in Englefield Green, Surrey, had begun his experiments in hydroponics and was growing carnations in tanks of gravel, the plants fed by nutrient solution via automatically switched pumps. These first experiments produced blooms a month earlier than similar cultivars grown in soil and a crop of some forty blooms per plant over the two-year flowering period. After the Second World War the Mullard Horticultural Engineering Company experimented with other materials, such as vermiculite, and marketed a suitable grade named Exflor, which they used to make a 50 percent mixture with fine silica sand.

Fred Hicks, of Embrook Nurseries, Wokingham, experimented with growing carnations in sand and gravel in raised concrete beds. His experiments were observed for the Royal Horticultural Society by

Dr. M. Tinckner, Keeper of the Laboratory at Wisley, and J. B. Stevenson of Colham Green Nurseries, Middlesex. It was found that cut flowers lasted about three days longer than those grown in soil, and that the soil-less–grown plants produced more blooms over the two-year growing period. John Dutton was not very impressed, however, and neither was Montagu Allwood, while Eric Engelmann said that when gardening became too much of a science he would retire to the backwoods and just live. For the other side of the picture Professor R. H. Stoughton, the Director of the Department of Horticulture at Reading University, who had collaborated with Captain Mullard, could not resist saying that those who considered such methods as interfering with nature ought to pull down their greenhouses, throw away their fertilizers and composts, and leave it all to nature, including the competition of those other plants called weeds. John Stevenson felt that the experiments were almost putting carnations back into their original habitat with poor soil-root anchorage and that the plants seemed to be enjoying it. He said the new system was growing blooms in winter as good as those normally produced in summer, and there were no weak stems or split calyces. I saw Fred Hicks's plants and remember watching him throw handfuls of dry fertilizer over the sand and watering it in.

In 1967 Fred Hicks wrote that in 1904 he was working for one of the first nurseries to import the American tree carnation, as the perpetual-flowering carnations were then known, into England. Cuttings were potted into 7-cm (3-in) pots and potted-on into 11-cm (4.5-in) pots; they were then stood outdoors on ash beds at the end of April and final-potted into 17-cm and 20-cm (7- and 8-in) pots in summer. At each potting they were potted as hard as possible, and in the final potting they were rammed with a wooden rammer to ensure the hardest possible potting. They were staked and tied, and all watering was done by watering can from a 40-gallon galvanized tank on wheels. Only chargehands were allowed to water; the tank was pulled by two boys. At that time foremen were paid 21 shillings per week, chargehands 18 shillings, and boys 5 shillings. Hours were 6 a.m. to 6:30 p.m. with one-half hour for breakfast and one hour for lunch. On Saturdays work ended at 5 p.m. and there were no paid holidays. Prices for blooms were 3 to 9 pence a dozen in summer and up to 30 pence a dozen at Easter and Christmas. (There were 240 pence to the pound in those days and 12 pence to the shilling.)

Another method of growing was from 7-cm (3-in) pots planted outdoors and dug up in September and planted into heated greenhouses, where they stayed until the following August. In later years the plants occupied greenhouses all year round for a period of two or three years. The beds were made up with good quality loam with the addition of stable manure, bonemeal, potash, and mortar rubble, when obtainable. The beds were trodden and rolled to make them as firm as possible; one had difficulty getting the trowel in when planting. Later it was realized that this firming was unnecessary, and beds were loosely filled with prepared soil and planting was done directly from the propagating bench and only firmed sufficiently to hold the plant in position until the roots took hold.

R. J. "Jack" Morton of Sunbury-on-Thames, whose small nursery was only a mile or so away from our own, experimented with carnations and other crops, growing them in sharp sand in pots. Jack was a most interesting man and we became good friends. He had been a ship's radio officer and was very clever with electrical appliances and always interested in innovations of that nature. I learned the technique of mist propagation from him; he had a most open nature and would teach anyone all he knew of any particular method or system, and he was always thorough and particular in all he attempted. I was impressed by his plants of all kinds grown in sand; his carnations and tomatoes *(Lycopersicon)* when fully grown rarely lost their lowest leaves. He was impressed by Fred Hicks's formula for dry fertilizer to be spread on top of the sand once every 7 to 10 days in summer and 15 to 18 days in winter and watered in by hosepipe or watering can. This fertilizer was trademarked SSS fertilizer—standing for "sand, soil, soluble"—and marketed in 1949 by Morton's firm, which became known as Horticultural Fertilisers and Sundries Ltd. with Richard Attenborough, later Sir Richard Attenborough, as a partner.

As previously mentioned, the National Carnation and Picotee Society and the British Carnation Society amalgamated in 1949 to become the British National Carnation Society. The British Carnation Society Patroness, H.R.H. The Princess Royal, became Patroness of the new Society, with George Monro of Covent Garden as its first

President. Some other perpetual-flowering carnation notabilities of the time included Stanley Lord of Shenley and Laurence J. Cook of Enfield, a writer and founder-member of the British Carnation Society, and many amateurs were active in exhibiting as well.

Developments Since the Amalgamation

Most carnation books published since the middle of the nineteenth century mention the names and home towns of a number of worthy florists, nowadays known as exhibitors; I too have mentioned them in the chapters on early history. But these early florists were those who were obliged to pull out faulty petals and dress their flowers and exhibit them resting on white paper collars with their calyces hidden in flat boxes. Paintings and drawings of their floral creations were criticized and ridiculed at the time as painted lies drawn with a compass. I have studied photographs of some of the best of the old cultivars and am convinced that such specimens would stand little chance in a novice's class of today. Old photographs also show plants in pots and outdoors in gardens with weak stems and such an abundance of lush foliage that they might have been grown in a bed of undiluted manure. Yet the books so revered these old florists that they are almost regarded as saints. Even as recently as the 1950s, when I started judging, some judges would lift up weak-necked blooms to see them and then award them prizes. The standard of flowers today is as good as it has ever been and, to judge from illustrations in old books, certainly better than that seen up to the early part of the twentieth century. I therefore consider it is high time that present-day hybridizers and exhibitors were accorded the recognition they have earned. It has been all too easy for writers to trot out the same old names repeated from the same old books; I know, or have known, most of the recent and present-day exhibitors and breeders I mention, and have judged their exhibits and seen their new cultivars as they have appeared.

The 1949 amalgamation of the National Carnation and Picotee Society and the British Carnation Society was effected smoothly enough, and fears that one society might dominate the other proved unfounded, although friendly rivalry continued to exist between border carnation enthusiasts and perpetual-flowering carnation enthusiasts, with each firmly believing theirs to be superior. The Grand Summer Show of 1949 was described by the newspapers as the best ever with record entries. The new society's gracious patroness, H.R.H. The Princess Royal, attended and inspected the border and perpetual-flowering carnations and pinks. On this special occasion *The Daily Mail* Gold Challenge Cup for the best scented perpetual-flowering carnation was won by H. G. Mason, of Hampton, with 'Hampton Pink', a rich salmon-pink self. C. Engelmann was very successful in the classes open to market growers, using such cultivars as 'Ashington Pink', 'Moonbeam', 'Northland', 'Peter Fisher', and 'Topsy'. The Allwood Brothers trade exhibit, with all types of *Dianthus* represented, was awarded a Large Gold Medal, and C. Engelmann was awarded a Gold Medal for its stand of perpetual-flowering carnations. Lindabruce Nurseries was awarded a Gold Medal for its trade exhibit of border carnations, which featured their own new introductions 'Lancing Lady' and 'Lancing Gem', both white-ground fancies, and 'Frances Sellars', a rose-pink self. The Cartwright Challenge Cup for a large exhibit of border carnations was won by F. W. Goodfellow of Aldridge, whose new scarlet self 'Royal Mail' was given an Award of Merit (AM). Other novelties from the same firm included 'William Newell' and 'Sprite', both white-ground fancies. In the spring show of 1950 the class for a market pack of carnation blooms, inaugurated by T. Harrison Chaplin, Sunbury-on-Thames, made its debut with twelve entries. Peter Chaplin's nursery was a short walk from mine and situated halfway between my nursery and Jack Morton's. I used to call in at Chaplin's to pick up a big bunch of fern foliage to use on my trade stands. A few fronds hanging over a vase would soften its distinct outline. Peter Chaplin designed an ingenious cardboard pack suitable for sending carnation blooms by post.

I began exhibiting in open classes for border carnations at the time of the amalgamation, and at the 1951 National Carnation Show I won the handsome Gilbert Greenall Memorial Trophy, which required ten cultivars in ten vases, one cultivar to a vase. Classes are less demanding nowadays. In those days the carnation show filled the entire Royal Horticultural Society Old Hall, border carnations in one half and perpetual-flowering carnations in the other. The wall spaces were filled with magnificent trade exhibits from such specialists as Montagu and George Allwood, James Douglas, Eric Engelmann, Lindabruce Nurseries, Horace Lakeman, F. W. Goodfellow, and John and Eileen Galbally, some of whom would also enter the open classes. At the 1953 National Show, where I won the open classes, Arthur Hellyer asked me to write an article for *Amateur Gardening*; I have been writing for that famous magazine ever since. I also wrote for *Gardening Illustrated*, *Popular Gardening*, and *Gardener's Chronicle*, all of which were printed in black and white in those days, and occasionally for a color-illustrated glossy magazine; I recall being asked to visit the sumptuous London office of *House Beautiful* magazine to view the large color transparencies around which I was to write my article. At a London show shortly after one of my articles appeared in *Gardening Illustrated*, Anthony Huxley greeted me with the words "I see you've arrived!" Puzzled, I replied that I had arrived at the show about an hour or so earlier. Anthony laughingly told me he was referring to the center-page spread in *Gardening Illustrated*. The following year, in 1955, I was invited to serve on the Joint RHS/BNCS Border Carnation committee, representing the Royal Horticultural Society. The committee in those days included, among others, Montagu Allwood, Gordon Douglas, and Charlie Fielder. Little did I think then that I would still be serving on it nearly forty years later, the only remaining member of that 1955 committee.

The most prestigious trophy for border carnations was the Cartwright Cup, first offered for competition in 1908, and valued then at 20 guineas. This open competitive class was for an exhibit of border carnations measuring 6 m × 2 m (20 ft × 6 ft) and was won by James Douglas in the first year and 15 times in succession thereafter. Allwood Bros. won it almost every year during the 1930s, then Lindabruce Nurseries of Lancing won it several times, as did F. W. Goodfellow of Aldridge and Matthew Kennedy of Darvel, Ayrshire. In 1956, following a long period during which the trophy had not been competed for, it was offered, together with a solid Gold Medal, for the best trade exhibit of border carnations and picotees at the National Carnation Show. There being no restrictions as to size, my wife and I put up a 9-m (30-ft), four-tier stand and won the cup and medal; the trophy was to be returned after one year and the medal to be paid for at cost price.

The year 1960, or thereabouts, saw the end of an era, when a number of leading exhibitors, some of whom employed gardeners and grew many more plants than the average exhibitor, retired from competition because of old age. Although more concerned with putting on trade exhibits, I would receive an SOS asking me to fill the open classes. With a few keen amateurs we held the fort until sufficient capable enthusiasts participated to make strong competition possible again. Successful exhibitors came from all over Britain, exhibiting such cultivars as 'A. A. Sanders', 'Alice Forbes Improved', 'Bookham Heroine', 'Clarabelle', 'Dorothy Robinson', 'Egret', 'Eudoxia', 'Fiery Cross', 'Frances Sellars', 'Harmony', 'Mendip Hills', 'Merlin Clove', 'Robert Smith', 'Sunray', and 'Thomas Lee'; the best picotees were 'Dot Clark', 'Eva Humphries', 'Fair Maiden', 'Firefly', 'Margaret Lennox', 'Santa Claus', and 'Togo'.

Records of the 1966 National Show reveal that I competed for all seven open-class border carnation trophies, won them all, and was unbeaten in all 22 classes entered. I should say my wife, Eileen, and I won them, for we always worked together. The National Summer Show of 1969 was held in Birmingham, instead of London, to give Midlands and northern growers a better chance to compete. Apart from being a flower show it was also a social occasion, many people meeting others who to them had previously been only names in prize-winners lists. Prominent among those present were George Cromarty, northern champion for many years and known locally as the "Cock o' the North," Ruby Goodfellow of Aldridge, Norman Simister and Reg Harris of Birmingham, W. F. (Bill) Dunn and Archie Fulton from Scotland, and Jack Humphries of Manchester, raiser of the peerless white-ground picotee 'Eva Humphries'.

At this time, when most other specialists seemed to have lost interest in breeding border carnations, Eileen and I decided to do less exhibiting and turn to breeding new cultivars, which soon began to find success on the show bench and at the Wisley trials. A new exhibitor, Peter Russell of Marlow-on-Thames, graduated from novice in 1977 to champion exhibitor in five short years, before he too turned to breeding new cultivars. By 1983, when I retired from business, I had bred and introduced seventy cultivars, and half of the Wisley trials plants consisted of my introductions—nearly half were Peter Russell's and the remainder were from Norman Simister and Steven Bailey.

Since the middle of the twentieth century, amateur growers have become increasingly involved in raising new cultivars of border carnations, some breeding their own and others buying seed. Some cultivars raised by amateurs and being shown successfully at the present time include 'Lord Nuffield' and 'Blue Ice', both from Stanley Stroud of Oxford; 'Jean Knight' and 'Nichola Ann', both from Ray Knight of Ollerton; 'Kathleen Sharp' and 'Ken Stubbs' from Ted Dungey of Luton; and 'Betty's Joy' and 'Spinfield Buff' from Peter Russell. By the 1990s other new exhibitors were making a name for themselves, both in London and in the north of England. Among the most successful were Jim Linnell of Northants, Keith Robb of Falkirk, exhibiting the popular Scottish cultivars, and Charlie Brown of Hartlepool—all with flowers equal to the quality of those of the old exhibitors of forty years earlier.

At the time of the amalgamation of the two societies in 1949, exhibitors of perpetual-flowering carnations favored the cultivars 'Ashington Pink', 'George Allwood', 'Marchioness of Headfort', 'Miller's Yellow', 'Northland', 'Peter Fisher', 'Pharaoh', 'Princess Irene', 'Royal Crimson', and 'Topsy'. The new scarlet self 'William Sim' had just started to appear in one or two vases during the 1950s, and within about ten years amateur exhibitors were finding 'William Sim' easy to grow well in spite of its very tall habit of growth, and Sim-type cultivars and their sports became prominent on the show benches. His Grace the Duke of Roxburghe, himself a keen exhibitor of these flowers, became the Society's new patron in 1969.

Most people thought the Sim cultivars would last forever, but continental breeders were working to produce cultivars unrelated to 'William Sim' and its derivatives, cultivars of shorter habit and a new disease-free vigor. At the same time, hybridizers in Great Britain, mainly amateurs, were crossing perpetual-flowering carnations, some using pollen from border carnations, and producing splendidly formed exhibition cultivars of shorter and sturdier habit, more suitable for their modest greenhouses. By 1976 the Sim carnations were being ousted from the show bench by such cultivars as 'J. M. Bibby', hybridized by J. M. Bibby by crossing perpetual-flowering carnations with border carnations, and 'Fragrant Ann', raised by John Neil of Derby, which has been a consistent prize-winner every year since it was introduced in 1953. Tom Bradshaw crossed 'J. M. Bibby' with 'Fragrant Ann' to produce 'Apricot Sue'. Bradshaw's F$_2$ hybrids with 'Apricot Sue' as one parent resulted in 'Royal Tribute', purple self, and 'Joanne', an absolutely stunning cerise-pink self. John Neil, who also produced 'Chanel', bought border carnation seeds from me, but he never mentioned what results he had obtained. He did, however, recommend other amateur enthusiasts of perpetual-flowering carnations to approach me for seeds, who told me they had seen John's garden full of splendid border carnations.

There then followed the recent introductions of Colin Short of Oldham (some of whose cultivars were obtained by European breeders for use in their hybridization work), Colin Stringfellow of Stockport, Bob Dickinson of Cumbria, and Brian Dean of Atherton. Many of their cultivars are described in Chapter 6. All these raisers have also been extremely successful exhibitors, as has Desmond Donaldson of Dumfries, winner of the coveted Daily Mail Gold Cup for five years in succession (1990–1994), beating all previous records for that trophy, before ill health forced his retirement. Meanwhile, professional breeders Maurice and Brian Woodfield, also raisers of many fine lupins *(Lupinus)* and delphiniums, introduced their own 'Jacqueline Ann', 'Vera Woodfield', 'Jess Hewins', 'Audrey Robinson', and many more successful exhibition cultivars.

Famous British Hybridizers

Four men who greatly influenced carnation growing were James Douglas of Great Bookham and his son, also James, who succeeded him as a brilliant breeder of border carnations, and Montagu and George Allwood of Haywards Heath, Sussex, who developed several new kinds of pinks and carnations.

JAMES DOUGLAS

James Douglas senior was apprenticed in 1851 to Andrew Tait's nursery at Kelso, and three years later worked for the Balfour family where he planted and layered flakes and bizarres for the grandmother of the then Prime Minister. When a young man of 23 years he worked for the James Veitch nursery at Chelsea. Three years later he became head gardener to Francis Whitbourn of Ilford and remained in his employ for over thirty years. In 1893, at the age of 56, James Douglas built his own nursery at Great Bookham, Surrey, specializing in auriculas and carnations. He had great success with his breeding of both subjects, and his supremacy was acknowledged by all. He was a member of the Royal Horticultural Society Council for nine years and served on every committee but one. He helped found the National Carnation and Picotee Society and the National Auricula Society (Southern Section) in 1876 and the RHS Orchid Group. James Douglas was awarded the Royal Horticultural Society Victoria Medal of Honour, and upon his death in 1911 the RHS journal acknowledged him as one of the greatest practical gardeners and florists in the country, and one who had for many years worked wholeheartedly on the Council of the Royal Horticultural Society and on committees as a judge and an examiner. He contributed articles to *Gardener's Chronicle* and *Gardener's Magazine* and wrote a number of books on various gardening subjects. At the age of 72 years he claimed he owed his long active life to rising at six every morning, summer and winter, a cold bath, and a sharp walk before breakfast, and not drinking or smoking.

JAMES DOUGLAS THE SECOND

James Douglas was succeeded by his son James, who continued breeding border carnations and auriculas. The carnations produced by the second James Douglas lived up to the standard set by his famous father; in fact, I consider many were superior to their forebears. Some would say he had superb material to work with, which is true, but I believe many of the cultivars raised by the second James Douglas have not been superseded since. Many have faded away, age having taken their toll; others may have been equalled, but not surpassed, cultivars such as 'Belle of Bookham', 'Bookham Fancy', 'Bookham Heroine', 'Bookham Perfume', 'Catherine Glover', 'Clunie', 'Eudoxia', 'Merlin Clove', 'Sunray', and 'Tosca'—ten cultivars with an average age of forty years and still growing well. Incidentally, the 1913 Douglas catalogue listed more than 100 cultivars of picotees, over 40 flakes and bizarres, 28 Malmaisons, 31 tree carnations, and over 200 self and fancy border carnations. There were also over 60 cultivars of pinks, 100 cultivars of auriculas, and over 20 cultivars of German iris. James Douglas also grew over 100 cultivars of double peonies.

The second James Douglas in turn was succeeded by his son Gordon, who continued the family tradition of raising quality border carnations and auriculas. The House of Douglas, famous for their border carnations, pinks, and auriculas, were also noted as producers of fine quality seeds. But their long reign eventually drew to a close, for in February 1967 Gordon Douglas wrote me to say "The Council has bought the whole of the Nursery and ground for a building estate by compulsory order, and not given me time to rebuild, so I am giving up Carnation growing at the end of April." The ensuing correspondence over the next two years between myself and Gordon Douglas concerned the difficulty that Douglas and his customers had in getting quality border carnation seed, and he frequently asked me to supply him with "the best I can." I continued to supply Gordon with seed for a year or two until eventually he passed the orders to me to deal with direct. He continued to grow auriculas professionally, which were his favorites.

THE BROTHERS ALLWOOD

Montagu and George Allwood, from Lincolnshire, set up their carnation nursery in Sussex in 1910. As youths they were employed together at a carnation nursery in Edmonton, London, before Montagu moved on to work at the Stuart Low nursery in Enfield, where he became the firm's carnation specialist when in his early twenties. Allwood Bros. quickly became a household name; the firm put up splendid trade stands at all the principal flower shows year after year for a long period of time, and their advertisements in the gardening magazines and the popular press kept their name and carnations before the public at all times. The Allwoods produced many fine new cultivars in all the various types of *Dianthus*, mostly successful and launched with great publicity, although sadly many have now faded into obscurity.

Dianthus allwoodii. The Allwoods will probably be best remembered for the introduction of their *Dianthus allwoodii*, a race of hybrid pinks obtained by crossing *D. plumarius* with perpetual-flowering carnations. No doubt some other people had crossed pinks with perpetual-flowering carnations—perpetual-flowering hybrid pinks were already in existence—but the Allwood brothers were the first to introduce them as a distinct hybrid race and give the race a collective name. Montagu Allwood wrote in the third edition of his book *Carnations and All Dianthus* (1947) that he set to work in 1910 to create *D. allwoodii* and it took nine years of crossing to produce it. Allwoods pinks are described further in Chapter 3.

Perpetual-Flowering Border Carnations. James Douglas introduced the new race of perpetual-flowering border carnations, which he bred from a cross between the true border carnation and the perpetual-flowering carnation. He raised them on a very large scale, and one of his cultivars, 'Hercules', obtained Award of Merit in 1911. But when a large number of plants collapsed one spring after a very severe frost, Douglas decided to discontinue crossing the two types and did not include them in his catalogue for 1913. The Allwoods introduced their perpetual-flowering border carnations in their 1913 catalogue, saying that others had claimed to have raised this new race previously. They discarded them in 1941 when compelled to do so by war restrictions.

Cottage Carnations. In 1932 Allwoods introduced their "Cottage" border carnations bred from cottage garden carnations, which were simply short-growing border carnations, such as the old brick-red cultivar 'Rifleman'. One outraged member quoted in the National Carnation and Picotee Society *Year Book* wrote, "I saw flowers just like 'Rifleman' win a first prize this year and everybody was disgusted, they were small, ragged and bursted." Montagu Allwood himself admitted in the same year book that "'Rifleman' could not compare with more modern kinds in any single respect." He believed that the superiority of the Cottage carnations lay in their hardiness, fearing border carnations were becoming "pampered pets" suitable only for the showbench, and he pressed for autumn-planted outdoor trials at the Royal Horticultural Society garden at Wisley to put them to the test.

In 1935 autumn-planted outdoor trials were instituted at the Wisley gardens, the border carnations planted out in the open field in autumn and judged when in bloom the following summer. Of the great number of cultivars at this first autumn-planted trial, 16 received AM, but these did not include any of the Cottage cultivars. Montagu Allwood wrote that the carnation experts were not impressed by the Cottage carnations and that these carnations themselves did not seem absolutely happy at being seen alongside other border carnations. Yet Allwoods' 1936 catalogue stated, "At the hardy carnation trials at Wisley our Cottage types proved without exception to be the best class of garden carnation." Their advertisements and catalogues proclaimed their race of super-hardy Cottage carnations to be virtually perpetual-flowering from June to October, which was certainly untrue of those grown at Wisley. In the first eight years of autumn-planted trials, seven border carnations were awarded First Class Certificate and 50 received Award of Merit. Of these 57 awards, only one went to a Cottage cultivar: 'Cottage Pride' obtained AM in 1943. Ironically, Allwoods' non-Cottage exhibition-type cultivars were successful in the trials, winning FCCs and AMs, while the Cottage cultivars were repeatedly passed over. Montagu Allwood wrote,

> Floral Committees have been of assistance to some extent in the past—in fact horticulture is better off with them than without them—but the fault of the floral committee is that they very rarely have any imagination; often their decisions are ruled by envy, so that their judgement is anything but infallible. (Allwood 1947)

Writing in the 1942 *Annual* of the National Carnation and Picotee Society, Allwood admitted that "the trials at Wisley have undoubtedly killed the old notion that the border carnation was a pampered pet grown in greenhouses for exhibition purposes." But gardening articles and books of the period continued to praise the Cottage carnations and perpetual-flowering border carnations, implying these were superior to and had superseded the "old border carnations." Border carnation specialists did not concur; they did not list the Cottage and perpetual-flowering border carnation cultivars, which eventually faded out. The old border carnations are still going strong.

Downs Carnations. Another group introduced by Allwoods at about the same time as the Cottage carnations, and heralded with much publicity, were the border carnations bearing the prefix "Downs." They were described as an improved, large-flowering strain and a great advance in border carnations, some blooms measuring 12 cm (5 in) across. A few cultivars of this type obtained AM after trial, one of which, 'Downs Cerise', is still in cultivation. Most were too full-petalled for the great outdoors, however, and hung their heads when the flowers were heavy with rainwater. Rainwater runs off normal border carnations because they have fewer petals.

Amateur Carnations. About 1948 Allwood Bros. introduced their "Amateur" carnations, another blend of perpetual-flowering and border carnations, aiming to combine the short bushy hardier habit, the shapely flower, and the delicate coloring of the border carnation with the perpetual-flowering characteristics. It was claimed that they could be grown in a cold (unheated) greenhouse and would flower from spring right through to autumn. The Amateur carnations ran for about 12 years, with novelties every year, and then faded out. It is most probable that some of the amateur hybridizers of that era used these cultivars, along with border carnations, in their breeding programs. Since the 1960s these have produced flowers with the smoother edges and colorings of the border carnations so that many of the modern cultivars seen on the show bench could easily be mistaken, at first glance, for well-fed border carnations. Trials of some of these new cultivars at Wisley have proved many of them to be fully perpetual-flowering.

Perpetual-Flowering Malmaisons. As the Amateur carnations went out, a new race called "Perpetual-Flowering Malmaisons" came in. Allwoods proclaimed, "We have now recaptured and improved on this unique type of Malmaison by retaining all its old virtues, but adding a perpetual-flowering habit." In 1957 'The Queen Mother' was introduced, and in 1958 'Apricot Queen' and 'White Queen' were added. 'Fragrant Queen' and 'Flaked Queen' appeared in 1959, but no Malmaison carnations appeared in the 1962 catalogue.

END OF AN ERA

Montagu Allwood died in 1958, aged 78, only five days after attending the British National Carnation Society summer show in London. George Allwood died in 1964. I can still remember the last time we chatted; he had been ill, but on feeling better told me how he had been prescribed a set of breathing exercises that had made a new man of him. I had never seen him quite so cheerful. He was a quiet man, not flamboyant like his brother "Monty." Someone once said Monty could have succeeded at anything, including being a ring-master in a circus. He was the supreme showman; his exhibit had to be the biggest and the best, and it always was. He enjoyed attending meetings, especially trials where the cognoscenti gathered to adjudicate on the merits or otherwise of the new carnations. He would write thanking me for mentioning his firm or cultivars in articles, sometimes calling my criticisms "fair comment."

Monty once gave me a plant of an apricot-ground fancy border carnation named 'Renoir', which, when I had built up a good stock a few years later, I included in my catalogue. To my great surprise and discomfiture it appeared in Allwood's catalogue that same year as their latest novelty.

One year my wife and I took our two very young schoolgirl daughters to a Royal Horticultural Society summer show. Monty met them on the dais, and was captivated. He asked them if they liked ice cream and brought out a half-crown. He also told them that whenever they saw him they were to go up and speak to him, and, tapping his nose, he said, "You'll always remember me, I'm Monty with the big nose." Who could forget those sharp, twinkling eyes and that rasping lisp.

Upon the death of Montagu, Robert Allwood, son of George and nephew of Monty, became manager of the business. I remember Robert's enthusiastic intention to infuse the business with a new energetic spirit. One evening when passing the nursery, Eileen and I called in, and Robert talked of his plans to revitalize the nursery. He invited us to see the new super-efficient boiler system then being installed. I recall his exuberance as he climbed up on top of the boiler and called down to us details of the technical facts and figures of the monster's capabilities; one of the many occasions I have regretted not having my camera handy.

I remember when the long-established family business of the House of Douglas ceased trading and the famous firm of Allwood Bros. finally passed out of family hands; one felt that the curtain had fallen at the end of an era. In fact, it proved to be merely the first act. In retrospect the carnation story of the first half of the twentieth century seems almost theatrical. Of course, all old people have nostalgic memories of their own "good old days"; no doubt the present time will become the good old days of the future. Many excellent cultivars are now being raised, and it is fortunate that there are sufficient older ones in cultivation for comparison to ensure a high standard is maintained. The modern trade exhibits at shows may not yet equal those of the old Allwood Bros., but the quality is there, if not the quantity.

The nursery continued on a smaller scale, trading under the name Allwood Bros., and in 1967 purchased all the stock and goodwill of the House of Douglas. Following the retirement of the owners in 1984 the business was acquired by Sue and David James, the daughter and son of two well-known mail-order nursery families dealing in other types of plants. Both are keenly interested in *Dianthus* and are enthusiastically searching for more of the older cultivars raised by Montagu and his brother George to add to those still available. They have already staged three Gold Medal exhibits in London and elsewhere in their first season. The curtain has risen on the second act.

Chapter 3

History of Pinks

There is always conjecture regarding the origin of the name pink. Some say it is derived from *pinkster* (the old Dutch word for Whitsuntide or Pentecost, during which many pinks may have been used in floral decorations for the Dutch religious festivals; see Ingwersen 1949), some say it referred to the petal edges, which originally were fringed as though snipped with pinking shears, while others say it referred to the flower's central zone, or eye, which contrasts with its paler ground color. The French, among the first to cultivate carnations, named the plants *ouillet*, meaning a small eye.

A question often asked is, "What is the difference between a pink and a carnation?" The answer is that they derive from different species. Garden pinks have been produced by hybridizing the species *Dianthus plumarius*, *D. chinensis*, and *D. gratianapolitanus*, whereas the border carnation was developed solely from *D. caryophyllus*. Annual carnations are the result of cross-hybridization of *D. chinensis* and the border carnation.

A simpler, although not technically accurate, answer is that a pink can be considered a scaled-down model of a carnation. The leaves, calyx, stem, root, and nodes of the pink are all identical to those of the carnation; the only real difference is in the flowers. Apart from being larger, the carnation flower has more petals than the pink's. The fancy carnations have colored stripes that contrast with the ground color, whereas fancy pinks in general have a contrasting central zone or eye. A few modern pinks do have stripes, the result of mixed breeding with carnations. Picotee carnations and laced pinks both may be described as "fancy," and there is an interesting difference between them. The picotee carnation has a margin of a contrasting color around the very edge of every petal, but the laced pink has a margin of a contrasting color just inside the edge of every petal. According to the old florists the width of the laced pink's contrasting band of color should be the same as that of the clear margin encircling it. Over 400 years ago pinks were variously called pynkes, soppes in wine, feathered gillofers, and small honesties.

Seventeenth-Century Pinks

Although regarded with affection, pinks were not highly esteemed as subjects for garden decoration until named cultivars began to appear. Right up to the eighteenth century pinks were mostly single flowered with but five or six petals; the few double-flowered cultivars were called feathered pinks. The following old pinks are mentioned for historical reasons; I doubt any of them genuinely exist today even though their names may appear in traders' lists. 'Fair Folly' (synonymous 'Constance Finnis') and 'Queen of Sheba' are painted lady types, which have single flowers, white with purple and pink markings and the undersides of petals flushed pink. My reasons for doubting their authenticity appear later in this chapter.

Eighteenth-Century Pinks

The eighteenth century saw a breakthrough in the breeding of garden pinks. A cultivar named 'New Dobson's', a pheasant-eyed type bred from *Dianthus plumarius*, was so distinctly superior that it was recommended as a cultivar for breeding purposes. White with a central eye of deep chocolate, it was the forerunner of the black and white pinks. About the year 1772 a seedling with a band of contrasting color around the edges of the petals, which were the same color as the central eye, was bred by James Major, gardener to the Duchess of Ancaster and named after her. This success was followed two years later by another from Major, from seed obtained from his 'Duchess of Ancaster'. Named 'Lady Stoverdale', it was of very fine form and considered to be the first of what became the laced pinks.

Breeding laced and black and white pinks became very popular with London, Lancashire, and Scottish growers. The London and Lancastrian growers bred laced pinks while the Scots in Paisley grew the black and white pinks, which did not have lacing. When the Scots obtained seeds from London they too produced laced pinks, and their laced pinks became known as Scotch pinks. Some confusion arose later when the name Scotch pinks was used to represent the black and white, unlaced cultivars. The laced pinks were all of white ground color with fringed or serrated petals, and they were very popular as exhibitors' flowers.

Other eighteenth-century pinks include 'Bat's Double Red' (1707), ruby-red; 'Cockenzie' or 'Montrose Pink' (1720), red with darker center, double; 'Musgrave's Pink' (1730), white with pale green eye, single; 'Delmonden Fairy' (1750), pink with scarlet eye; 'Little Old Lady' (synonymous 'Chelsea Pink') (1760), white, laced crimson, double; 'Inchmery', pale pink; 'Paisley Gem' (1798), white, laced purple; 'Dad's Favourite', white, laced maroon-purple, discovered by A. J. Macself, one-time editor of *Amateur Gardening*, in a Northumberland garden, also thought to have originated in Scotland; and 'William Brownhill', white, laced maroon, semi-double.

Nineteenth-Century Pinks

Early in the nineteenth century the first "rose-leaved" laced pinks appeared—that is, pinks with almost smooth-edged petals—and some of these were of pink ground color. Thomas Davey, of King's Road, Chelsea, in addition to breeding his own cultivars with the prefix "Davey's," introduced many fine laced pinks bred by amateur enthusiasts, but none of these is available today. 'Davey's Juliet' and 'Davey's

Bolivar' were illustrated in Robert Sweet's *The Florists Guide* about 1828; however, as with the carnation flakes and bizarres of that period, these were paintings, not photographs, and all were depicted with perfect circular shape and markings.

Some popular nineteenth century pinks are still obtainable. Most have a strong scent and a weak calyx and are those I remember growing half a century ago. They bloom for a week or two in early summer and are not repeat-flowering. These old cultivars, which should not be stopped but allowed to grow naturally, include 'Earl of Essex', rose-pink with a darker central zone, petals fringed, and a calyx that invariably splits, and 'John Ball', white, laced purple, and double, bred by Dr. Alan McLean and introduced by Turner and Son, who also introduced 'Mrs. Sinkins' (1868), white with pale green center, double, strong perfume. So many different white pinks have been labelled 'Mrs. Sinkins' that it is not possible to guarantee authenticity, but all clones are similar in one respect—they really burst the calyx, as do 'Paddington', amaranth-rose, zoned pansy-purple, double, bred by Thomas Hogg, and 'Sam Barlow', white with a bold deep purple center, compact habit, and fringed petals.

Mule pinks, so-called because the plants are sterile—that is, do not produce seed—were also introduced around the middle of the nineteenth century. These were the result of crossing the sweet william, *Dianthus barbatus*, with *D. plumarius*. They have cluster-heads of double flowers, are long-flowering, and sweetly scented, with green foliage. One of the most popular, 'Emil Paré', with rose-pink flowers, hybridized by Andre Paré in Orléans, France, in 1840, is still available today.

Twentieth-Century Pinks

HERBERT'S PINKS

Some of the finest pinks ever seen were bred by C. H. Herbert of Acocks Green, Birmingham, during the first thirty years of the twentieth century. He also produced some very fine border carnations. Herbert's pinks were sometimes called *Dianthus herbertii*. One of the earliest was 'Progress' (pre-1909), mallow-purple with a darker eye, double, and clove-scented. I grew his cultivars 'Bridesmaid', shell-pink with scarlet center; 'Model', light pink with deep red center; and 'Queen Mary', rose-pink with a crimson center. Now only 'Bridesmaid' still exists, and it has been used extensively in breeding. These plants were better propagated by layering than by cuttings. Herbert's pinks are discussed more later in this chapter.

ALLWOODS PINKS

The pinks hybridized by Montagu Allwood have had the greatest influence on modern garden pinks. They are variously described as perpetual-flowering, as flowering from May to October, and as flowering from May until the frosts. I call them remontant, as they have two or three flushes of bloom during summer and autumn. Allwood wrote (1947) that he set to work in 1910 to create a plant that was perpetual-flowering during the entire spring, summer, and autumn, and he had crossed 'Old Fringed', a semi-double, fringe-petalled, white self garden pink, with a perpetual-flowering carnation. This group of plants was given the collective name *Dianthus allwoodii*. Almost all modern pinks have parents connected with the *D. allwoodii* group; what puzzles me is that, among the many *Dianthus* seedlings I have bred from plants in this group, I have never come across a 3-ft tall freak, nor have I ever heard of any other breeders having done so. One would expect to find some increased height as evidence of perpetual-flowering carnation influence among the progeny.

Montagu Allwood wrote in an article published in 1950 that he had crossed *Dianthus allwoodii* with Herbert's pink 'Progress' to obtain his Show pinks group of *D. allwoodii*. 'Progress' was bred before 1909 and was described by James Douglas as a very fine perpetual-flowering cultivar, very free-flowering. Some Allwoods pinks still grown and shown are 'Denis', deep pink self; 'Diane', salmon-pink sport from 'Doris'; 'Doris', salmon-pink with scarlet eye; 'Eileen', a single of white ground color with a large crimson central zone; 'Helen', deep pink self; 'Joy', carmine-pink self; 'Laced Hero', white, laced purple; 'Laced Joy', rose-pink, laced crimson; 'Prudence', pale pink ground, laced crimson; and 'Show Beauty', deep rose-pink with bold maroon eye.

IMPERIAL PINKS

Herbert's pink 'Bridesmaid' became the most sought-after exhibitors' cultivar and the one most used for breeding. Around 1950 Charles Fielder of Lindabruce Nurseries used it to produce his 'Lancing Supreme' of similar coloring, pink with a deeper central eye. Fielder told me all the top breeders were using 'Bridesmaid'. He produced many fine exhibitors' pinks, but never considered calling them *Dianthus fielderii*. Instead he named them Imperial pinks, hybridized by crossing *Dianthus allwoodii* with Herbert's pinks. Some of his best-known still grown and shown are 'Carlotta', claret colored; 'Crimson Ace'; 'Freckles', dusky salmon, flecked red; 'Iceberg', white self; and 'Winsome', rose-pink with faint crimson center. Some Imperial pinks do not root easily from cuttings, a trait inherited from Herbert's pinks; in fact, Fielder layered all his pinks into the 10- and 12-cm (4- and 5-in) pots in which they were grown. 'Lancing Supreme', his best cultivar, was very successful on the show bench—that is, until Allwood's 'Doris' came along. They were similar in color, but 'Lancing Supreme' had the better show qualities, especially the form of the flower. Yet 'Doris' won more prizes, probably because it was shown more often. I feel sure that the reason for this was that 'Doris' rooted more easily from cuttings than 'Lancing Supreme'. Many of the Imperial pinks and Herbert's pinks are no longer grown. Allwoods pinks have also declined in popularity, but not to the same extent.

DOUGLAS PINKS

Douglas pinks, produced by James Douglas around 1930, were laced pinks of the old florists' type. 'Daisy' was pink with blood-red center; 'May Blossom', shell-pink with crimson center; 'Mohican' was of deep salmon-red, laced crimson; and 'Selma' was red with maroon center and laced crimson. A whole series of Douglas pinks was named after wild birds, such as 'Chaffinch' and 'Wagtail', but I believe all have now disappeared.

DIANTHUS WINTERII

The species of pinks known as *Dianthus winterii* was bred by Sydney Morris of Norwich, who died before seeing the results. Gordon Winter of Wramplingham continued the work, and the first named cultivars were introduced by Gibson and Amos of Cranleigh, Surrey. Some were 'Henry Back' and 'Mrs. Back', 'Betty Norton' and 'Cherry Norton', and 'Norah'. I believe 'Betty Norton' (c. 1929), deep rose with maroon center, to be the sole survivor; this cultivar has been misprinted as 'Betty Morton'.

HIGHLAND PINKS

A large number of pinks hybridized by P. S. Hayward of Clacton-on-Sea was introduced in the 1930s, all with the prefix "Highland" and mostly of the alpine type. Of these, plants of 'Highland Fraser' are still available, as are seeds of this group, bearing the name Highland Hybrids (Plate 22).

MODERN LACED PINKS

In about 1950 the laced pinks, those with a central eye and lacing around the petals, were still grown for garden display and use on the show bench. But these were mainly the older cultivars, which had one short flowering period. The Allwoods produced a few using their *Dianthus allwoodii* cultivars, which were longer-flowering and generally more floriferous. A London barrister, F. R. McQuown, took up breeding laced pinks as a hobby and some of his cultivars were introduced by Allwood Bros. with the prefix "London." Some of these are 'London Brocade', pink, laced purple; 'London Delight', pink, laced purple, semi-double; 'London Lovely', white, laced crimson, semi-double; and 'London Poppet', pink, laced ruby-red. I consider 'London Brocade' to be his best cultivar, and since no one seemed anxious to introduce it commercially I did so myself. It went on to obtain a First Class Certificate after trial at Wisley.

I began breeding seedlings from the old fragrant white self 'Mrs. Sinkins' starting in the 1950s. Next I tried crossing rock garden pinks, and I succeeded in producing many pretty little plants, but achieved nothing spectacular. However, to my surprise, I found among the rock garden plant seedlings a semi-double, white-ground laced pink, eventually listed by Steven Bailey and named 'Truth'. I selfed this plant, impregnated it with its own pollen, and obtained a good number of pinks of all shapes and sizes. One stood out from all others: a profusely petalled laced pink, pure white with deeply fringed petals having lacing of the same crimson-purple color as its parent. It was of compact habit with short stiff stems, very vigorous, and it invariably burst its calyx. Its petals hung together well, however; the flower did not blow as 'Mrs. Sinkins' does. And its scent was as good as, in fact I would say stronger than that of 'Mrs. Sinkins'. This arrangement of the petals and their bold lacing meant it just had to be named 'Can-Can'. It propagated easily and so became quite popular. When it was about ten years old we moved house and nursery; it was mid-winter, and the severe weather denied us the pleasure of moving our plants in the leisurely manner we had intended. We never did find our stock plants of 'Can-Can', and our efforts to locate a few from friends proved unsuccessful. Some years later the Patron of the British National Carnation Society, The Marchioness of Salisbury, kindly allowed us to search her *Dianthus* gardens at Cranborne, Dorset, but to no avail. 'Can-Can' had disappeared without trace.

After many years of concentrating on breeding border carnations I again turned to laced pinks, and I selfed 'London Brocade' to obtain seeds. The progeny was very mixed, nothing exciting, and I crossed the siblings year after year, always with very mixed results. Often I would sow all the seeds of one pod from a selected seedling and plant them in one bed so that they could then become open-pollinated, just as the old florists did before planned crossing was understood. In 1984 I found a flowering seedling I liked, two, in fact, in the same bed that were almost identical. I kept them, and the cuttings taken from them, separate from each other. I kept a main stock of one and named it 'Becky Robinson'—after the daughter of a young friend, a little tot of three years who set her cap at me with great determination. 'Becky Robinson' obtained highest honors at the Royal Horticultural Society Wisley trials and excelled on the show bench; in fact, it was exhibited nation-wide on more occasions than all other cultivars in its category put together.

The unnamed identical twin cultivar of 'Becky Robinson' was not distributed in Britain, but it was not denied its share of glory. My younger daughter, Helena Hitchcock, who was a landscape gardener and designer in Kelowna, British Columbia, Canada, was on the committee of a local Heritage Conservation movement, which sought to preserve early Canadian buildings and gardens. Close to her home was a ranch named Guisachan situated near Lake Okanagan in the Okanagan Valley. The ranch was owned by Lord and Lady Aberdeen around the turn of the century. In 1988 the restored Guisachan property was to be opened as a Heritage Park, and my daughter Helena was commissioned to re-create the flower gardens, which had been quite famous in their day. The present Lady Aberdeen had been invited to conduct the opening ceremony, and Helena thought it would be a nice touch if some well-known rose specialist could be persuaded to name a new rose after Lady Aberdeen. I thought it likely that one might jump at the suggestion, but it was not to be—the firm I approached wanted thousands of pounds. What about the Douglas carnation 'Guisachan' then? I explained that this cultivar had long since been laid to rest. Well, how about a nice new laced pink like 'Becky Robinson'. I did have just such a pink, too much like 'Becky Robinson' to be introduced in England, and promised to export some plants as soon as possible. I posted a dozen rooted cuttings and a score of unrooted ones, labelled 'Lady Aberdeen', to a well-known Kelowna nursery. When these bloomed the nursery was delighted at the flowers' clear markings and strong scent. I understood the intent was to not only grow these in the Guisachan garden but also eventually to sell plants in aid of the Guisachan Park Heritage scheme. I learned later that plants were selling like hot cakes. Lord Aberdeen, who with his wife had officiated at the Guisachan Park opening ceremony, asked me to supply him with flowers of 'Lady Aberdeen' because, as a professional botanical artist, he had been asked to design a commemorative plate that was also to be sold in aid of the Heritage scheme.

Another of my seedlings bred from 'Becky Robinson' and therefore closely related to 'Lady Aberdeen' is now portrayed in an even more famous commemorative plate. In autumn 1992 the honorary secretary of the British National Carnation Society told me of a lady artist who was seeking a *Dianthus* having a name with royal or coronation connections. The artist, Margaret Stevens, Fellow of the Society of Botanical Artists, told me it was for her design for the Royal Horticultural Society 1993 Chelsea Plate, the subject of which was to be a Coronation Bouquet commemorating the Queen's forty-year reign. I could find no existing *Dianthus* with such a name, but I sent Margaret Stevens a photograph of my newest laced pink seedling, saying if she liked it she could use it and name it herself. So it became 'Coronation Ruby', plants of which were graciously accepted by Her Majesty The Queen for her silver border in Buckingham Palace gardens.

CASTLEROYAL LACED PINKS

The Castleroyal laced pinks were a group of fine laced pinks produced by John Douglas of Wokingham between 1967 and 1975, and they won him many prizes at the British National Carnation Society national shows during that period. 'Castleroyal Emperor', white laced velvet-crimson, and 'Castleroyal Sceptre', white-ground laced red, were his most successful cultivars. Mostly they were rather leggy, producing few sideshoots, and so were not easy to propagate. They are seldom seen nowadays.

WYATT'S PINKS

Some very fine garden pinks bred by Cecil Wyatt since the 1970s have been introduced by David Hitchcock of Three Counties Nurseries, Bridport, Dorset. This firm is noted for its splendid Gold Medal exhibits of pinks at the Chelsea Flower Show and many others throughout Britain. Some of the best Wyatt cultivars include 'Haytor White', a white self; 'Jenny Wyatt', shell-pink; 'Monica Wyatt', pink with magenta eye; and 'Valda Wyatt', lavender with deeper center. All these cultivars are excellent for exhibiting at flower shows as well as being very good garden plants.

STEVEN BAILEY PINKS

In the 1980s Steven Bailey, founder of the well-known specialist perpetual-flowering carnation firm bearing his name, commenced hybridizing pinks with the objective of producing short compact plants excellent for garden decoration. The firm's Gold Medal trade exhibits can be seen at the Royal Horticultural Society Chelsea Flower Show and at numerous other large shows throughout Britain. Currently available cultivars include 'Nan Bailey', white self; 'Dad's Choice', white with a claret center; 'Sway Candy', pink, heavily striped rose-magenta; 'Sway Gem', crimson self; 'Sway Mist', lilac-pink with mauve eye; and 'Sway Pearl', white self. The nursery, based at Sway, Hampshire, and now in the capable hands of Steven's son, Stef Bailey, also supplies other nurseries and garden centers in addition to their own retail trade.

H. R. WHETMAN PINKS

The pinks of H. R. Whetman are among the most recent introductions and may be purchased from many garden centers. Mainly of the long-stemmed cut-flower type, cultivars may be seen at the Royal Horticultural Society Wisley Trial Gardens, where a number have received the RHS Award of Garden Merit AGM(H4)—H4 indicates that the plants are completely hardy (see Chapter 13). These include 'Devon Dove', white, semi-double; 'Devon Glow', magenta; 'Devon Maid', white with magenta eye; and 'Devon Wizard', rich cyclamen-purple with ruby-red center.

The firm of H. R. Whetman and Son has been growing pinks for the past fifty years, and it was largely responsible for developing pinks as a cut-flower crop under glass, and later polyethylene tunnels, in Devon in the late 1960s, a trade that has since spread steadily throughout the United Kingdom. The mother-plants are grown in insect-proof houses by the Nuclear Stock Association at Littlehampton, Sussex, which ensures that the stock is free of both viral and wilt diseases.

WHATFIELD PINKS

Whatfield pinks are a group of free-flowering dwarf pinks suitable for rock garden use, produced by Mrs. Joan Schofield since 1959 by hybridizing alpine plants with *Dianthus deltoides*, *D. neglectus*, and *D. erinaceus*. A dozen cultivars were listed in the fifth supplement to the *In-*

ternational Dianthus Register, many of which are commercially available, all bearing the prefix "Whatfield." It is proposed that a trial of these should be held at the Wisley garden in the near future to assess their suitability for the coveted AGM(H4).

SUCCESSFUL AMATEUR BREEDERS AND EXHIBITORS

Several keen amateurs have taken up the exciting hobby of breeding new cultivars, many of which have been grown in the Wisley trials and have received the AGM award. Jack Radcliffe, of Romford, has four to his credit: 'Louise's Choice', 'Marg's Choice', 'Rhian's Choice', and 'Sheila's Choice'. These are all also prize-winning cultivars. Syd Hall, of Nottinghamshire, is another prolific breeder and successful exhibitor of new cultivars of pinks, all of which have the prefix "Oakwood." Gerald Kiddy, a retired farmer from Ipswich, has introduced several cultivars with the "Suffolk" prefix, including the prize-winning 'Suffolk Pride', rose-pink with a darker eye, and the pink self 'Suffolk Summer', which received the AGM(H4) award at Wisley. Commercially available plants of these and of other breeders can be found in the list of pinks cultivars in Chapter 4.

Some Pinks of Doubtful Origin

Many of the old pinks previously mentioned are no longer obtainable. Some are listed in catalogues, but not all can be guaranteed to be genuinely old. Researching their origin can be a fascinating journey, as I discovered when starting on that trail. Interest became intrigue as one clue led to another or sometimes came mysteriously to a dead end, making it difficult to sort fact from fiction. I remember George Allwood telling me how he had advertised for propagating material of the true 'Mrs. Sinkins', and of the fifty samples received no two were alike. I grew 'Mrs. Sinkins' over forty years ago when I lived at Hampton Hill, and large quantities were grown then around the Feltham and Hampton areas of Middlesex for sale at Brentford Market. I assumed mine to be of the original clone. When I bred seedlings from 'Mrs. Sinkins' I found some had a small bright crimson eye. The late Charles Cox, a friend and carnation enthusiast, knew Mrs. Sinkins's son Frank very well, and he and Arthur Turner, son of the famous nurseryman of Slough who introduced 'Mrs. Sinkins', told Charles most of its history, which included the fact that 'Mrs. Sinkins' used to have a lovely splash of crimson on the fringed petals but which disappeared in later years. This information appeared in a letter to *The Times* nearly seventy years ago. I have a book about a hundred years old in which appears a sepia photograph captioned "Border Pink Mrs. Sinkins," and the contrasting eye on the pictured flower is quite distinct. Any white pink that had scent and split the calyx would be sold as 'Mrs. Sinkins', just as any crimson carnation with a scent would be sold as 'Old Crimson Clove'. I have seen flowers with the latter name on trade stands, ranging in size from garden pinks to full-blown perpetual-flowering carnations. 'Crimson Clove', a semi-double carnation, originated in England and was lost to cultivation until reintroduced from Holland early in the seventeenth century. I have known traders' stands where flowers of laced cultivars like 'Paisley Gem', 'Dad's Favourite', and others were totally different from those on neighboring stands. 'Casser's Pink' is sometimes shown with a pale washed-out pink color, nothing like the original bright rich red self plant introduced and sent to Wisley by R. S. Oatley. I used to visit Oatley's nursery at Wallington, Surrey, to buy plants of it. Oatley would give my young schoolgirl daughters small flowering pots of *Kalanchoe*. I remember him telling me there were white and pink forms of 'Casser's Pink' and that they all originated in Germany.

I have seen 'Paddington' and 'Sam Barlow' at shows recently and these appeared to be genuine to me. But I have doubts about 'Paisley Gem'. The chronicle of the development of these doubts is something of a horticultural detective story, and it may not be out of place here. I have endeavored to present the facts in this chronicle as they have come to me, as objectively as possible. It is for the reader to decide if my doubts are reasonable or not.

'PAISLEY GEM'

It has been written that the Paisley growers exhibited only in the Paisley area of Scotland; Sacheverell Sitwell wrote of the Paisley pinks in his 1939 work *Old-fashioned Flowers*, stating that not a drawing is left of these. It is also written of the legendary exhibits of these laced pinks that they were never named and no records kept of the show results. The exhibitors of Paisley, so the story goes, grew their plants only from seeds and did not propagate them from cuttings or layers. Did the Paisley enthusiasts find their plants difficult to propagate, or were they just miffy? The first *International Dianthus Register* (1974) describes 'Paisley Gem' only as dark red, a self, and the British National Carnation Society *Pinks Register* (1953) does not include it at all. This seems strange when one considers that the chief compiler, the late F. R. Mc-Quown, specialized in breeding and exhibiting laced pinks and wrote about them extensively. C. Oscar Moreton, in his book *Old Carnations and Pinks* (1955), states that 'Paisley Gem' was raised before 1798 by a John Macree of Longniddry and had grown in the garden of Macree's great-grandson ever since. He writes that George M. Taylor of Long-niddry had rescued about a dozen varieties of Paisley origin, and that 'Paisley Gem' was another of Taylor's finds. But an article by David Stuart that appeared in *The Garden*, journal of the Royal Horticultural Society, in January 1985, entitled "Was There a Paisley Pink?", is very convincing. Stuart says that his own garden is quite near Longniddry and that he hoped to find there some of the Paisley pinks collected by Taylor. Having tried, and found the garden "empty," he says he now wonders whether there was a distinctive Paisley pink at all and questions whether today's 'Paisley Gem' is actually old, because eighteenth-century laced pinks had fringed petals, and pinks with smooth-edged petals did not appear until about 1830.

An article published in 1842 defines the differences between northern and southern types of laced pinks; David Stuart says 'Paisley Gem' is clearly a northern type of pink, but after a reasonably thorough search of the period (in Scottish periodicals) he had "not come across any suggestion that there was a particularly Scottish sort of pink, let alone one emanating from Paisley." David Stuart says the story of the Paisley pink seems to have originated with the Rev. Ferrier, a writer who was said to have been President of the Paisley Florists Society, which might suggest a reason for his undue enthusiasm for local flowers. Stuart says the Society still exists (though its members are now more interested in vegetables) but has lost its late-eighteenth- and early-nineteenth-century records. Stuart also quotes that great florist James (George) Lightbody, of nearby Falkirk, who wrote in 1853 to the *Scottish Florists and Horticultural Journal* to say that there was no "Scottish achievement with Seedling Pinks." David Stuart writes, "Taylor himself had published several books on old plants and seems to have been remarkably successful in finding old plants (including amusing things like a double martagon lily, a double black pansy and so on)." An auricula-enthusiast friend wrote wondering if the above appeared to suggest that G. M. Taylor had been something of a horticultural fraudster; however, he also very kindly sent me a copy of Taylor's obituary published in the *Gardener's Chronicle*, 15 January 1955. It referred to Taylor's vast knowledge of horticultural matters and the great respect accorded him by a very wide circle of friends. Especially appreciated by American readers was his book *The Little Garden*. The obituary continues,

> Always an able apostle of the ability of our forebears to grow good flowers, he waxed particularly enthusiastic with historical groups of amateurs, such as the Paisley Weavers, whose interest and ability to breed new Auriculas, Pinks and Tulips captivated his mind. He endeavoured to follow them and produced some very fine plants. He became a crusader in his search for valuable plants which were lost to cultivation and succeeded in finding not a few, in which achievement he took a pardonable pride. A zealous exponent of truth, ever watchful that correct information was given, he lived a valiant life never failing to speak his mind in any company. He was an individualist who could show by his pen what can be accomplished by one entirely fearless, sure he could face any criticism by reason of his immense store of information.

Taylor seems to have been a most formidable character; obviously there had been criticism of him at times. He was proud of having found many lost plants (as was C. Oscar Moreton, who also found lost plants). In an article contributed to *The Gardener's Album* in 1954, the year of his death, Taylor wrote that the Paisley weavers sent to London for seeds of pinks in favor there.

The plants raised from seed produced amongst others laced pinks and the cultivation of these was entered upon with the characteristic enthusiasm of the artisans. This was attended with such success that the cultivars were soon distributed all over the country, and they were recognised to be better than all others.

Taylor repeated, "The laced pinks of the weavers of Paisley were reckoned to be the finest in cultivation at that time." And yet no surviving illustrations, records of names, or show results have ever been found. In the same article Taylor wrote of laced pinks, "one or two plants were discovered in old gardens, and working upon these a new race has now been evolved equal in every respect to the grand old pinks of the weavers." This is accompanied by a photograph of a pink that Taylor describes as,

> A fine example of such a pink, and it was raised in my garden— after ten years of breeding—from plants actually grown at Paisley. It was one of many, and there will soon be a fine new strain of these beautiful things.

No mention here of his having rediscovered 'Paisley Gem', nor of his having "rescued about a dozen cultivars of Paisley origin," as Moreton's book would have us believe. The British National Carnation Society's historians, Audrey Robinson and Syd Wilson, say Moreton's book is the only known reference to the name of the 'Paisley Gem' discoverer. My auricula-enthusiast friend points out that since no names, illustrations, or show results of Paisley pinks had been found before Moreton's book was published, how could anyone have discovered an old cultivar named 'Paisley Gem'?

To return to the article in *The Garden* in 1985, David Stuart mentions an elderly lady friend of Taylor who had contacted him and who knew all about Taylor's pinks. She said there were lots of Paisley pinks, 'Paisley Gem', 'Paisley Weaver', 'Paisley Delight', 'Evelyn Taylor', and more, and that "they all came from the same pod"; also that she hadn't had room for them recently and had given them to a friend, but her friend lost them all the following winter.

Summarizing the evidence, George Taylor wrote that one or two plants were discovered in old gardens, and from his ten year's work on them in his own garden there had evolved a new race equal in every respect to the grand old pinks of the Paisley weavers. He had named them all, including 'Paisley Gem', with the prefix "Paisley," except for

'Evelyn Taylor', which was surely named after a relative of his. And all this in the twentieth century, possibly mid-century, which would not have interested Oscar Moreton, who was obsessed with *old* plants. I knew him, we swapped plants and met a few times at the famous Douglas nursery at Great Bookham.

Moreton wrote that the cultivar is "the most perfect example of a laced pink that I have ever seen." Yet in the past three years, during which a total of 250 stems of white-ground laced pinks were successfully exhibited at carnation shows all over the country, only one of these was named 'Paisley Gem'. It cannot be said that it is difficult to obtain plants of this name, for no fewer than six reputable nurseries list it, possibly more. Either 'Paisley Gem' has deteriorated beyond recognition or the plants available nowadays are not of the original cultivar. There are doubts that 'Paisley Gem' originated before 1830, at which time there were two different types of laced pinks. The southern type had far fewer petals than the northern type, so displayed the contrasting eye and lacing to better advantage than did the high-domed, very double northern type. Southerners called the northern pinks "mops," while northerners referred to southern pinks as being merely semi-double. The photograph of G. M. Taylor's laced pink that accompanied his article published in 1954 shows it to be of the northern type, very full-petalled. The petal edges are notched, as is the pattern of the lacing, and the flowers would stand little chance of winning a prize in a modern carnation show. Yet Taylor considered it "a fine example" and promised there would "soon be a fine new strain of these beautiful things." Since his 'Paisley Gem' was one of these "beautiful things," one must consider it was of the same type, full-petalled with notched edges, and therefore bearing no resemblance whatever to the painting in Moreton's book, which is clearly a southern type of laced pink. So what is, or was, the pink in the book? My guess is that it is not old at all.

I sought the assistance of my friend Syd Wilson of Newcastle-on-Tyne, historian to the British National Carnation Society, whose assistance is also acknowledged in the *International Dianthus Register*. Moreton's book says his list of some 250 cultivars therein was taken from lists of about 1819 onwards, yet 'Paisley Gem' is not included in those lists. Moreton names all the books he consulted, yet he is the only one to have written about 'Paisley Gem', and he failed to give any reference. Syd Wilson spent a day and a half ploughing through old catalogues to no avail. 'Paisley Gem' was not listed by Turner or by Thomas Ware between 1840 and 1880. It was not listed by Thomas Hogg, nor by Cutbush, Campbell, Thyne, Forbes, or any Scottish or Irish grower of the period. Nor was it mentioned in the *Account of Flower Shews* of 1826 for Oxford, Chelmsford, Cheshire, Lancashire, and Yorkshire; these lists of show cultivars name the first eight exhibits in order of merit in each class. The earliest catalogue Syd Wilson found to contain 'Paisley Gem' is that of Ramparts Nurseries in 1982; yet this cultivar, "the most perfect example of a laced pink" Moreton had ever seen, had been in Moreton's possession since before 1955 when his book *Old Carnations and Pinks* was published. Surely some enterprising trader would have snapped it up long before 27 years had elapsed. One now wonders whether Moreton's 'Paisley Gem' and Ramparts' version were one and the same cultivar. My own plants labelled 'Paisley Gem' purchased a few years ago are identical to those labelled 'William Brownhill' bought at the same time, and they do not resemble either picture of these cultivars in Moreton's book.

'MUSGRAVE'S PINK'

'Musgrave's Pink' is recorded in the first *International Dianthus Register*, with 'Green Eyes', 'Musgrave', 'Charles Musgrave', and 'C. T. Musgrave' as synonyms. It is listed as a white self, single with a green center, and raised by Charles T. Musgrave in 1936 with an Award of Merit as a garden plant in 1946. 'Musgrave's Pink' was introduced commercially by George Allwood, who wrote that he found it in a Henfield, Sussex, private garden and was told it had been presented to the owner of the garden by Mr. Musgrave who raised it, and "We named it 'Musgrave's Pink' when we distributed the stock." Will Ingwersen (1949) wrote, "We owe the present abundance of it in gardens to the great gardener whose name it at present bears." Also, "Mr. Musgrave VMH has propagated and distributed it to such good purpose during the past ten or twelve years that it is now firmly established in cultivation." C. Oscar Moreton wrote, "Though apparently a seedling it must have been a reversion to a much older strain, for paintings as early as 1730 show a flower almost identical." Although he conceded it was "apparently a seedling" and only "almost identical" to flowers in some old paintings, this was sufficient for the second edition of the *International Dianthus Register* to record its date of raising as c. 1730 and for Charles T. Musgrave's name as raiser to be omitted. Hundreds of "almost identical" paintings of the *Mona Lisa* are in existence, and more in course of production, but all are distinct and not interchangeable.

'DELMONDEN FAIRY'

The story with 'Delmonden Fairy' is similar to that of 'Musgrave's Pink'. The first edition of the *International Dianthus Register* indicates Dr. D. M. Amsler of Hawkhurst, Kent, to be the raiser of this cultivar in 1945. According to C. Oscar Moreton, it

> was found growing in the garden of an old manor house at Delmonden, Kent. It might almost be mistaken for 'Bridesmaid' except that the flower is a little smaller. It is almost certainly of ancient origin and is very similar to the description of a pink raised by a Kentish gentleman about 1750. (Moreton 1955)

"Almost certainly" and "very similar to the description of" are hardly conclusive proof. What a coincidence that 'Delmonden Fairy' is stated in the first edition of the *International Dianthus Register* to have been raised by Dr. Amsler (a Kentish gentleman) but is then supposed by Moreton to have been raised by another Kentish gentleman two hundred years earlier. On the strength of Moreton's supposition the entry in the second edition of the *Register* states the date of raising as c. 1750.

That it might almost be "mistaken" for 'Bridesmaid' is a more useful clue to its origin. Herbert's 'Bridesmaid' had the largest flower (6 cm [2.5 in] diameter) of all his cultivars, which are similar in that most have a pink ground color and a scarlet or crimson central eye. This leads to an interesting fact: the entry for 'Delmonden Fairy' in the British National Carnation Society's *Pinks Register* (1953) states, "Shown 1945 by Dr. D. M. Amsler, Hawkhurst, Kent. Very similar to 'Mrs. Gifford Woolley' which see." This is the only entry in that Register (except where a cultivar is a synonym or belongs to a species or group) in which the flower's description is not included, but the reader referred to the entry of a different cultivar. Obviously the compilers were saying 'Delmonden Fairy' is 'Mrs. Gifford Woolley' (which is a Herbert's pink and similar to 'Bridesmaid'). This is a far more plausible supposition than Moreton's "old cultivar raised by a Kentish gentleman about 1750." Incidentally, 'Mrs. Gifford Woolley' is to be found in both RHS Registers as 'Mrs. Clifford Woolley'.

HERBERT'S PINKS

The pinks bred by C. H. Herbert, sometimes called *Dianthus herbertii*, were considered to be the finest of all, with large, perfectly formed flowers. They were propagated more successfully by layering than by taking cuttings. This led some people to suggest that border carnations had been used in their breeding, which Herbert consistently denied. I remember the rumors that people had seen pinks at Herbert's nursery growing 4 feet (1.2 m) tall and had concluded that perpetual-flowering carnations had been used in their breeding. I have never had greenhouse-grown border carnations grow to a height of 4 feet. Writing of laced pinks in 1926 (and printed in the National Carnation and Picotee Society *Annual* of 1930) Herbert stated,

This gradual development has been brought into existence by the care and devotion of the old florists. These men set up a standard of excellence as a guide for the raisers and exhibitors which brought into cultivation the more beautiful laced flowers. These men loved the flowers they cultivated. Some are disposed to smile at the whims and fancies of these men, whose ideals were the perfection of the flowers they grew. They worked till they made the pink a flower of high standard, conforming to the rules laid down for its improvement.

Writing to James L. Gibson, carnation specialist and writer, Herbert said,

When I started fertilising pinks . . . I only had two plants in 5-inch pots. These were the florists' laced type, one purple-edged and the other red. After crossing these I got enough seed to make a small bed, and when the seedlings flowered, there were some very fine sorts. One came quite distinct from any of the others, having very strong stems, the flowers of a rosy-purple color with a darker base. This I named 'Progress'. One day when looking over some plants of 'Progress' I saw a flower flaked with another color, which gave me the idea of trying to get different shades. I fertilised that flower with its own pollen and got a few seeds, but when the seedlings bloomed, I got a breakaway in color from the parent, and then used the pollen from the seedlings on the parent again. This gave me the start of my varieties, and of course I keep on getting new seedlings every year, but it is most difficult to obtain seeds from these varieties. I have quite a new feature coming along. This is pink with red lacing and very stiff stems, producing from ten to fifteen flowers on each stem. I think this will introduce quite a new type, and am sending you a photo of my first one. I have christened it 'Unique'.

P.S. All my pinks are pure, with no other pollen has been used. If any other was used, such as carnations, we should no doubt lose the delightful fragrance, which I consider one of the greatest charms of the pink, which is hardly surpassed by any other flower. All the varieties are quite hardy, good growers and free-flowering. I have them in flower from May until the autumn. Buds formed late in the year often live through the winter and open in the spring. (Gibson 1949)

Nearly half a century later the doubts persisted. In a letter dated February 1975 that appeared in an article in the 1991 British National Carnation Society *Year Book*, Charles Fielder wrote,

I well remember speaking to the late C. H. Herbert at a National Carnation and Picotee Society summer show in the late twenties on the very subject, he then did assure me no border carnation was ever used in his crosses. I believe him, none was used intentionally. However, I personally do think border pollen carried by bees, insects or even wind, naturally got into the strain.

Jack Waldron worked at Allwoods and went to Birmingham on his firm's behalf to obtain plants from Herbert for crossing with Allwoods' plants. In a letter from February 1975 and quoted in the same 1991 *Year Book*, Waldron stated that he was "told by Mr. Herbert that he used border pollen on his pinks and one of the varieties he used was 'Butterfly' which he raised himself and was like a small 'Harmony'."

F. R. McQuown provided some defense of Herbert's pinks.

Modern experts often believe that Herbert's Pinks arose from a cross with a border carnation, but those who knew Mr. Herbert say that he was a truthful man and always denied this, asserting that they came purely from the old laced pinks. I personally think that Mr. Herbert revived by selection the border carnation habit which had probably been bred into pinks from border carnations about a century before. Though now unimportant, this group is mentioned because it has played a decisive part in producing the modern exhibition pinks. (McQuown 1955)

Herbert himself wrote, "I was personally congratulated by their Majesties the King and Queen for my exhibit of pinks at the Royal Horticultural Society's show at Chelsea on May 24th 1921."

In an article entitled "Stray Notes" written for the British National Carnation Society 1988 *Year Book*, I stated,

That fine Scottish carnation grower Robert Kennedy, whom I knew briefly and for whom I have great respect, described C. H. Herbert as the epitome of all that was gentle and gentlemanly and says "There never moved among flowers a more gracious and courteous spirit than the late C. H. Herbert."

FURTHER DOUBTS

An article in the *Hardy Border Carnation Annual 1948* states that 'Fenbow's Clove', the nutmeg clove carnation, "originally planted in 1652 by an ancestor of the present owner Colonel Fenbow, was discovered last year." I am puzzled by this gap of three centuries; carnations have but one main stem and one single root system. Did no one propagate it? A rooted cutting or layer can develop into a 50-cm (20-in) diameter plant in two years. In three hundred years, at the same rate of growth, a plant would measure about 9 meters (30 feet) across. One would not need to discover it, one would trip over it. Perhaps the answer is seen in a book by Sophie Hughes, a national collection holder of old *Dianthus*, wherein a charming picture of a vase of *Dianthus* is captioned, "A few named varieties in your garden will give rise to many self-sown progeny like these."

The article goes on to state that a number of old pinks still awaits discovery "where the very old plants have been allowed to remain century after century undisturbed." I cannot believe this; I planted a seedling, a vigorous, short-growing laced pink, now grown in many countries, and apart from taking a few cuttings in its first year, left it to grow undisturbed. After ten years the flowers, stems, and foliage had deteriorated to such an extent that the plant just had to be pulled out. Oscar Moreton reminds his readers that in 1820 Thomas Hogg advised that pinks should never be suffered to remain longer than two years in the same spot and ground, without either change of soil or situation; yet Moreton contradicts this by saying, "Hence it (the pink) has lingered on undisturbed in cottage and farmhouse gardens so that many old cultivars have come down to us today." He continues,

> One of the objects of this book is to encourage others to join in the interesting and exciting search for hitherto lost cultivars. This is a fascinating pursuit, but it does of course need some knowledge of the older forms and familiarity with illustrations and paintings of the last three centuries.

Imagine self-appointed authenticators let loose on modern cultivars of popular garden plants. Consider how many roses, chrysanthemums, dahlias, lupins, delphiniums, daffodils, etc., they would find to be "almost identical," "almost certainly," "very similar to the description of," "appears to resemble closely," "believe this to be identical," "has all the appearance of," "it may well be," and so on. Plant registers and plant lists would all be altered to include the new, much older dates of raising, introduction, and more. Imagine the breeder of a splendid new cultivar being told he is not the originator because his plant was raised a couple of hundred years earlier.

As an example, some of my own laced pinks have recently been planted in two crematoriums, where they will remain, possibly undisturbed, for some years, and most probably also spread seed. Germinated plants of these could range from single five-petalled to semi-double or double flowers. Colors could vary from different shades of pink, to white with a central eye or zone, to beautifully marked laced types. From my own experience, these could very well resemble pinks of an earlier century. In years to come, someone could chance upon them, compare them with photographs in old books, and decide they have found one of the pinks of a bygone age.

At this stage I wish to quote the following words from a writer who feared his criticism might be seen as "invective."

> There are basically two kinds of journalism. Investigative journalism, an American invention, starts with the *a priori* assumption that a given group of people are corrupt and sets out to prove it. The other kind, arising from a much older tradition of English writing, is campaigning journalism, whereby through the written word you campaign for a situation to change.

With respect to my American friends, I hope this discussion will be taken as an example of the latter and not the former!

I am concerned because some plant traders latch on to the trend and present their plants as antiques. A recent catalogue lists 'Charles Musgrave', 'Bat's Double Red', 'Dad's Favourite', and 'Inchmery', among others, as "Antiques and Heirlooms." Many keen gardeners carried away by the vogue and catalogue blurb could well be disappointed with the performance of these treasures. I have seen large clumps of old-fashioned pinks bearing only one or two flowers; I find some old cultivars produce very few flowers compared with those of the modern, repeat-flowering type.

Some specialists have used the same name again upon the demise of a well-known cultivar, without seeing anything wrong in the practice. This does confuse matters, even though done without that intention. I remember a summer day many years ago when my wife Eileen and I visited a nursery to see what was new or interesting for an article I was to write. I was impressed by a fine batch of yellow-ground fancy border carnations that I recognized as 'Edenside Fairy', bred by James Douglas. I complimented the grower on their quality and asked how he had managed to grow them with unsplit calyces, the cultivar being notoriously prone to that defect. He let me into a secret, saying that although the flowers were exactly like those of 'Edenside Fairy', except for the calyx, they were in fact not of that cultivar, but a new cultivar of their own. Since 'Edenside Fairy' was such a good seller and no one would believe it was not that cultivar, there seemed no point in giving it another name. The famous garden pink 'Doris' was preceded by another 'Doris', named by the same breeders twenty years earlier. And James Douglas named a pink 'Bridesmaid' even after using Herbert's pink 'Bridesmaid' for breeding. So one can never be sure of names and dates of so-called old cultivars, or even of some not-so-old.

I note that some catalogues list modern repeat-flowering pinks in with the old-fashioned cultivars, describing all as Tudor laced and old-fashioned pinks, and advising these should not be stopped. This is quite wrong; the old-fashioned pinks should not be stopped, but the repeat-flowering type must be stopped to induce a bushy, free-flowering habit of growth. It is therefore wrong to group them together under one heading. I remember a nursery that used to exhibit at flower shows the Show pinks raised by Allwood Brothers, which all had the prefix "Show," such as 'Show Achievement', 'Show Ideal', 'Show Pearl', and 'Show Portrait'. Since some gardeners refuse adamantly to have anything whatever to do with exhibiting, the nursery staged the blooms on their trade exhibits with very short stems and actually omitted the prefix "Show" on their labels and in their catalogues. The names became simply 'Achievement', 'Ideal', 'Pearl', and 'Portrait'. I do not imply that all traders are rogues; most are honest, hardworking, and completely trustworthy. But growing and selling plants is a highly competitive business, as I learned from nearly fifty year's experience, and advertising must be persuasive to be effective.

National Council for the Conservation of Plants and Gardens

A group of *Dianthus* experts met on 7 June 1993 to attempt to authenticate a number of old cultivars. Graham Pattison was in charge of the proceedings, held in truly delightful surroundings at the garden of National Dianthus Collection Holder Sarah Franklyn's home by the River Thames at Richmond Green in Surrey. Those present, apart from Eileen and myself, included Dr. Alan Leslie, Registrar for the *International Dianthus Register*, Collection Holders J. Marshall, Mrs. S. M. Tracey, and Mrs. Sophie Hughes, author Richard Bird, Arthur and Audrey Robinson, and Fred Smith, representing the British National

Carnation Society, and nursery specialists David Hitchcock and Mark Trenear.

Set out on the lawn under the mighty trees stood a long table covered with jam jars, each containing a few specimen stems of pinks, some fairly modern, others thought to be very old. The guests were seated on garden chairs, mercifully shaded by giant parasols. Sophie Hughes was quite excited by the occasion, comparing it to the "florists' feasts" of a century or two ago. Some experts had illustrated books open and I have to confess my heart sank when I saw Moreton's *Old Carnations and Pinks* about to be used as an authoritative source of reference. Some guests had brought flowers for naming, others had cultivars they hoped were named correctly.

Each specimen from the table was passed around for comment on the correctness or otherwise of the name it bore; some were right, some wrong, and some remained in doubt. A consensus of opinion was sought regarding cultivars thought to be very old, but it was agreed that with some cultivars such a consensus was no guarantee of authenticity. It was felt, however, that, right or wrong, it would be a step forward if nurseries could all agree to sell the same cultivar under one agreed name only. Some specimens of a laced pink said to be 'Dad's Favourite' were of that cultivar, some others were not. I was on safe ground here, having color slides of that cultivar taken a long time ago when flowers of it seen on the various trade exhibits all looked alike. My specimen of 'John Ball' was identical to that brought by a nursery specialist, so he went home happy. Another cultivar that caused much debate was the old favorite 'Mrs. Sinkins'. Many different specimens were passed around, and it was difficult to decide which, if any, was the original. With tongue-in-cheek, I also took a flower of one of our new seedlings that I had intended to discard, but to which my wife Eileen had taken a fancy. It was very similar to the one accepted by all of us as 'Sops-in-Wine' (the double form), and some knowledgeable guests preferred my flower to that of the named cultivar. Is this how some ancient cultivars manage to look so young? I wondered how long it would be before my new seedling became linked with Geoffrey Chaucer. Sophie Hughes laughingly nicknamed it 'Mrs. Galbally's Sops-in-Wine' and it has, I learn, since been catalogued and will be registered under that name. I remember one pathetic little flower being passed around several times without eliciting any comment. When all the other flowers had been paraded the chairman made one last desperate effort to extract some response, asking "What are we to do with this one?" After a brief silence, Audrey Robinson advised "Put it on the compost."

Two weeks later at a Royal Horticultural Society Joint Trials committee meeting at Wisley, both Audrey and I brought up the question of whether the 'Mrs. Sinkins' plants in the trials were genuinely of that cultivar. At the second visit of the committee towards the end of July, when 'Mrs. Sinkins' was still in full bloom a month later than would normally be expected of that cultivar, Audrey proposed, and it was agreed, to obtain plants from other sources for comparison.

I remember we both joked as we laughingly helped each other up the grassy slopes away from the trials field. Sadly, just a few weeks later, Audrey lost her life in a road accident. My wife and I had known her for over thirty years; she was very fond of pinks, old and new, and was most knowledgeable regarding the history of the older cultivars. She wrote reports on shows and trials and, with Syd Wilson, was historian for the British National Carnation Society. Their joint assistance is acknowledged by Dr. Alan Leslie on the first page of the *International Dianthus Register*.

Chapter 4

Pinks Cultivars

Classification of Types and Descriptive Summaries

For the purposes of this list pinks are divided into five groups: old and old-fashioned type pinks, rock garden pinks, laced pinks, exhibition pinks, and garden pinks. Cultivars that have proved especially useful for exhibiting are classified as exhibition pinks. Some laced pinks are also useful for exhibiting. Cultivars classified as garden pinks are those that do not fit into any of the other four categories. All five types make good garden plants.

Most pinks have serrated petals, deeply laciniated on some old cultivars, and so finely serrated on most exhibition cultivars as to be almost smooth-edged. All flowers are double, except where stated otherwise. Many pinks have a sweet perfume. With regard to the appearance, it is not always easy to convey in writing the precise markings on petals or the subtleties of color variations, particularly with some of the older cultivars. Flowers vary from 3.5 to 6 cm (1½ to 2½ in) diameter.

The raiser's name and date of raising or introduction follow the description, taken, wherever possible, from the *International Dianthus Register*. However, it is not possible to guarantee that all dates are strictly accurate. The symbol ® following a cultivar name indicates that it is protected by Plant Breeders' Rights; this subject is fully discussed in Chapter 13, Breeding New Cultivars.

The following list of names is intended to be a guide to the more popular and important cultivars, but is not a comprehensive list of all available, which would be impossible to include in this book. Abbreviations are as follows:

AM(e): Award of Merit exhibition RHS
AM(g): Award of Merit garden RHS
AM(r): Award of Merit rock garden RHS
FCC(e): First Class Certificate exhibition RHS
FCC(g): First Class Certificate garden RHS
FCC(r): First Class Certificate rock garden RHS
AGM(H4): Award of Garden Merit RHS (H4 designation
    not included prior to 1992)

OLD OR OLD-FASHIONED TYPE PINKS

'Allspice'. Very attractive single. Magenta with fringed overlapping petals edged and lightly splashed white. Scented. Compact growth. Believed to be 17th century.

'Bat's Double Red'. Semi-double, with fringed flowers. Strawberry-red with darker marks towards the center. Free-flowering. T. Bat, early 18th century.

'Beauty of Healey'. White with crimson-maroon lacing. Single and double forms exist. Straggly growth, weak stems. Named after a Yorkshire village. W. Grindrod, 19th century.

'Bridal Veil' (Plate 9). White with maroon-crimson eye. Deeply fringed, frilly petals, and burst calyx. Strongly scented. Early-flowering. 17th century.

'Brympton Red' (Plate 10). Single, curved overlapping petals. Deep rose with darker zone and edging. Scented. Pre-1960.

'Casser's Pink'. Dark red self, semi-double. A very free-flowering mule (sterile) pink. Scented. FCC(g) 1955. R. S. Oatley, pre-1952.

'Cockenzie'. Also known as 'Montrose Pink'. Deep pink with deeper center. Heavily fringed petals. Clove-scented. Circa 1720.

'**Constance Finnis**' (Plate 12). Synonymous 'Fair Folly'. Single, white with striking deep rose-purple central bar and lacing, giving appearance of two white eyes on each petal. Scented. Painted lady type. C. S. Finnis, pre-1969.

'**Coste Budde**'. Single, white zoned, laced reddish purple. Scented. Valerie Finnis, 1978.

'**Dad's Favourite**' (Plate 14). White, laced ruby-red. Synonymous 'A. J. MacSelf', named for the man who discovered it growing in an old garden. AM(g) 1949. Said to be a very old cultivar.

'**Earl of Essex**'. Rose-pink, small dark zone, deeply fringed petals. Invariably splits its calyx. Sometimes confused with 'Pink Mrs. Sinkins' and 'Excelsior' in the trade. 19th century.

'**Emil Paré**' (Plate 19). Cluster-heads of double salmon-pink flowers. Long-flowering. Strongly scented. A mule pink. A. Paré, 1840.

'**Inchmery**'. Delicate pale pink self. Long flowering season. Clove-scented. Neat habit. AM(g) 1946. AGM 1962. 18th century.

'**John Ball**'. White, laced purple-violet. Strongly scented. Alan McLean, mid-19th century.

'**Lady Granville**'. Semi-double, white zoned, laced deep red. Large fringed petals. Slightly scented. 1840.

'**Messines Pink**'. Clusters of miniature salmon-pink flowers on short stems with pale green sweet-william foliage. An old mule pink. Raised in France, pre-1933.

'**Mrs. Sinkins**'. White with deeply fringed petals. Very full blowsy appearance, invariably splits its calyx. Very short flowering period. Heavily clove-scented. Many plants offered today under this name may not be the true cultivar. FCC 1880. J. Sinkins, 1868.

'**Musgrave's Pink**'. Single, white with distinct pale green eye. Large, irregularly toothed petals. Scented. Numerous synonyms. AM(g) 1946. C. T. Musgrave, 1936.

'**Old Fringed**'. Single, small pale mauvish pink flowers fading to white with age. Deeply fringed petals. Dainty appearance, slender stems. Very free-flowering. Scented. 17th century.

'**Old Velvet**'. Deep velvety red with narrow pale pink edge. Scented. Old, origin unknown.

'**Paddington**'. Pale rosy pink, deep maroon center, deeply fringed petals. Clove-scented. AM(g) 1946. T. Hogg, 1830.

'Paisley Gem' (Plate 27). White, laced deep purple. Scented. Said to be a very old cultivar (see discussion in Chapter 3).

'Pheasant's Eye'. Small white flower with purple center, deeply fringed. Strongly scented. A number of single and double forms exist with the same name. Pre-1671.

'Pink Mrs. Sinkins'. Large, fringed, heavily scented flowers, which split the calyx. Pale pink sport of 'Mrs. Sinkins'. Also sometimes listed as 'Earl of Essex' and 'Excelsior'. C. Turner, pre-1908.

'Queen of Henri' (Plate 28). Deep rose-pink, heavily laced reddish purple, with two pink splashes on each petal. Long-flowering. Scented. Old-fashioned painted lady type. Modern pink.

'Queen of Sheba'. Single, ivory-white, laced and flaked magenta, with central magenta bar on each petal. Small fringed petals. Scented. Painted lady type. 17th century.

'Rose de Mai'. Lilac-pink. Early- and repeat-flowering. Scented. Plant forms a compact mat but with a tendency to spread. Circa 1820.

'Sam Barlow'. White, zoned deep maroon-purple, fringed petals. Large frilly flowers. Clove-scented. AM(g) 1946. 19th century.

'Ursula le Grove' (Plate 29). Synonymous 'Old Feathered'. Single, deeply fringed white flower with large reddish purple central zone surrounding white throat. Random reddish purple flakes and feathered appearance add further to the distinctiveness of this cultivar. Early 17th century, rediscovered by C. Oscar Moreton and named after his daughter.

'White Ladies'. White self, with serrated petals and split calyx. Sweetly scented. Often confused with 'Mrs. Sinkins'. Old, unknown origin.

'William Brownhill'. White, laced maroon. AM(e) 1950. W. Brownhill, late 18th century.

ROCK GARDEN OR ALPINE PINKS

'Annabelle'. Purplish pink self. Scented. FCC(r) 1971. T. Carlisle, pre-1957.

'Baby Blanket'. Single, bright pink with darker eye. Clove-scented. Sage-green foliage. Registered as 'Far Cry', but renamed 'Baby

Blanket' in the United States. Available also in New Zealand. Keith Hammett, 1987.

'Ben Gascoigne' (Plate 7). Single, deep rose with darker eye, overlapping petals. Excellent shape. Very similar to 'Betty Norton', a *Dianthus winterii* pink. Derek Gascoigne, 1985.

'Berry Burst' (Plate 8). Single flowers of raspberry-pink with splash of red at the center. Sweetly scented. Gary Eichhorn, 1988.

'Betty Norton'. Single, rose with maroon center. Good form. Scented. G. Winter, pre-1929.

'Bombardier'. Bright scarlet-crimson self. Very floriferous. S. T. Byatt, pre-1963.

'Brigadier'. Tyrian-purple self. Long-flowering. AM(r) 1966. S. T. Byatt, pre-1965.

'Elizabeth'. Fuchsine-pink, zoned garnet-lake. Strongly scented. FCC(r) 1960. S. T. Byatt, pre-1955.

'Essex Witch'. Semi-double, fringed petals, pink with darker pink center. Sweetly scented. Pre-1983.

'Fusilier'. Single, rose-red, zoned crimson. Scented. FCC(r) 1967. S. T. Byatt, pre-1955.

'Grenadier'. Dark red with deeper zoning. Clove-scented. FCC(r) 1968. S. T. Byatt, pre-1963.

'Hidcote'. Single, rose-red self. Strongly scented. L. Johnson, pre-1964.

'Highland Fraser'. Single, pale pink, laced and zoned maroon. Scented. P. S. Hayward, circa 1930.

'Inshriach Dazzler'. Single, carmine-pink, with buff reverse on petals. J. Drake, pre-1979.

'Joan's Blood'. Single, deep blood-red, darker center. AGM(H4) 1992. J. Elliott, pre-1975.

'Kesteven Chamonix'. Single, red-purple, laced purple. AM(r) 1973. A. E. Robinson, 1971.

'La Bourboule'. (Frequently mis-spelled La Bourbille.) Tiny pink flowers. Very dwarf habit. Scented. AGM(H4) 1993. Pre-1949.

'Little Jock'. Semi-double, maroon, crimson eye. Scented. AM(r) 1930. J. Gray, pre-1930.

'Mars'. Bright crimson self. Scented. Allwoods, pre-1934.

'Maureen Patricia' (Plate 25). Single, magenta-rose with wide crimson zone and deeply serrated petals. J. Galbally, 1989.

'Nyewood's Cream'. Single, tiny white flowers rising from low-growing hummocks of light green foliage. E. S. Lyttel, pre-1933.

'Oakington'. Purple-pink self. Very free-flowering. Alan Bloom, 1928.

'Pike's Pink'. Pale pink, cerise eye. Scented. FCC(r) 1972. AGM (H4) 1992. J. Pike, pre-1965.

'Spencer Bickham'. Single, large pink flowers with red eye. Dwarf. AM 1906. R. Veitch, circa 1900.

'Spotty'. Also sometimes spelled 'Spottii'. Bright rose-red, edged and spotted silver. Dwarf and long-flowering. Fleming Bros., pre-1984.

'Tiny Rubies'. Small, double rose-red flowers, on 10-cm (4-in) stems. Neat foliage. Pre-1984.

'Waithman's Beauty'. Single, ruby, splashed pink. Scented. Low-growing plant. Also known as the clock-faced pink because of its regular hour-like markings. R. Kaye, pre-1967.

'Whatfield Gem' (Plate 30). Pink, laced maroon. Very compact. Mrs. J. Schofield, 1970.

'Whatfield Joy' (Plate 31). Single, lilac-pink with darker eye. Mrs. J. Schofield, 1967.

'Whatfield Magenta'. Single, magenta self. Scented. Mrs. J. Schofield, 1984.

'Whatfield Ruby'. Single, deep red with darker eye. Long-flowering. Scented. Mrs. J. Schofield, 1984.

LACED PINKS

'Becky Robinson' (Plate 6). Camellia-rose, laced ruby-red. Clove-scented. Excellent form. FCC(e) 1984. FCC(g) 1984. AGM(H4) 1992. J. Galbally, 1982.

'Coronation Ruby' (Plate 13). Persian-rose, heavily laced ruby-red. Clove-scented. AGM(H4) 1994. J. Galbally, 1991.

'Dad's Favourite'. Old laced pink; see under Old or Old-Fashioned Type Pinks.

'Frances Isabel'. Pale rose, laced deep crimson. Scented. Compact growth. AM(g) 1983. AGM(H4) 1994. H. V. Calvert, 1972.

'Gran's Favourite' (Plate 20). White, cerise-pink lacing. Scented.

Compact growth. AM(g) 1982. AGM(H4) 1993. Mrs. D. Underwood, 1966.

'Helena Hitchcock' (Plate 21). Pure white, laced rosy purple. Clove-scented. Slender stems. Good for plantings in wall crevices and hanging baskets. J. Galbally, 1990.

'John Ball'. Old laced pink; see under Old or Old-Fashioned Type Pinks.

'Kaleidoscope'. Semi-double, creamy white with maroon eye and lacing. Sweetly scented. Registered and available in New Zealand as 'Kiwi Magic'. Keith Hammett, 1985.

'Laced Hero'. White, laced purple. Scented. Allwoods, 1947.

'Laced Joy'. Rose-pink, laced crimson. Floriferous. Clove-scented. FCC(g) 1984. Allwoods, 1947.

'Laced Monarch'. Large pink flowers, laced maroon-purple. A strong-growing bushy plant for the garden. AM(g) 1978. Allwoods, 1972.

'Laced Romeo'. Creamy white, laced chestnut-red. Allwoods, 1963.

'London Brocade'. Pink, laced purple. Scented. Neat habit. FCC(g) 1971. F. R. McQuown, pre-1961.

'London Delight'. Pink, laced purple. Scented. AM(g) 1963. F. R. McQuown, pre-1960.

'London Glow'. Dark crimson, laced pale lilac. Strongly scented. AM(g) 1948. F. R. McQuown, pre-1944.

'London Lovely'. Semi-double, white, laced deep red. Scented. F. R. McQuown, 1944.

'London Poppet'. White, flushed pink and laced ruby-red. FCC(g) 1962. F. R. McQuown, 1946.

'Louise's Choice'. Light purple-pink, laced deep purplish red. Scented. AGM(H4) 1994. J. Radcliffe, 1989.

'Paisley Gem'. Old laced pink; see under Old or Old-Fashioned Type Pinks.

'Pink Swirl'. Single, delicate light pink with slightly deeper central eye and edging, giving swirling appearance. Long-flowering. Clove-scented. Available in the United States and New Zealand. Keith Hammett, 1990.

'Prudence'. Pale pink, laced crimson. Scented. FCC(g) 1961. Allwoods, pre-1953.

'**Tamsin**'. Lavender-pink, laced purple. Clove-scented. Petals slightly toothed. Excellent for cutting. AGM(H4) 1994. J. Galbally, 1991.
'**Toledo**'. Deep pink, laced dark crimson. Compact. Good garden cultivar. Roy P. Tolley, 1972.
'**William Brownhill**'. Old laced pink; see under Old or Old-Fashioned Type Pinks.

EXHIBITION PINKS

'**Allen's Ballerina**'. Pure white self. Scented. Compact. D. Thomas, 1984.
'**Becka Falls**'. Scarlet-red self. Clove-scented. Compact. C. Wyatt, 1977.
'**Bovey Belle**'. Deep purple self. Scented. AM(g) 1984. AGM(H4) 1994. C. Wyatt, 1973.
'**Carlotta**'. Claret self. Strongly scented. Not repeat-flowering, so do not stop. C. H. Fielder, 1946.
'**Chetwyn Doris**' (Plate 11). Salmon-pink, flecked and striped ruby. Scented. Sport from 'Doris'. R. and T. Gillies, 1986.
'**Cranmere Pool**'. White, tinged pink, overlaid red. Lightly scented. Dwarf habit. FCC(g) 1987. AGM(H4) 1994. C. Wyatt, 1984.
'**Crimson Ace**'. Crimson self. AM(e) 1967. FCC(g) 1975. C. H. Fielder, 1967.
'**Diane**'. Salmon-pink self. Scented. Sport from 'Doris'. AGM(H4) 1996. Allwoods, 1964.
'**Doris**' (Plate 18). Salmon-pink with scarlet eye. Very free-flowering. Scented. FCC(g) 1956. AGM(H4) 1992. Allwoods, pre-1945.
'**Eileen**'. Single, white, large crimson central zone. Clove-scented. Allwoods, 1927.
'**Haytor White**'. White self. Scented. AM(e) 1980. AM(g) 1982. AGM(H4) 1993. C. Wyatt, 1971.
'**Helen**'. Deep pink self. Scented. Compact growth. FCC(g) 1966. Allwoods, pre-1948.
'**Houndspool Cheryl**'. Light crimson self. Scented. Sport from 'Houndspool Ruby'. AGM(H4) 1994. J. Whetman, 1980.
'**Houndspool Ruby**'. Rose-pink with red center. Scented. Sport from 'Doris'. FCC(g) 1987. AGM(H4) 1992. J. Whetman, 1977.

'**Iceberg**'. White self. Scented. FCC(g) 1956. C. H. Fielder, 1950.

'**Joy**'. Carmine-pink self. Free-flowering. AGM(H4) 1995. Allwoods, pre-1965.

'**Kesteven Kirkstead**' (Plate 23). Single, white with red-purple eye. Scented. AM(e) 1983. FCC(g) 1988. AGM(H4) 1993. A. E. Robinson, 1981.

'**Lincolnshire Poacher**'. Single, lavender-pink with maroon eye. Clove-scented. FCC(g) 1991. AGM(H4) 1992. J. H. T. Pepper, 1982.

'**Marg's Choice**'. Light salmon-pink self. Early and continuous blooming. Excellent for cutting and for exhibition. AGM(H4) 1993. J. Radcliffe, 1989.

'**Monica Wyatt**' (Plate 26). Cyclamen-pink with magenta eye. Very free-flowering. Scented. Compact growth. FCC(g) 1986. AGM (H4) 1992. C. Wyatt, 1981.

'**Oakwood Bill Ballinger**'. Pink ground, streaked red. S. Hall, 1985.

'**Oakwood Billy Boole**'. Pale pink, slightly streaked and heavily ticked salmon-red. Scented. Light green foliage, compact habit. Free-flowering. S. Hall, 1990.

'**Oakwood Erin Mitchell**'. Shapely white self. Petals slightly fimbriated. Scented. S. Hall, 1991.

'**Oakwood Gillian Garforth**'. Clear crimson self. Petals slightly toothed. Free-flowering habit. Strong stems. AGM(H4) 1996. S. Hall, 1992.

'**Oakwood Romance**'. Magenta self. AGM(H4) 1996. S. Hall, 1988.

'**Oakwood Rose Parker**'. Deep pink with maroon eye. Light green foliage and compact habit. Floriferous. S. Hall, 1990.

'**Old Mother Hubbard**'. Pink, flecked deeper pink. Scented. Sport from 'Doris'. FCC(g) 1989. AGM(H4) 1992. R. Hubbard, 1984.

'**Rhian's Choice**'. Rich bright crimson self. Silvery foliage. Very popular with exhibitors. AGM(H4) 1993. J. Radcliffe, 1992.

'**Sheila's Choice**'. Rich deep magenta self. Long strong stems. AGM(H4) 1994. J. Radcliffe, 1992.

'**Show Beauty**'. Deep rose-pink with bold maroon eye. Scented. FCC(g) 1966. Allwoods, pre-1939.

'**Strawberries and Cream**'. Creamy white, splashed with two shades of pink. Scented. Very stiff stems. C. Wyatt, 1984.

'**Valda Wyatt**'. Lavender-pink with deeper center. Scented. Vigorous, compact growth. FCC(g) 1983. AGM(H4) 1992. C. Wyatt, 1977.

'**Zoe's Choice**'. Pink, splashed and boldly striped red. Very attractive flower. AGM(H4) 1996. J. Radcliffe, 1993.

GARDEN PINKS

'**Alice**'. Ivory-white with crimson eye. Scented. FCC(g) 1969. Allwoods, 1930.

'**Allen's Maria**'. Cochineal-pink with paler edging. Lightly scented. Compact habit. D. Thomas, 1986.

'**Anniversary**'. Shell-pink. Compact growth. S. Bailey, 1987.

Bailey's Yellow Delight®. Clear yellow self. The long-awaited color break. Long-lasting cut-flower cultivar. S. Bailey, 1990.

'**Cherryripe**'. Cherry-pink self. FCC(g) 1964. C. H. Fielder, pre-1959.

'**Claret Joy**'. Bright crimson self. Free-flowering. Scented. Sport of 'Joy'. AGM(H4) 1995. D. Thomas, 1985.

'**Constance**'. Pale pink, deep pink central eye. Free-flowering. Lightly scented. FCC(g) 1977. Allwoods, pre-1955.

'**Dad's Choice**'. White with claret eye. Lightly scented. Very compact. S. Bailey, 1989.

'**Daily Mail**'. White with deep maroon eye. Lightly scented. S. Bailey, 1988.

'**David**'. Bright scarlet self. Strong clove-scent. Stout stems. Good cut-flower cultivar. FCC(g) 1979. Allwoods, pre-1970.

'**Denis**'. Very deep pink self. AM(g) 1963. Allwoods, pre-1959.

Devon Cream® (Plate 15). Chrome-yellow with light magenta flecks. A new color break for pinks. H. R. Whetman, 1986.

Devon Dove®. White, green eye, fringed petals. Scented. Compact growth. AGM(H4) 1992. C. Wyatt, 1986.

Devon General®. Deep red self. Long-flowering. AGM(H4) 1996. H. R. Whetman, 1990.

Devon Glow®. Magenta self. Strongly scented. Compact growth. AGM(H4) 1993. H. R. Whetman, 1986.

Devon Maid® (Plate 16). White with magenta eye. Compact habit. AGM(H4) 1993. H. R. Whetman, 1991.

Devon Wizard® (Plate 17). Rich cyclamen-purple with ruby-red center. Strongly clove-scented. AGM(H4) 1995. H. R. Whetman, 1987.

'Freckles'. Dusky salmon-pink, flecked red. Scented. Compact growth. AM(g) 1962. C. H. Fielder, 1934.

'Haytor Rock'. Pale pink, heavily streaked bright red. Scented. AGM(H4) 1995. C. Wyatt, 1979.

'Ian'. Deep crimson self. Free-flowering *Dianthus allwoodii* pink. Allwoods, 1938.

'Jenny Wyatt'. Shell-pink self. Free-flowering. Strongly scented. Tall. C. Wyatt, 1985.

'Letitia Wyatt'. Blush-pink self. Clove-scented. Compact growth. AM(g) 1984. AGM(H4) 1995. C. Wyatt, 1981.

'Little Ben' (Plate 24). Semi-double. White with rich purple edging, wide central zone, and central bar to each petal, resembling a clock face. J. Galbally, 1992.

'Nan Bailey'. White self. Lightly scented. Compact growth. FCC(g) 1989. S. Bailey, 1985.

Pink Monica Wyatt®. Delicate pale pink with scarlet center. Scented. A sport of 'Monica Wyatt'. H. R. Whetman, 1993.

'Rose Joy'. Rich rose self. Free-flowering. Scented. Sport of 'Joy'. AGM(H4) 1994. T. A. Percival, 1983.

'Spot On'. Single, white with distinctive large deep maroon eye. Long-flowering. Available in the United States and New Zealand. Keith Hammett, 1990.

'Susan'. Lavender-pink with purple eye. Scented. Compact growth. An early *Dianthus allwoodii* pink. Allwoods, 1917.

'Sway Belle'. White, overlaid purple. Scented. S. Bailey, 1988.

'Sway Candy'. Pink, heavily striped carmine. S. Bailey, 1988.

'Sway Gem'. Crimson self. Lightly scented. Compact growth. S. Bailey, 1986.

'Sway Mist'. Misty lilac-pink, mauve eye. Lightly scented. Compact growth. S. Bailey, 1987.

'**Sway Pearl**'. Pearly white self. Scented. Short compact growth. S. Bailey, 1991.

'**Thomas**'. Brick-red with dark central eye. Early *Dianthus allwoodii* pink. Allwoods, pre-1931.

'**Widecombe Fair**'. Pastel pink self. Good perfume. Compact habit. Much admired by floral artists. AGM(H4) 1995. C. Wyatt, 1974.

Chapter 5

Border Carnation Cultivars

Classification of Types and Descriptive Summaries

Border carnations are divided into selfs, white-ground fancies, yellow-ground fancies, apricot-ground fancies, fancies other than those of white, yellow, or apricot ground, picotees, and cloves. Selfs have flowers of one clear color in a range of white, yellow, apricot, pink, scarlet, crimson, heliotrope-gray, purple, and old rose. White-ground fancies have a ground color of white, decorated with stripes, flakes, ticks, or splashes of a contrasting color or colors. Some also have an edging to the petals of the same color, sometimes a fine, wire edge and sometimes a broad or heavy edge. Yellow-ground fancies have a yellow ground color and are marked with stripes, flakes, etc., of a contrasting color or colors, or they have the fancy coloring blending with or suffusing the ground color instead of contrasting with it. Apricot-ground fancies have a ground color of buff apricot, orange-apricot, golden-apricot, or coppery apricot. These are mostly flushed or suffused with other colors such as mauve or lavender-gray, some having additional splashes of scarlet. Apricot-ground fancies used to be included with the yellow-ground fancies for exhibition purposes, but most nurseries list them as "other fancies." So many exhibits were disqualified because of the confusion, I campaigned for apricot-ground fancies to be classified as a distinct type, despite the fact that few such cultivars were available at the time. Fancies other than those of white, yellow, or apricot ground are usually referred to as "other fancies." These are mostly of heliotrope-gray or pink ground color and used to be called "nondescripts" or "motleys."

Picotees generally have smaller flowers than other types and are of more slender growth with daintier foliage. White-ground picotees are pure white with a pink, scarlet, crimson, or purple margin to every petal. The heavy-edged forms have a margin about 3 mm (0.125 in) wide, the medium-edged a narrower margin, and the light-edged ones have a very fine margin. Even finer is the wire edge of some excellent show cultivars. The ground color should show no marks or spots other than the margin on the petals, although even the best exhibition cultivars sometimes have such imperfections. Yellow-ground picotees are similar to white-ground picotees in most respects; a deep yellow ground is more desirable than a pale yellow one. The ground color should show no marks or spots of another color, although it is generally accepted that yellow-ground picotees are not quite up to the standard expected of the white-ground picotees. Other-ground picotees are of more recent origin and so far have not impressed. These are mostly of pink ground color but none of a really pleasant shade of pink, in my opinion. No doubt improved cultivars will appear in due course.

Many carnations possess scent, but cloves are those hardy border carnations that happen to be endowed with that distinct perfume we call a clove scent. Show schedules usually contain a few classes for clove-scented carnations. Quality of scent is difficult to judge in a show marquee or hall, therefore this asset is not taken into account comparatively. Judges accept a known clove cultivar without question, but suspect all others might not possess the elusive and desirable perfume.

The following list of names is intended to be a guide to the more popular and important cultivars, but is not a comprehensive list of all available, which would be impossible to include in this book. The various self types are listed first, followed by the fancy types. In the descriptive notes the raiser's name and date of raising or introduction follow the description. It is not possible to guarantee that all dates are strictly accurate. Cultivars that are particularly recommended for exhibition is also indicated, although many others are also useful for this purpose. Abbreviations are as follows:

AM(e): Award of Merit exhibition RHS
AM(g): Award of Merit garden RHS
FCC(e): First Class Certificate exhibition RHS
FCC(g): First Class Certificate garden RHS
AGM(H4): Award of Garden Merit RHS

APRICOT SELF

'Apricot Dream'. Raised in New Zealand and available also in the United States. Keith Hammett, 1984.
'Clunie'. A soft apricot of excellent form and vigorous habit of growth. Recommended for exhibition. AM(g) 1975. J. Douglas, 1957.
'Consul'. Bright flame-apricot flowers held on short stiff stems. Compact growth habit. AM(g) 1951. R. Bath, 1934.
'Eileen O'Connor' (Plate 37). Golden-apricot blooms of good form on very stiff stems. Compact growth habit. FCC(g) 1991. AGM(H4) 1993. J. Galbally, 1980.
'Lustre'. Light apricot. Vigorous growth. Allwoods, 1959.
'Spinfield Buff'. An unusual shade of apricot. FCC(g) 1991. AGM (H4) 1994. P. Russell, 1985.

CRIMSON SELF

'Bookham Perfume'. Rich crimson blooms. Clove-scented. J. Douglas, 1939.
'Christopher Tautz'. Crimson. Good form, tall stems. Recommended for exhibition. AGM(H4) 1995. P. Russell, 1981.
'Crimson Velvet'. Well-formed flowers of deep crimson. Vigorous habit of growth. S. Stroud, 1968.

GRAY SELF

'Blue Ice'. Lilac-gray self. Recommended for exhibition. S. Stroud, 1988.

'**Grey Dove**' (Plate 40). Perfectly formed blooms of glistening heliotrope-gray. A compact grower with stiff stems. Recommended for exhibition. AM(e) 1979. FCC(g) 1984. J. Galbally, 1974.

'**Lavender Clove**'. Large clove-scented flowers on long stiff stems. A popular old cultivar. L. A. Lowe, 1932.

OLD ROSE SELF

'**Belle of Bookham**'. An early-flowering cultivar with very fine large flowers. Needs good growing to produce strong stems. Recommended for exhibition. AM(g) 1947. J. Douglas, 1937.

'**Leiden**'. Large flowers. Vigorous plant that does well in the open garden. FCC(g) 1969. S. Bailey, 1956.

'**Maisie Neal**'. Large well-formed blooms on long stiff stems. Good outdoors and on the show bench. AM(e) 1980. FCC(g) 1988. AGM(H4) 1994. J. Galbally, 1980.

PINK SELF

'**Exquisite**'. Bright rose-pink blooms of good form. Sport from 'Afton Water'. J. Douglas, 1942.

'**Kathleen Hitchcock**'. Rose-pink flowers on short stiff stems. Recommended for exhibition. AM(e) 1979. FCC(g) 1988. J. Galbally, 1973.

'**Portsdown Clove**'. Deep shell-pink. Clove-scented. Hayward's Carnations, 1955.

'**Spinfield Bridesmaid**'. Pale pink, of compact habit. Recommended for exhibition. AGM(H4) 1994. P. Russell, 1990.

SCARLET SELF

'**Alfriston**' (Plate 32). Scarlet flowers of excellent form on a plant of compact habit. Recommended for exhibition. AGM(H4) 1994. J. Galbally, 1972.

'**Fiery Cross**'. Bright scarlet blooms of good form on short stiff stems. FCC(g) 1971. J. Douglas, 1949.

'**Flanders**'. Large well-formed flowers on stout stems. Early-flowering cultivar of vigorous habit. AM(e) 1985. FCC(g) 1988. AGM(H4) 1994. J. Galbally, 1974.

'Richard Pollak'. A vigorous plant with flowers of exhibition quality. AM(e) 1984. AM(g) 1987. J. Galbally, 1973.

'Scarlet Fragrance'. Fine scarlet. Clove-scented. AM(g) 1959. Allwoods, pre-1950.

WHITE SELF

'Driven Snow'. Pure white. Registered as 'Herald' and renamed in the United States. Raised and available in New Zealand. Keith Hammett, 1976.

'Eudoxia'. Good cultivar of strong growth habit. Recommended for exhibition. J. Douglas, 1958.

'Lily Lesurf'. Large blooms of good form. J. Galbally, 1970.

'Nichola Ann'. The most popular exhibition white. Recommended for exhibition. FCC(e) 1981. AM(g) 1983. AGM(H4) 1996. R. Knight, 1976.

'Whitesmith'. Glistening white clove of excellent form. Compact growth. AM(e) 1972. FCC(g) 1975. AGM(H4) 1992. J. Galbally, 1972.

YELLOW SELF

'Aldridge Yellow'. Large canary-yellow blooms of good form. Compact habit of growth. Recommended for exhibition. AM(e) 1951. F. W. Goodfellow, 1951.

'Golden Cross' (Plate 39). Short compact plant with sweetly scented flowers of fine form on stiff stems. AM(e) 1972. FCC(g) 1975. AGM(H4) 1995. J. Galbally, 1972.

'Sunray'. A vigorous plant with large flowers of good form. J. Douglas, 1953.

APRICOT-GROUND FANCY

'Betty's Joy'. Apricot, edged and suffused deep orange-red. Recommended for exhibition. P. Russell, 1988.

'**Chris Crew**'. Deep apricot, edged orient-red. A good garden cultivar of compact habit. AGM(H4) 1994. J. Galbally, 1981.

'**Doris Galbally**' (Plate 35). Well-formed flowers of golden-apricot and marked bright pink. J. Galbally, 1973.

'**Forest Sprite**'. Buff apricot, flaked cerise. A good free-flowering garden cultivar. FCC(g) 1985. S. Bailey, 1972.

'**Kathleen Sharp**'. Apricot, heavily marked scarlet. Recommended for exhibition. E. Dungey, 1979.

'**Sandra Neal**' (Plate 48). Golden-apricot with broad flakes of deep rose-pink. Large flowers of good form. Recommended for exhibition. FCC(g) 1983. AGM(H4) 1992. J. Galbally, 1972.

'**Spinfield Happiness**'. Soft apricot, suffused pink. AGM(H4) 1995. P. Russell, 1992.

'**Taff Glow**'. Buff apricot, suffused deep rose. Recommended for exhibition. T. Brotherton, 1978.

WHITE-GROUND FANCY

'**Alfred Galbally**'. White, edged and heavily striped ruby-red. Strongly clove-scented. Good form. AM(e) 1981. AM(g) 1983. J. Galbally, 1977.

'**Alice Forbes Improved**'. White, striped rosy mauve. Although an older cultivar, this is still very popular with exhibitors. Recommended for exhibition. FCC(g) 1937. G. D. Murray, 1926.

'**Bryony Lisa**' (Plate 33). White, edged and marked rosy carmine. Vigorous plant with flowers of excellent form. AM(e) 1981. FCC(g) 1984. AGM(H4) 1994. J. Galbally, 1977.

'**Claire Tautz**'. White, heavily edged and flecked purple. AGM(H4) 1996. P. Russell, 1979.

'**David Saunders**' (Plate 34). Clove-scented flowers of white, edged and marked ruby-red. Good form and compact habit. AM(e) 1980. FCC(g) 1984. AGM(H4) 1994. J. Galbally, 1977.

'**Forest Treasure**'. A good garden plant with white flowers flecked red-purple. AM(g) 1976. S. Bailey, 1968.

'**Hazel Ruth**' (Plate 42). Pure white, boldly striped blood-red. Of good form and free-flowering. AM(g) 1991. AGM(H4) 1994. J. Galbally, 1980.

'Irene Della-Torré'. Pure white, evenly marked fuchsia-pink. Clove-scented blooms on tall stout stems. Vigorous growth. AM(e) 1980. FCC(g) 1984. AGM(H4) 1992. J. Galbally, 1980.

'Jean Knight'. White, heavily edged and ticked purple. Recommended for exhibition. AM(e) 1985. AGM(H4) 1994. R. Knight, 1974.

'Merlin Clove'. Pure white, heavily edged and striped purple. Strong clove-scent. Recommended for exhibition. FCC(g) 1947. J. Douglas, 1928.

'Riccardo'. White, boldly marked red. Good form. Short compact habit. AM(e) 1980. AM(g) 1989. AGM(H4) 1994. J. Galbally, 1980.

'Sean Hitchcock' (Plate 49). White, heavily edged and marked garnet-lake. Blooms of good form on long stems. AM(e) 1981. AM(g) 1983. J. Galbally, 1980.

'Something Special'. White flowers marked light purple. A popular clove-scented exhibition cultivar. Recommended for exhibition. D. Kellett, 1977.

'Tamsin Fifield'. White flowers, evenly feathered cherry-red. Good form and with stout stems. AM(e) 1981. FCC(g) 1983. AGM(H4) 1994. J. Galbally, 1981.

'Tosca'. White, edged and ticked scarlet. Recommended for exhibition. J. Douglas, 1964.

'Uncle Teddy' (Plate 50). Pure white, edged and boldly striped purple. Large blooms of good form on short stiff stems. FCC(g) 1991. AGM(H4) 1994. J. Galbally, 1970.

YELLOW-GROUND FANCY

'Andrew Morton'. Yellow, lightly striped red. A popular Scottish cultivar. Recommended for exhibition. M. Kennedy, 1945.

'Angelo'. Yellow, edged and marked deep purple. Recommended for exhibition. J. Douglas, 1964.

'Bookham Fancy'. Bright yellow flowers edged and ticked purple, on short stiff stems. J. Douglas, 1952.

'Brian Tumbler'. Yellow, edged and striped rose-red. Recommended for exhibition. A. Fulton, 1974.

'Catherine Glover'. Bright yellow flowers, edged and barred scarlet, on short stiff stems. Recommended for exhibition. J. Douglas, 1939.

'Howard Hitchcock' (Plate 43). Shapely flowers of bright yellow, edged and evenly striped rosy red. Vigorous habit of growth. Recommended for exhibition. AM(g) 1987. AGM(H4) 1994. J. Galbally, 1981.

'Ken Stubbs'. Yellow, edged and striped scarlet. Recommended for exhibition. FCC(e) 1980. E. Dungey, 1979.

'Maudie Hinds' (Plate 44). Bright yellow, lightly splashed deep pink. Short compact growth. Good garden cultivar. J. Galbally, 1971.

'Yorkshireman'. Large blooms of bright yellow, edged and marked scarlet. Compact growth habit. AM(g) 1962. Miss R. Goodfellow, 1960.

OTHER FANCY

'Afton Water'. Soft pink, flaked deep rose. FCC(g) 1947. J. Douglas, 1934.

'Eileen Neal' (Plate 36). Well-formed clove-scented flowers of heliotrope-gray color, flaked and striped purple. Compact habit of growth. J. Galbally, 1980.

'Harmony'. Heliotrope-gray, flaked cerise. Finely formed flowers. Compact habit. Recommended for exhibition. AM(g) 1937. FCC(e) 1937. Allwoods, 1934.

'Leslie Rennison'. Orchid-purple overlaid rose-pink; gives a sheen to the petals. Strong clove-scent. Tall. AM(e) 1942. FCC(g) 1953. R. Thain, 1942.

'Lord Nuffield'. Perfectly formed flowers of silvery gray, flaked pink. Compact habit of growth. Recommended for exhibition. AM(g) 1971. S. Stroud, 1966.

'Mendip Hills'. Well-formed blooms of blossom-pink, flaked scarlet. Vigorous habit of growth. AM(g) 1968. FCC(e) 1971. S. J. Cook, 1954.

'Michael Saunders' (Plate 45). Well-formed and sweetly scented blooms of heliotrope-gray, flaked rich rose-pink, on long stems. FCC(g) 1981. J. Galbally, 1972.

'**Peter Wood**' (Plate 47). Large, shapely flowers of light pink, flaked bright red. Compact habit of growth. Recommended for exhibition. FCC(e) 1984. FCC(g) 1988. AGM(H4) 1992. J. Galbally, 1980.

'**Stanley Stroud**'. Silvery gray, flaked crimson. Clove-scented. S. Stroud, 1972.

WHITE-GROUND PICOTEE

'**Eva Humphries**' (Plate 38). Glistening white, wire-edged purple. Perfectly formed picotee. Recommended for exhibition. FCC(e) 1947. J. Humphries, pre-1946.

'**Filigree**'. White, edged crimson. Prize-winner in New Zealand. Available also in the United States. Keith Hammett, 1980.

'**Mary Robertson**'. White, wire-edged purple. Popular exhibition picotee. Recommended for exhibition. AM(e) 1971. A. Fulton, 1969.

'**Natalie Saunders**' (Plate 46). Pure white, medium-edged lavender-pink. Compact habit. AGM(H4) 1996. J. Galbally, 1985.

'**Rudheath Pixie**'. Pure white, heavy-edged rose-pink. Recommended for exhibition. W. Ingley, 1987.

YELLOW-GROUND PICOTEE

'**Hannah Louise**' (Plate 41). Yellow, heavy-edged scarlet. Short stems and compact growth. Recommended for exhibition. FCC(g) 1987. AGM(H4) 1995. J. Galbally, 1974.

'**Margaret Lennox**'. Yellow, heavily edged rose-pink. Long stems. Late-flowering. Recommended for exhibition. AM(e) 1912. J. Douglas, 1910.

'**Santa Claus**'. Yellow, medium-edged crimson-purple. Long stems. Recommended for exhibition. Also good for the garden. FCC(g) 1962. Phillips and Taylor, 1907.

PINK-GROUND PICOTEE

'**Jane Coffey**'. Whitish pink with purple edge. S. Stroud, 1987.

Chapter 6

Perpetual-Flowering Carnation Cultivars

Classification of Types and Descriptive Summaries

Perpetual-flowering carnations were produced for the cut-flower market long before they were used by exhibitors at flower shows. The hundreds of cultivars derived from the legendary scarlet self 'William Sim' have mostly disappeared, but the few still available continue to perform well and are listed below. Perpetual-flowering carnation cultivars popular today are mostly of shorter habit of growth and have flowers of superior form to those of Sim-type carnations.

There was a time when fancy cultivars were shown in with selfs, but show schedule compilers have adopted an approach similar to that used for border carnations, and the fancy (variegated) types now have classes of their own. Perpetual-flowering carnations are divided into selfs, apricot-ground fancies, lilac or lavender fancies, pink- or red-ground fancies, white-ground fancies, yellow-ground fancies, and other color fancies. The fancy cultivars have stripes, ticks, or bars of a contrasting color or colors, and they are beginning to rival the border carnations in their diversity. There are a few picotee-type cultivars, edged with a contrasting color, which resemble descriptions of early-eighteenth-century picotees—they have spots and small additional ticks of the edge color imposed upon the ground color. These were classified as fancies until 1994, when the British National Carnation Society introduced separate picotee classes for exhibition purposes, with some resulting confusion in classification.

The following list of names is intended to be a guide to the more popular and important cultivars, but is not a comprehensive list of all available, which would be impossible to include in this book. The various self types are listed first, followed by the fancy types. The raiser's name and date of raising or introduction follow the description. It is not possible to guarantee that all dates are strictly accurate. The symbol ® following a cultivar name indicates that it is protected by Plant Breeders' Rights; this subject is fully discussed in Chapter 13, Breeding New Cultivars. Cultivars that are specially recommended for cutting and exhibition is also indicated, although one could say that almost all the cultivars listed are quite useful for both purposes. Abbreviations are as follows:

AM(e): Award of Merit exhibition RHS
FCC(e): First Class Certificate exhibition RHS
FCC(m): First Class Certificate market-use RHS
AGM(H1): Award of Garden Merit RHS

CRIMSON SELF

Crimson Tempo®. Rich crimson. Good buttonhole flower. Sport of Tempo®. Recommended for cut-flower use. A. Baratta, 1995.

'Jess Hewins'. Popular exhibition crimson. Free-flowering. Clove-scented. Recommended for exhibition. Woodfield, 1986.

LIGHT PINK SELF

'Crowley Sim'. Light pink. Free-flowering. Tall. Sim sport. Recommended for cut-flower use. Crowley, 1950.

'Gala'. Light pink with deeply serrated petals. N. Baratta, 1989.

'Joanne's Highlight' (Plate 63). Light pink. Very popular exhibitor's cultivar. Sport from 'Joanne'. Recommended for exhibition. H. Wilcock, 1986.

'Mary Jane Birrel'. Light pink. Recommended for exhibition. C. Stringfellow, 1984.

'Queen's Reward'. Light pink. Popular exhibition cultivar. Recommended for exhibition. C. Short, 1982.

Ramona®. Light pink. Popular color for bouquets and floral arrangements. Recommended for cut-flower use. N. Baratta, 1989.

DEEP PINK OR CERISE SELF

'Canup's Pride'. Cerise. Recommended for exhibition. Raised in Canada, pre-1974.

Dona® (Plate 59). Deep pink with finely cut petal edges. Recommended for cut-flower use. I. Breier, 1989.

'Joanne' (Plate 62). Very fine form. Scented. Undoubtedly the most popular of this color group. Recommended for exhibition. T. Bradshaw, 1974.

Manon®. Deep salmon-pink. Serrated petals. Recommended for cut-flower use. G. Nobbio, 1972.

PURPLE OR LAVENDER SELF

'Carolyn Hardy'. Pale lavender, sweetly scented. Short. Recommended for exhibition. Woodfield, 1990.

'Joan Randall'. Lavender-pink. Free-flowering. AM(e) 1993. Woodfield, 1990.

'Joe Vernon'. Outstanding deep purple. Compact. Most popular show cultivar in this group. Recommended for exhibition. C. Short, 1974.

'Lavender Lady'. Very good form. Scented. Free-flowering. An old cultivar but still very popular for exhibition. Allwoods, 1959.

SCARLET SELF

Indios®. Bright red. Recommended for cut-flower use. AGM(H1) 1995. N. Baratta, 1982.

'**J. M. Bibby**'. Bright scarlet, large flowers, good form. R. Bibby, 1957.

Nelson®. Bright scarlet. Good form. G. Nobbio, 1987.

'**Robert Allwood**'. Bright scarlet. Large full flowers. Short bushy habit. FCC(e) 1934. Allwoods, 1931.

'**Royal Scot**'. Brilliant scarlet, good form. AGM(H1) 1995. Woodfield, 1986.

'**Scania**'. Bright scarlet. Sport from 'William Sim'. Flowers well in winter. Tall. Recommended for cut-flower use. L. Hakansson, 1955.

'**Scarlet Joanne**' (Plate 67). Smooth-edged petals. Scented. Very popular exhibition scarlet. Sport from 'Joanne'. Recommended for exhibition. H. Wilcock, 1984.

WHITE SELF

'**Crompton Princess**'. The most popular white exhibition cultivar. Smooth-edged petals. Recommended for exhibition. C. Short, 1985.

Delphi®. Pure white of very good form. Petals slightly serrated. Recommended for cut-flower use. P. Kooij and Zonen, 1985.

'**Fragrant Ann**'. Heavily clove-scented. Short growth. Very successful show cultivar. FCC(e) and FCC(m) 1980. AGM(H1) 1992. J. Neil, 1952.

'**John Faulkner**'. Large flowers on very stiff stems. Recommended for exhibition. FCC(e) 1992. AGM(H1) 1992. Woodfield, 1989.

'**Northland**'. White. Good form. Recommended for cut-flower use. W. Sim, 1939.

'**V. E. Jubilation**'. Pure white, very free-flowering. Recommended for exhibition. AM(e) 1995. Woodfield, 1990.

'**White William Sim**'. Tall. Sport from 'William Sim'. The most widely grown commercial cultivar. Recommended for cut-flower use. Terlouw, pre-1949.

YELLOW SELF

'**Crompton Bride**'. Apricot-yellow. Recommended for cut-flower use. C. Short, 1991.

Liberty®. Light yellow with smooth-edged petals. Recommended for cut-flower use. A. Baratta, 1992.

Murcia®. Bright golden-yellow. Serrated petals. Sport from Raggio di Sole®. Recommended for cut-flower use. P. Kooij and Zonen, 1985.

'Rosalind Linda'. Lemon-yellow, slightly serrated petals. Recommended for exhibition. Woodfield, 1986.

Salamanca® (Plate 66). Bright yellow flowers of excellent form. Recommended for exhibition. P. Kooij and Zonen, 1990.

'Vera Woodfield'. Deep yellow. Vigorous growth. Tall. Popular exhibition cultivar. Recommended for exhibition. FCC(e) 1984. Woodfield, 1982.

OTHER SELF COLORS

'Cream Sue' (Plate 57). Cream. Sport from 'Apricot Sue'. Very popular exhibition cultivar. Recommended for exhibition. W. Jeggo, 1979.

Pax®. Cream. Petals slightly serrated. Medium height. Recommended for cut-flower use. A. Baratta, 1991.

Prado®. Lime-green. The first "green" carnation. Recommended for cut-flower use. P. Kooij and Zonen, 1991.

Sympathy®. Rich orange, almost smooth-edged petals. Recommended for cut-flower use. G. Nobbio, 1991.

'Tangerine Sim'. Bright orange. Tall. Good winter cropper. Sport from either 'Skyline' or 'Harvest Moon'. Recommended for cut-flower use. C. Mann, 1956, or E. McLellan, 1957.

Valencia®. Described as a bronze-yellow. Serrated petals. A sport from Raggio di Sole®. Recommended for cut-flower use. P. Kooij and Zonen, 1982.

APRICOT-GROUND FANCY

'Alan Hardy'. Maize-apricot, wire-edged and flecked orange. Very free-flowering. Recommended for cut-flower use. AM(e) 1994. Woodfield, 1992.

'Ann Unitt' (Plate 52). Apricot, flushed mauve and rose-pink. Bushy habit. Recommended for exhibition. AM(e) 1993. AGM(H1) 1995. Woodfield, 1990.

'Apricot Sue'. Apricot, lightly marked cerise. Popular exhibitor's cultivar. Recommended for exhibition. T. Bradshaw, 1972.

'Dunkirk Spirit' (Plate 60). Orange-apricot, lightly flecked red. Short. Commemorating the 50th anniversary of the historic evacuation of Dunkirk. Recommended for exhibition. AM(e) 1991. FCC(e) 1993. AGM(H1) 1993. Woodfield, 1988.

Malaga®. Apricot-orange with flame-red markings and toothed petals. Recommended for cut-flower use. AGM(H1) 1995. A. Baratta, 1982.

Raggio di Sole®. Described as an orange self, but slightly marked deeper orange, so exhibited in orange fancy class. Very fine cultivar. Recommended for cut-flower use. G. Nobbio, 1975.

LAVENDER OR LILAC FANCY

'Admiral Crompton'. Pale lilac, ticked and edged purple. Popular with exhibitors. Recommended for exhibition. C. Short, 1978.

'Janelle Welch'. Pale lilac ground, edged and heavily overlaid with crimson-purple markings. Clove-scented. Recommended for exhibition. B. Dean, 1989.

'Little Dianne' (Plate 64). Pale lilac, edged and spotted purple. AM(e) 1990. Woodfield, 1987.

Pierrot® (Plate 65). Lilac-pink, spotted and picotee-edged purple. Scented. Recommended for exhibition. AGM(H1) 1995. N. Baratta, 1985.

'Tony Langford' (Plate 68). Lavender, edged and flecked carmine-crimson. Recommended for exhibition. C. Short, 1986.

PINK- OR RED-GROUND FANCY

'Bob's Highlight'. Pale pink, flecked and striped cerise. Popular with exhibitors. Recommended for exhibition. R. Dickinson, 1992.

'Colin's Shot Salmon'. Soft salmon-pink, flaked and ticked deep rose. Scented. Recommended for exhibition. C. Short, 1984.

Dark Tempo®. Lavender-pink with purple edge and flecks. Sport of Tempo®. Recommended for exhibition. A. Baratta, 1995.

'**Ron's Joanne**'. Light cerise with light pink markings. Sport from 'Joanne'. Popular with exhibitors. Recommended for exhibition. R. Peaty, 1987.

'**Woodfield's Jewel**'. Pale pink, edged and flecked maroon. Recommended for exhibition. Woodfield, 1986.

WHITE-GROUND FANCY

'**Audrey Robinson**' (Plate 53). White, heavily edged and marked deep purple. Large blooms. Clove-scented. Recommended for exhibition. AM(e) 1989. Woodfield, 1987.

'**Betty's Choice**'. White. Edged, flecked, and striped pink. Strongly scented. Recommended for exhibition. R. Dickinson, 1992.

'**Clara's Lass**' (Plate 56). White, edged and ticked red. Scented. Sport from 'Clara'. By far the most popular of the white-ground fancies. Recommended for exhibition. C. Short, 1982.

'**Crompton Classic**' (Plate 58). White, edged and marked purple. Recommended for exhibition. C. Short, 1987.

'**Jacqueline Ann**'. White, flecked rose-pink. Scented. Short. Very popular exhibition cultivar. Recommended for exhibition. FCC(e) 1978. AGM(H1) 1992. Woodfield, 1970.

'**Joanne Taylor**'. White, flecked red-purple. Recommended for exhibition. C. Stringfellow, 1985.

YELLOW-GROUND FANCY

'**Clara**' (Plate 55). Yellow, edged and flecked red. Scented. Smooth-edged petals. A very attractive flower. By far the most popular in this color group. Recommended for exhibition. C. Short, 1978.

Havana®. Chrome-yellow with light magenta flecks. Very attractive flower, with almost smooth-edged petals. Recommended for exhibition. N. Baratta, 1994.

Incas®. Yellow, edged and flecked purple, with smooth-edged petals. Recommended for exhibition. A. Baratta, 1992.

Tundra®. Bright yellow, heavily edged and occasional flecks of scarlet. Smooth-edged petals. Recommended for exhibition. A. Baratta, 1995.

OTHER COLOR FANCY

Arevalo®. Bright purple, paling at edge. Recommended for cut-flower use. P. Kooij and Zonen, pre-1982.
'Can Can'. Synonymous 'French Can Can'. Rosy purple, paling to lavender edge. Short. Very serrated petals. M. van Staaveren, 1982.
'Crompton Wizard'. Fuchsine-pink, flaked ruby-red. Recommended for exhibition. C. Short, 1986.
'Doris Allwood'. Described in raiser's catalogue as salmon-cerise, heavily shaded heliotrope, but is not exhibited in the class for pink- or red-ground fancies. Scented. Short stems. Recommended for exhibition. AM(e) 1936. Allwoods, 1935.
'Purple Frosted'. Light purple, edged white. Scented. W. Holley, 1962.
'Storm'. Heliotrope-gray fancy. Scented. Short stems. Recommended for exhibition. Avonmore Nurseries, pre-1967.

WHITE-GROUND PICOTEE

'Charlotte' (Plate 54). Pure white, picotee-edged pink. Recommended for exhibition. A. Baratta, 1989.
'Rendez-Vous'. White, heavily edged and occasional purple flecks. Recommended for exhibition. A. Baratta, 1992.
Tempo®. White, wire-edged and flecked ruby-red. Recommended for exhibition. A. Baratta, 1992.

YELLOW-GROUND PICOTEE

'Ann Franklin'. Primrose-yellow, wire-edged and flecked maroon. Recommended for exhibition. AM(e) 1994. Woodfield, 1992.
Ivonne® (Plate 61). Yellow, picotee-edged salmon-red. Recommended for cut-flower use. A. Baratta, 1988.

Chapter 7

Malmaison Carnations

Although very fashionable among the wealthy as well as nursery-men around the end of the nineteenth century, Malmaison carnations were out of fashion by the middle of the twentieth century, seemingly lost to cultivation. Malmaisons, however, are once again available from carnation specialists as a result of a few private collections that continued to grow these "collector's items."

The Malmaison carnation was so named because of its resemblance to the Bourbon rose 'Souvenir de la Malmaison'. For a long time there was much confusion as to the time and place of its origin. Writing in the 1892 National Carnation and Picotee Society's *Carnation Manual*, F. W. Burridge, an eminent correspondent, asked if there was anyone alive who could tell the origin and history of the Malmaison carnation. He wrote that it had been popular in British gardens for many years and suggested that perhaps our Continental friends who made a speciality of Malmaison carnations might enlighten our insular ignorance as to the birth and parentage of so beautiful a flower.

La Malmaison was the name of the château that became the home of Napoleon Bonaparte and the Empress Joséphine. La Malmaison (literally, "bad house") is a translation of the original thirteenth-century name of the place where the château was built. It is near Reuil, 8 km

(5 miles) from Versailles and 14 km (9 miles) from Paris. Joséphine bought the château in 1789 when she was the wife of Alexandre, Vicomte de Beauharnais, and made what was to become a beautiful and famous garden. Her husband was executed during the Revolution and she married Napoleon Bonaparte in 1796. But the marriage was not fruitful, and in 1809 Napoleon divorced Joséphine because she did not bear him a son. She retained her title of Empress and, with two million francs per annum, continued to live at her home at La Malmaison until she died in 1814, about three weeks before her 51st birthday. Her château at Malmaison is now a museum, but the original gardens of some 240 hectares (600 acres) now occupy only 6 hectares (15 acres).

Thomas Hogg wrote in his book published in 1820, "Empress Joséphine, wife of Napoleon I, had an admirable collection of yellow picotees at Malmaison." However, colored illustrations of that time reveal these to be what are now known as yellow-ground fancy carnations. The first true yellow-ground picotees were not raised until 1858. Towards the end of the nineteenth century James Douglas wrote that the origin of the Malmaison carnation seemed lost in obscurity, and he suggested that it likely might have originated at La Malmaison, seeing that carnations were such a favorite there. But the Malmaison carnation is not as old as generally supposed.

Although originally thought to have been named for the Empress and grown in her famous garden by the botanist Bonpland, the Malmaison carnation did not appear until 1857, over forty years after Joséphine's death. A seed-mutant from the remontant carnation, it was raised in a garden near Paris by M. Laisné, and named 'Souvenir de la Malmaison'. Its flowers are larger than those of the remontant carnation and its habit of growth quite distinct. The plant is compact, the stems very thick, and the foliage much broader and curlier than that of the remontant type. In Great Britain it became 'Souvenir de la Malmaison Old Blush'. In 1864 William Young of Edinburgh passed some plants to David Thomson of Archerfield. In 1870 a bud-mutant appeared, the blush-pink flowers ornamented with rosy pink stripes. John Cowe, of Luffness House, East Lothian, secured the sport, which was named 'Lady Middleton'. In 1875 a second sport appeared, in Musselburgh, Scotland, a salmon-pink form that was named 'Souvenir de la Malmaison, Pink' and sometimes called 'Lord Rothschild'. It became very fashionable indeed when it was called 'Princess of Wales' after the princess who was to become Queen Alexandra. About a year after this, another sport of 'Old Blush' appeared, and was named 'Souvenir de la Malmaison, Crimson'. To add to the confusion of names, a deep salmon-pink sport of 'Princess of Wales' was named 'Souvenir de la Malmaison, Rothschild's Variety'.

These Malmaison carnations did not produce seeds, but they did provide a very small amount of pollen, which was used for crossing with border and perpetual-flowering carnations. Martin Ridley Smith raised many very fine cultivars using border carnations, including the first yellow self, 'Yaller Gal'. This is now lost to cultivation, but his white self 'Thora' is still grown. This cultivar is blush-pink in the bud stage but becomes white as the flower matures. Other early cultivars were 'Duchess of Westminster' (Plate 69), a rosy salmon self raised by Mr. Barnes, head gardener to the Duke of Westminster, and described as an early-flowering cultivar of great beauty with true Malmaison foliage, and useful for winter flowering; 'Maggie Hodgson', crimson, raised by Mr. Coles, gardener to R. Measures, of Streatham; and a Belgian cultivar, 'Mme. Arthur Warocque', which had small bright scarlet flowers and bloomed at Christmas. Around the year 1890 a J. Jennings wrote that he had a plentiful supply of carnation flowers all the year round and had border carnations, 1200 tree carnations, 1400 of the rose-pink 'Miss Joliffe', and 3500 Malmaisons. In 1906 a seed-mutant appeared amongst perpetual-flowering carnation seedlings raised by H. Burnett of Guernsey. This was the first perpetual-flowering Malmaison carnation, and their breeding was taken up by several other hybridizers, but all these cultivars seem now to have disappeared.

Cultivation of Malmaison carnations is similar to that for perpetual-flowering carnations but with greater care. (Cultivation is described in more detail in Chapter 9.) They prefer a drier, slightly warmer greenhouse atmosphere than perpetual-flowering carnations and require more shade in summer. It has been said that Malmaisons could not possibly be grown in an unheated greenhouse and that these are difficult enough even in a heated greenhouse. They are notoriously capricious and very slow-growing, but were they always so miffy? Some light is cast by a gentleman who saw them in their infancy. In 1926 Lord Lambourne, when President of the Royal Horticultural Society, wrote the foreword to the first edition of Montagu Allwood's *Carnations and All Dianthus*. He wrote,

> My earliest acquaintance with the carnation dated from 1856, when my dear mother, Mrs. Mark Wood, received a cutting of the Blush Carnation from Lady Middleton of Birdsall, her great friend. I remember we grew it in an unheated house close by the door up against the wall for many years, covering it up with newspaper during the winter.

The 1856 date is interesting in that the generally accepted date of the raising of the "Blush Carnation" is 1857.

Malmaison carnations have very large flowers and what many once considered to be splendid form. They do have a delicious clove perfume, but I cannot agree regarding their form. En masse, they make a splendid sight when in full bloom (Plate 71), but individually, in my opinion, they are blowsy. The one exception is my own favorite, the 'Duchess of Westminster', which is less like the original Malmaisons than most because of the perpetual-flowering carnation influence in its breeding. Upon inspection of Malmaison carnation flowers, with the object of breeding from them, I came to the following conclusions. With 'Princess of Wales', a sport of 'Old Blush', the flower comprises a cluster of 16 small flowers. The calyx does not enclose the cluster, nor does it burst. The sepals divide naturally and open out to form a star-shaped chalice. All the flowers have styles and surround a cluster of filaments in the center of the bloom. Their stamens appear to contain viable pollen; the ovaries contain no female seeds.

'Duchess of Westminster' (perpetual-flowering carnation × Malmaison carnation) (Plate 69) has a typical calyx that encloses the base of the flower and normally does not burst. Within the calyx are three smaller flowers that surround the main central bloom. All have petals and styles, but the filaments are insignificant and the stamens carry no pollen. The ovaries contain unfertilized female seeds.

It would seem that the Malmaison carnation 'Old Blush' and its sports could be used as male (pollen) parents only, while 'Duchess of Westminster', and probably others of its type, could be used as female (seed) parents only.

Montagu Allwood wrote in 1947,

The greatest of them all was the Malmaison, and especially the cultivar 'Princess of Wales', which, like so many other plants and flowers of that period, have long since passed into the shadows. No one regrets more than I the passing of the Malmaison and especially that old aristocrat, 'Souvenir de la Malmaison Old Blush', so fragrant, so beautiful a shade of glowing flesh pink, and so handsome.

Fortunately, their passing was not permanent, for 'Old Blush', 'Duchess of Westminster', 'Thora', and 'Tayside Red' are still grown extremely well at the Royal Horticultural Society Wisley garden in the care of Ray Waite, the Glasshouse Superintendent. The only information I have regarding 'Tayside Red' is that it was introduced pre-1916 (Plate 70).

The National Trust for Scotland has a National Collection of Malmaison Carnations at Crathes Castle, Banchory, Kincardineshire. David MacLean, the Head Gardener, told me that a lot of interest is shown in them, and that people write to him asking questions about Malmaisons. He says that I may mention that people are welcome to see them there. He also very kindly sent me the following notes:

> The Malmaison Carnations we have here at Crathes are 'Blush Pink', 'Duchess of Westminster', 'Thora'—all pink—and 'Tayside Red'. We also have one called 'Princess of Wales' but this seems to be the same pink as the 'Duchess of Westminster'. We usually take cuttings in July/August (I may say the cuttings can be temperamental and we have been known to take a second batch). They are potted up into 3-in [8-cm] pots and left till the spring. Then they are potted into 5-in [12-cm] pots. Once they are pot-bound in 5-in pots we pot into 7- or 8-in [17- or 20-cm] pots using a rough mixture with a little lime-rubble. The plants are then pinched regularly, staked and tied and should come into flower the following spring. We disbud to obtain the large flowers. The one problem with Malmaisons is that the flowers tend to burst open so to keep a good firm flower we have been known to put an elastic band behind the bud. We also find the Malmaisons need a fairly cool and shaded house in summer. Too much sun burns the foliage white. We feed well with a high-potash feed during the flowering period.

As Mr. MacLean says, 'Princess of Wales' is very similar in color to 'Duchess of Westminster', but flowers of the latter are of greatly superior form. 'Princess of Wales' naturally resembles 'Old Blush' in flower form because it is a sport from it; 'Duchess of Westminster' is not a true Malmaison carnation but a cross between a Malmaison carnation and a perpetual-flowering carnation.

In 1989 I was given ten unrooted cuttings of 'Duchess of Westminster', ten because "they can be difficult to root!" In any event they all rooted, and I potted them into 8-cm (3-in) clay pots, then potted-on into 15-cm (6-in) pots and kept them in a very small unheated greenhouse, where they experienced temperatures down to −6°C (21°F). The great storm of late January 1990 blew out half the glass, which was not replaced until a fortnight later, although the gales were then still serious. By early March, however, one of the plants had a crown flower and four half-open buds, but no sideshoots, and another had a large crown bud with three other buds to follow, plus four side-shoots. The remaining seven plants all had four to six strong sideshoots but no signs of buds. I notice that whenever a bud is removed, another from the same axil seems to take its place. This seems unusual, although I remember it sometimes occurs with the perpetual-flowering carnation 'Fragrant Ann'.

I was recently given unnamed cuttings in return for 'Duchess of Westminster', and these turned out to be 'Princess of Wales' and 'Tayside Red'. I also exchanged a plant of 'Duchess of Westminster' for one called 'Marmion', said to have been in one family for many years. The *International Dianthus Register* states that it was raised by H. Burnett in 1906 and received an Award of Merit in 1907. It is described as cherry ground, margined white, and clove-scented. The flower is attractive, though small by Malmaison standards, and the foliage much daintier than that of the type.

Six years after receiving the cuttings of 'Duchess of Westminster', young plants propagated from the original plants continued to thrive in an unheated greenhouse. They have survived frosts every winter to date, and they still continue to bloom into November each year. Perhaps they are not as "miffy" as some people think.

Malmaison carnations are no longer regarded as a museum piece, a collector's item; two or three carnation specialists now list these in their catalogues and a national collection holder specializes in them (see Appendix II).

Chapter 8

Cultivation of Garden Carnations and Pinks

Carnations Commonly Grown from Seeds

Although almost all carnations are technically perennial or biennial, most garden types sown from seeds are treated as annuals—that is, grown to flower in the same year the seeds are sown. Since these garden types flower in garden borders, plants grown for sale in nurseries and garden centers are sometimes described as border carnations, although this is quite inaccurate because border carnations is the accepted title for the named cultivars of truly perennial garden carnations. The true border carnations, which have evolved through five centuries of breeding, are propagated by layers or cuttings from existing plants. They are listed in specialist growers' catalogues and named in the *International Dianthus Register*. Those carnations grown from seed as annuals are usually correctly called annual carnations.

ANNUAL CARNATIONS

A very wide range of carnations are grown from seeds, and for almost all it is recommended that they be treated as half-hardy annuals, raised in gentle heat early in the year and planted out when danger of frost has passed. The Chabaud strain of carnations is the most well known of the annual carnations (Plate 72). They are an improved form of the Marguerite carnations, growing 50 cm (20 in) tall and available in many carnation colors; a dwarf Chabaud carnation is also available. The Marguerite carnation is a hybrid group descended from *Dianthus chinensis*, the Indian pink, and the perennial border carnation. Believed to have originated in Sicily, it was introduced to England in 1889 as useful for flowering in autumn and winter. It is interesting to note that the Marguerite carnations and the forebears of the perpetual-flowering carnations are believed to have originated from a similar source: crosses between the Indian pink and the perennial border carnation.

The Marguerite carnation is not truly hardy and usually exhausts itself by continuous flowering. Plants are generally grown from seeds and are treated as annuals. Seeds should be sown very early in spring, planted outdoors in early summer, then lifted in early autumn and planted in a warm greenhouse to flower in the winter. They are also often grown in pots in a warm greenhouse throughout the year. Pot-grown plants tend to flower the same year the seeds are sown.

Various strains and series have been developed by seedsmen. The Double Triumph strain comes in mixed colors, grows about 60 cm (24 in) tall, and can be sown in late spring to flower in early summer of the following year. Early Dwarf Vienna, a group suitable for bedding, grows about 38 cm (15 in) tall, is scented, and may also be grown as a perennial. The Enfant de Nice strain grows about 45 cm (18 in) tall, bears scented flowers in mixed colors, and is good for cutting. The Fantasie et Flamand strain comes in various colors, mostly striped and flaked, and grows 60 cm (24 in) tall. 'Fleur de Camille' has well-formed flowers, freely produced, and is about 50 cm (20 in) tall. The Lillipot series of first-generation (F_1) hybrids, including 'Lillipot Scarlet' and 'Lillipot Rose', grows 23 cm (9 in) tall and may be used as bedding or as pot plants; they can be grown as both annuals and biennials. The Marguerite Malmaison series has very large flowers in a wide range of colors and is about 38 cm (15 in) tall. The Luminette series, an F_1 hybrid, has bright scarlet flowers and stout stems and is about 60 cm (24 in) tall.

The Dwarf Double group of F_1 hybrids from Sakata, Japan, has large flowers in a good range of colors, grows to only 30 cm (12 in) tall, and can be used for bedding, as a cut flower, and as a pot plant. 'Peach Delight' has medium-sized, pinkish apricot flowers on strong stems 60 cm (24 in) tall. The F_1 hybrid Knight series of carnations, only 30 cm (12 in) tall, is good for bedding out or growing in pots, and also can be useful for cutting. Separate selections of the Knight series are available in rose, crimson, scarlet, white, orange-picotee, and crimson-picotee colorings. Mixed seeds are also available in this very early-flowering type, which blooms within five months after sowing the seeds. A group of German origin called the Minarette series is similar to the Knight series in all respects except that it is not an F_1 hybrid. Bambino Mixed is a series with double, scented flowers in a very wide range of colors. Only 20 cm (8 in) tall, it is suitable for bedding and may also be grown as a pot plant.

DIANTHUS FOR SUMMER BEDDING

Almost all cultivars for summer bedding are derived from *Dianthus chinensis*, a species that is not completely hardy. Seeds are sown in midwinter in a heated greenhouse, potted singly into small pots, and then planted out in early summer when all danger of frost has passed.

Plants of most cultivars cover themselves completely with flowers, many as large as 5 cm (2 in) in diameter. The self-colored cultivars are favored for special bedding schemes; I personally find the fancy-colored cultivars more attractive. The Baby Doll strain is popular, only 15 cm (6 in) tall and in a mixture of colors. Double Gaiety Mixed is a strain with deeply fringed petals, grows 30 cm (12 in) tall, and is good for cutting. 'Fire Carpet', an F_1 hybrid, is 20 cm (8 in) tall and has 5-cm (2-in) diameter flowers. The Magic Charms series has large, fringed flowers in mixed colors and grows 20 cm (8 in) tall. 'Merry-Go-Round', which has large pure white blooms with a scarlet center, is 15 cm (6 in) tall. The Persian Carpet Mixed series, 10 cm (4 in) tall, has cushions of flowers in white, pink, and scarlet and is a good rock garden plant. 'Snowfire' (F_1) is a most striking cultivar, bearing flowers of pure white with a scarlet eye and growing 20 cm (8 in) tall. Telstar Crimson is another F_1 series and grows 25 cm (10 in) tall.

The Princess, Rosemary, Ideal, and Parfait series are other popular dianthus for summer bedding. Award-winning cultivars seen at Wisley trials include 'Princess Salmon, 'Princess Scarlet', 'Princess White, and 'Rosemary White', all from California, United States, and 'Ideal Crimson' from Avoine, France; all received the RHS Award of Merit. 'Rosemary Mixture' (Plate 75) was Highly Commended, as were 'Raspberry Parfait' (Plate 74), an F_1 hybrid bearing bright crimson flowers with a deeper crimson eye, and 'Strawberry Parfait' (F_1), pink with scarlet eye, both 15 cm (6 in) tall.

SOWING AND PLANTING ANNUAL CARNATIONS AND DIANTHUS

Seeds of annual carnations and dianthus should be sown in midwinter in trays in John Innes seed compost or soil-less or peat-free equivalent (see Chapter 10), made level and fairly firm. Given a temperature of 15 to 21°C (60 to 70°F), seeds should germinate in seven to ten days. I prefer to sow them singly, about 1 cm (0.5 in) apart in the rows, after having sprinkled silver or fine sand over the surface of the compost. I also find it useful to press furrows about 2.5 cm (1 in) apart into the sand with a plastic plant label, which causes some of the sand to run into the furrows. The black seeds are more easily seen on the sand and the sand base probably assists germination (Figure 8-1). I then sprinkle sand over the seeds, only just enough to cover them, and place the tray into a larger tray containing a little water, removing it when the sand begins to show that moisture from below has reached the surface. Seed trays should not be placed where they might be subjected to sunlight or strong winds. A light spray over with a diluted copper fungicide, such as Cheshunt Compound (copper sulphate and ammonium carbonate), will ensure against damping-off diseases that would cause stems to rot and seedlings to collapse. Cover the tray with paper or a sheet of glass to conserve moisture, but remove this cover altogether when seedlings begin to show through. Spray occasionally to keep the compost moist.

The baby leaves, or cotyledons, are broad and rounded, unlike the true sword- or strap-shaped leaves. When the first true swordlike leaves appear, ease the seedlings gently with a small dibber (dibble) and lift them by the cotyledons with thumb and forefinger. Pot into 5-

Figure 8-1. Seed sowing: fine sand on surface, cover seeds lightly.

cm (2-in) pots of John Innes potting compost number 1 (JIP 1) or soil-less or peat-free equivalent, ensuring that the surface of the compost finishes just under the cotyledons. If planted too deep, the stem may rot; if planted too shallow, the stem may buckle as the leaves grow and put on weight. When well rooted, pot on into 9-cm (3.5-in) pots of JIP 1 compost or soil-less or peat-free equivalent and plant out 30 cm (12 in) apart in beds prepared as for border carnations and pinks (see Spring Planting, later in this chapter) in late spring or early summer when all danger of frost has passed.

Carnations such as the Grenadin strain, the Tige de Fer (iron stem) types, and Teicher's strain are often considered perennial or biennial (and sometimes as half-hardy annuals or perennials), and these should be sown in early summer. After sowing and germinating the seed in the usual way, pot on into 9-cm (3.5-in) pots of JIP 1 compost or soil-less or peat-free equivalent and plant out in autumn in beds prepared

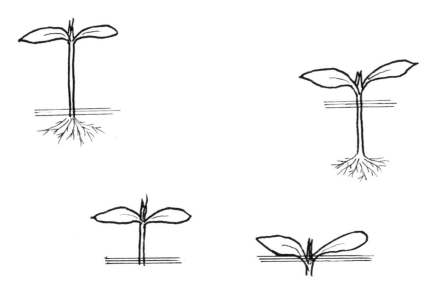

Figure 8-2. *Top left:* carnation seedling; *top right:* pricked out to correct depth; *bottom left:* too high; *bottom right:* too low.

as for border carnations to flower the following summer. The Grenadin strain of carnations has flowers somewhat similar to those of perpetual-flowering carnations, whereas the flowers of the Tige de Fer and Teicher's types are more like those of border carnations in appearance. All grow to a height of about 60 cm (24 in).

DIANTHUS BARBATUS

Dianthus barbatus, sweet william, is a short-lived perennial usually grown as a biennial. Sow seeds in late spring or early summer in the garden border and thin or transplant as soon as possible. Plant seedlings outdoors 30 cm (12 in) apart in autumn in a sunny spot, where they will flower the following summer.

ROCK GARDEN PINKS

Rock garden pinks consist mainly of hybrids resulting from the improvement of natural species, chiefly *Dianthus alpinus,* with more recent introductions brought about by the cross-breeding of *D. allwoodii* with several other species, including *D. alpinus*, *D. caesius*, and *D. arenarius*. Cultivation is similar to that described for the species in Chapter 1, except that the modern hybrid cultivars need rather more generosity in the matter of plant food because of their longer flowering habit, usually from early summer till autumn. Old stable manure or spent mushroom compost could be incorporated into the soil before planting. Pot-grown plants will benefit from the occasional balanced liquid feed, as described later in this chapter.

Acidity and Alkalinity

The soil for pinks and carnations should be about neutral, but this is not imperative, for they are tolerant of some variation in pH. Most gardens are suitable, but since it has always been said that pinks and carnations prefer lime, some gardeners scatter a powdering on the soil surface in spring, after tidying up their plants by removing the fallen leaves that invariably collect about them during the winter. Hydrated lime is usually applied in the autumn or winter, although ground chalk, carbonate of lime, or ground limestone may safely be used at any time of the year.

Soil testing kits are useful for testing the pH of the soil, pH being a coefficient relating to the degree of acidity or alkalinity of the soil. A pH of 7 represents neutral, neither acid nor alkaline; a higher pH represents the degree of alkalinity and a lower the degree of acidity. Pinks and carnations will happily tolerate a soil condition with a pH between 6.5 and 7.5.

The story that pinks and carnations love "limy soil" is as untrue as that about roses loving a clay soil. Over-liming is dangerous because it chemically locks up plant foods that, although present in the soil, cannot be taken up by the plants. A soil testing kit indicates the soil pH and gives instructions on how much lime to apply to raise an acid soil to the neutral condition. Where a test is not made one could apply lime at 55 g per sq m (2 oz per sq yd) to ground that has not been limed very recently and at 110 g per sq m (4 oz per sq yd) to ground that has not been limed for many years. However, in a new garden where the history is not known, it would be wiser to invest in a soil testing kit, not only to get it right but also for peace of mind. Old mortar rubble is so often mentioned as being good for pinks and carnations that one might imagine they could not survive without it. Really old mortar rubble contains some lime, but some mortars have ingredients that could be harmful to plant life.

Growing Border Carnations and Garden Pinks

That great plantsman and garden designer William Robinson of Gravetye Manor, Sussex, writing around 1890, considered the border carnation should be looked at as a garden flower as well as a subject for the show bench. As printed in the 1892 *Carnation Manual*, Robinson wrote,

> Acres of mean little sub-tropical weeds that happen to possess a colored leaf—*Coleus, Alternanthera, Perilla*, etc. occupy much of the ground which ought to be true flower-gardens, but which is too often set out in tile patterns, and with plants without fragrance, beauty of form, or even the charm of association.

He considered it "not enough" that the beautiful show carnation be grown in greenhouses.

> A great many people who may not have the skill, the time, or the means necessary for the growth of the finest florists' flowers, would yet find the strong and brilliant self carnations delightful in their gardens in summer and autumn, and even in winter, for the carnation, where it does well, has a fine color-value of foliage in winter, which makes it most useful to all who care for beautiful color in their gardens.

William Robinson described his method of massing carnations of various colors, mostly planted in informal groups of twenty to fifty. "So far as hardiness is concerned we had no trouble," he wrote, adding "the harder the winter, the happier the flower." He mentioned the beautiful effects of color by associating with carnations other gray-foliaged plants such as lavender *(Lavandula)* and rosemary *(Rosmarinus officinalis).* Robinson also wrote of the garden in Suffolk where Lord de Sausmarez entrusted him with the remodelling of what was considered to be the most famous bedding-out garden in England.

> I determined to plant to a great extent, with the Carnation, Tea Rose, Tufted Pansy, Lavender, Rosemary and all the beautiful and hardy plants available. Very many of the finest Carnations were used, and with most excellent effect. The beds were simple and bold, and we had large masses, in groups, of the finest self Carnations known.

He found rabbits and hares to be the worst enemies of carnations, and in one hard winter, when food was scarce, several thousand carnation plants disappeared. After that, by thoroughly fencing about 3 hectares (7 acres) around the house, he had no further trouble. He conducted extensive experiments at Gravetye Manor with Arthur Herington, who found pheasants to be as destructive as rabbits and hares.

Plants of true border carnations, the named cultivars, are hardy perennials (zone 5) and they are produced by layers or cuttings from existing plants. Garden pinks and the true border carnations will grow almost anywhere except in a bog or wood. They prefer full sunshine but will tolerate shade for part of the day. They prefer their own company to having other large plants growing close to them, which would restrict the flow of air about them and compete for light. They can be grown in a damp situation provided the bed is raised 8 or 10 cm (3 or 4 in) above the general soil level to assist drainage, ensuring that the plants' roots are not perpetually waterlogged. Garden pinks and border carnations may be used as dot plants amongst other neatly growing plants, or set out in small groups in a mixed border. Where there is space the most effective way is to give them a bed to themselves. I grow mine as edging plants around beds of roses, with the carnations flowering between the early summer and autumn flushes of the roses, and the pinks' flowering coinciding with the rose flushes.

BORDER CARNATIONS AND GARDEN PINKS FROM SEED

Border carnation plants can be grown from seed, but they will not breed true from seed; in fact, a large proportion of seedlings from named cultivars produce both single and bullheaded flowers, as well as many others that are quite worthless. This method generally is used only by breeders to obtain new cultivars, and it is also a hobby with some amateur carnation enthusiasts. Most plants grown from seed rarely resemble either of their parent cultivars.

Seeds of border carnations may be sown in March or April in John Innes seed compost or a soil-less or peat-free equivalent. Bottom heat is not essential but does get the seedlings off to a quick start. With fresh seed, germination takes only a few days in heat and a week to a fortnight without it. Prick out into boxes about 5 cm (2 in) apart or pot up into 5-cm (2-in) pots in JIP 1 or a soil-less or peat-free equivalent. Pot on into 9-cm (3.5-in) pots, and when well rooted but before they become pot-bound, plant out in the open border about 30 cm (12 in) apart. A few seedlings may bloom that same summer, usually strong vigorous plants bearing single-petalled flowers, which can be discarded immediately. The majority will flower the following summer and give many hours of pleasurable anticipation for about a month. Those considered worthy may be layered in the soil or lifted carefully and potted into a fairly large pot for layering and kept in a greenhouse, or under a glass- or polyethylene-covered frame.

As with border carnations, the named cultivars of garden, laced, and exhibition pinks do not breed true from seed. Although a few may have flowers similar to those of their parent plants, the majority will be an interesting mixture of both single and double flowers. They are sown in the same way and given the same treatment as border carnation seeds, but most should flower in their first season.

It is also worth mentioning here that seeds of carnations and pinks are brittle and easily cracked. They should therefore be handled with care.

PREPARING THE GROUND

Well cultivate the ground to the depth of a spade, incorporating bulky humus in the form of well-rotted manure, well-broken-down garden compost, used mushroom compost, crumbly leafmold, or granulated peat. Peat should first be moistened otherwise it may dry too quickly and blow away. Used potting compost is very useful, but not any that has contained diseased plants of any kind. Bonemeal is a slow-acting plant food popular with amateur enthusiasts and provides phosphorus to promote root growth, as well as a small amount of nitrogen to encourage steady growth. It can be stirred or hoed in to a depth of 7.5 to 10 cm (3 to 4 in), allowing 85 g per sq m (3 oz per sq yd). Crushed cinders and coarse grit help to improve porosity. Level the soil and, if dry, tread it firmly, otherwise wait until the soil dries out.

AUTUMN PLANTING

Rooted layers or rooted cuttings of carnations and pinks should be planted out in early autumn to give them sufficient time to become established before winter. Allow 38 cm (15 in) between carnation plants or 45 cm (18 in) where it is intended to increase stocks by layering after they have flowered. Rooted cuttings of pinks should be spaced 30 cm (12 in) apart. These distances allow room for the plants to increase in size and fill up the ground between them in their second and third years. They do continue growing far longer but will become woody and somewhat straggly, so it is better to keep them for two or three years and then replace them with healthy young plants. I keep some plants far longer in my own garden, however, cultivars that remain very compact and do not straggle, and these produce hundreds of blooms. Where grown for cut bloom for home decoration, carnations can be planted 30 cm (12 in) apart and pinks 20 cm (8 in) apart in the kitchen garden or allotment plot.

Whether plants are of your own cultivating or bought from a carnation specialist they should be inspected to ensure their roots are not dry. Make planting holes with a trowel, allowing ample space to accommodate the roots comfortably. Should the soil be dry, fill the holes with water. When the water has disappeared, dust with HCH (lindane) in each hole to deter soil pests, wireworms in particular. My own soil consisting mainly of clay and stones, I fill the space about the plants' roots with used potting compost. It is most important that the stem joint carrying the plant's lowest pair of leaves finishes just above soil level. Make the soil about the roots quite firm by pressing in with your fingers, and stake any tall plants with a short stick and a sweet-pea ring or twist-tie to prevent damage by winter gales. Where this is not done the plant may be rocked by strong winds, thereby making a hole about the stem that fills with water and could cause stem-rot. The water in the hole about the stem may freeze during the winter and so damage the stem irreparably. During winter, examine the plants periodically; any that have been pushed out of the ground by frost action should be refirmed as soon as the ground thaws. Do not protect plants with straw, bracken, etc., which would prevent a free flow of air about them.

SPRING PLANTING

Border carnations and pinks that have become established in pots during the winter should be planted out in spring. This should be done before the plants become pot-bound, or they never recover from the check to growth caused by this condition. The use of rooted layers and cuttings is not recommended for spring planting, as there is not sufficient time for them to become established to bloom only three months after planting. Enthusiasts who wish to plant in spring pot their rooted layers and cuttings into 10-cm (4-in) pots in autumn (Figure 8-3); these make up into fine specimen plants by spring. Mail-order nurseries use smaller pots for convenience of packing and economy in mailing charges. So for spring planting it pays to buy rooted layers and cuttings in autumn and pot them into 10-cm (4-in) pots.

The ground should be cleared before spring planting begins, but not cultivated too deeply. In well-worked garden soil a good going-over with the hoe should suffice, and a balanced fertilizer, one having approximately equal ratios of nitrogen (N), phosphorus (P), and potassium (K), should be incorporated at 83 g per sq m (3 oz per sq yd). A newly developed plant food product called Bio Friendly Fish, Blood and Bone, claimed to be 100% natural, is a preferable option to the oft-recommended Blood, Fish and Bone. Fortified with rock potash, its analysis is N6%, P5%, and K4%, and it can be used at 70 g per sq m (2 oz per sq yd) from spring to autumn. Make holes with a trowel and, if necessary, dust them with HCH (lindane) to destroy soil pests such as wireworms. The well-tried, old-fashioned method of inserting pieces of cut potato into the soil to trap wireworms is a natural alternative (see

Figure 8-3. *Left:* rooted layer; *right:* layer potted.

Chapter 12). If the soil is dry, fill the hole with water and wait until the water disappears before planting out. Also before planting out, water any plants that appear to be dry, otherwise their roots may stick to the pot-wall causing them to be damaged or, worse still, the root-ball to collapse.

Knock plants out of their pots by placing a hand over the top of the pot with the plant's stem held between two fingers. Holding the base of the pot with the other hand, turn it upside down and tap the pot rim sharply with the handle of a trowel or rim of a bucket. Set plants firmly in the ground with finger pressure, making sure that the top of the root-ball is flush with the soil surface, and water in if the soil is dry. A short stick is sufficient support for carnations until a month or so later when this should be replaced by a slim 75-cm (30-in) stake and the plant's stem secured with a sweet-pea ring.

SOIL CULTIVATION

Early in spring, established plants seem to come alive, with new shoots pushing forth from every leaf axil. Do not fill in any spaces near carnations and pinks with other plants that when fully grown would compete with them for light. Such plants as *Dahlia* and chrysanthemums *(Dendranthema)* are small when planted, but they quickly grow into very large plants.

Hoe shallowly among autumn-planted plants, incorporating a balanced fertilizer such as Gromore at 83 g per sq m (3 oz per sq yd) or Bio Friendly Fish, Blood and Bone at 70 g per sq m (2 oz per sq yd). Regular hoeing keeps weeds down, keeps the soil aerated, and conserves soil moisture during hot weather. The plants' silvery gray foliage is set off to advantage against the dark background of well-cultivated soil after a summer shower. However, it must always be remembered that their roots are very shallow, therefore hoeing must not be too deep nor too close to the stems. Although it is true that hoeing conserves soil moisture, there comes a time when the soil becomes so dry that the plants have to be watered. One-half liter (1 pint) of water is not too much for a young plant; a large plant may require 1 liter (2 pints). The plants' happy appearance after a good watering indicates their appreciation.

STAKING

Flower stems elongate very quickly towards the end of spring. Thin stakes 75 cm (30 in) long support carnation stems that will grow between 50 and 60 cm (20 and 24 in) tall. Secure stems to canes with sweet-pea rings; older plants can have their flower stems enclosed and supported by small galvanized-iron-wire circular hoops fastened to stakes. These can be obtained from garden sundriesmen or made up from 16-standard-wire-gauge wire from a hardware shop. Some people dislike seeing bamboo canes in outdoor beds; I use thin prunings of *Buddleia* and *Philadelphus*. Twiggy sticks are useful for supporting short-stemmed carnations and some of the modern, taller stemmed pinks. Alternatively, for plants in their second and third years of flowering in the garden, many less-obtrusive types of stakes are now available, which should be placed in position before stems start to elongate. These will give all the support needed, without the necessity for the "forest of canes" sometimes described by garden writers. These critics have probably only seen carnations grown by dedicated exhibitors whose concern is for perfect blooms and stems rather than a natural garden appearance.

PEST CONTROL

Few pests do serious damage to garden carnations and pinks, but some are a nuisance. Standard methods of control for such pests are mentioned briefly below, but the subject is dealt with in more detail in Chapter 12.

Aphids, mostly greenfly, can physically cripple a plant that becomes really infested; they suck sap from the leaves, causing them to curl up and become distorted. Another reason to control greenfly at all times is that they can transmit viral diseases from infected to healthy plants by sucking the sap and inoculating healthy plants, just as mosquitoes infect humans with malaria. Fortunately greenfly are comparatively easy to control compared with some other pests. Pirimicarb (Miracle Rapid) sprays control aphids without harming bees, ladybirds, and lacewings.

In summer in Britain the tortrix moth spins a web and gums up a plant's leaf tips, where it deposits its eggs, which turn into tiny green caterpillars. These chew their way down into the center of the shoot and are most destructive. They are very wriggly and lively, and easily squashed when handled.

Another moth whose caterpillars do mischief is the lychnis moth, which deposits its eggs in or near the calyx. This caterpillar makes its way into the calyx and feeds on the contents, leaving the calyx a hollow shell. Sometimes the caterpillar eats petals and even ripe seeds along with the unfertilized seeds. The small orange tortrix moth can sometimes be seen towards dusk, but the lychnis moth is very shy and seems to be truly nocturnal.

The frog-hopper or cuckoo-spit invades stem axils and sucks the sap like the greenfly. The spittle is as unsightly as it is on lavender *(Lavandula)* bushes, but this pest is as easily controlled as greenfly.

Thrips are a nuisance. The eggs are laid on the tips of the sepals of the calyx before the petals are fully formed. The tiny insects suck the pigment from the petals as they grow, so that when the flower blooms it shows blank scars where there should be color. Thus a red flower shows disfiguring white spots and blotches.

Pirimiphos-methyl sprays (Miracle Sybol) or malathion control all the pests mentioned above. Slugs, snails, and the carnation maggot, nuisance pests of outdoor carnations and pinks, are fully dealt with in Chapter 12, where the above pests are also dealt with in more detail, as are alternative methods of natural pest control.

FEEDING OUTDOOR PLANTS

Assuming that some manure was incorporated in the pre-planting preparation of the soil and a dressing of balanced fertilizer applied in the spring, plants in their first season should not require further sustenance. Two- and three-year-old plants, however, may well require some assistance. I recommend two monthly feeds commencing in spring. Soot and water mixed, and horse, sheep, or cow manure diluted in water are still used. The animal-based liquid manures are usually considered to be of the correct strength when diluted to the color of weak tea. However, most people now buy from shops or garden centers modern products, of which there is a bewildering choice. The advantage of some of these modern plant foods is that apart from the three main elements—nitrogen, phosphorus, and potassium—they also contain minor and trace elements, which are also essential to healthy plant growth. The granular or powdered forms are sprinkled around the plants in early spring, hoed into the surface, and watered in. Those of liquid form are diluted with water and may be applied to the plant roots by watering-can. Rates of use and dilution are given on the packet or bottle; however, outdoor-grown border carnations and garden pinks are not gross feeders and do not require the repeated application of liquid fertilizer that is recommended for annual bedding plants. One, or at most two, liquid feeds, applied in spring and early summer, should be sufficient, otherwise those shoots that should become the following year's flower stems will themselves run to flower, leaving few or no shoots for the future.

The proportions of the plant-food elements nitrogen, phosphorus, and potassium are stated on the packet or bottle as N for nitrogen, P or sometimes P_2O_5 for phosphorus, and K or K_2O for potassium, expressed as percentages of the whole. Where present, the proportions of the minor and trace elements are also mentioned, including magnesium (Mg), manganese (Mn), molybdenum (Mo), copper (Cu), iron (Fe), boron (Bo), zinc (Zn), and cobalt (Co). Various types of fertilizers are available for special purposes: some plants require a high nitrogen analysis, some high phosphorus, and others high potassium. Carnations and pinks usually prefer what is called a balanced fertilizer—one that contains all three elements in approximately equal proportions—although when the plants begin to spindle for bloom they benefit most from a high-potash liquid feed to assist in the production of strong stems and buds. Modern repeat-flowering pinks will benefit from the application of a teaspoonful of dried blood worked in around each plant after the first full flush of flowering to encourage further flowering stems to develop. They should also be dead-headed regularly for the same reason. If cuttings are to be taken to increase or replenish stocks, it would be advisable to take these before feeding in this way, otherwise potential cuttings could elongate for flowering. Border carnations and pinks should not be fed during the autumn and winter months.

STOPPING

Some pinks should be stopped and some others never stopped. Modern pinks of repeat-flowering habit are stopped when very young by breaking or pinching out the growing tip of the main stem. This induces lateral breaks, or sideshoots, to grow from the leaf axils, which lie at the base of a leaf where it joins the stem. When stopping, make sure that a part of the stem is removed, not just the leaf tips, because if the growing tip is not removed it will continue growing.

Pinks cultivars that are not repeat-flowering are usually called old-fashioned pinks; not a good name because some new cultivars have the same old-fashioned habit of flowering once only, usually in early summer. Typical once-flowering pinks are 'Mrs. Sinkins', 'Paddington', 'Excelsior', and 'Sam Barlow'. This type must not be stopped but allowed to grow naturally. Some people imagine that all laced pinks are old-fashioned; they certainly are not. The older white-ground laced pinks like 'Dad's Favourite', 'Paisley Gem', 'William Brownhill', and 'John Ball' have only one flowering period, but there are now many newer, repeat-flowering laced pink cultivars. It is also advisable to stop some of the stems of second- and third-year modern pinks before they flower to encourage new shoot production for the following year.

Border carnations should *not* be stopped, as is done with the perpetual-flowering type of carnation. Border carnations and perpetual-flowering carnations have quite different habits of growth. The perpetual-flowering type produces one main stem that has axillary shoots high up on that stem, so in order to make the young plant grow into a bush the growing tip of its stem is pinched out when it is only about 10 cm (4 in) tall. This induces four to six sideshoots to grow from the remaining axils, thereby producing a bushy plant, with the sideshoots growing on to become flowering stems. Stems of border carnation plants, on the other hand, each have six to twelve sideshoots growing from the base naturally without having to be induced. Pinching out the top of the stem would almost certainly prevent it from flowering that summer, although sideshoots on some very vigorous cultivars might possibly flower in the autumn. Since autumn flowers almost always damp off and become mildewed, they are no consolation for the loss of flowers that those same shoots should have produced the following summer. The only time I would stop a border carnation would be when a rare plant sends up a single flowering stem without sideshoots. Preventing flowering might induce sideshoots for propagation and thereby rescue the plant from extinction. In his *The Florist's Vade-Mecum*, published in 1683, Samuel Gilbert advised,

> Some July flowers in summer shoot up but with one stem or stalk, without any layer; if you suffer it to blow, the root dies, therefore if you have no more of that kind, suffer it not to flower, but timely cut off the spindle that it may sprout anew, which preserves the root.

DISBUDDING

Disbudding is discussed in detail under Border Carnations and Pinks Under Glass, but plants grown for the garden may also be disbudded. Young carnation plants in the garden are best left undisbudded, except for the small bud that grows beside the crown bud. This bud should be removed because sometimes it pushes the main bloom to one side, but it must not be removed before it can be handled easily, otherwise the main bud could be damaged. Plants in their second year of flowering benefit from moderate disbudding, leaving three or four buds per stem to mature; three-year-old plants could have all buds taken out, save the crown bud on each of their many stems. Buds should not be removed all at once because this could cause the calyces to split. Pinks should be left to grow naturally with all their buds and thus are not disbudded.

EARLY AND MID-SUMMER ATTENTIONS

Pinks start to flower in early summer and border carnations in mid-summer. Encourage repeat-flowering in modern pinks by dead-heading—that is, removing dead blooms and cutting their stems hard back when they have finished flowering. Carnation stems must be watched over and secured to their stakes to keep them growing straight. Give the plants a spraying or dusting with insecticide before buds are too far advanced, so as not to spoil the flowers.

Enthusiasts always become impatient when the buds show color; not surprising since it takes two to three weeks from the time the petals break through the tip of the calyx to the time the flower is fully open. It is even more tantalizing with new cultivars, and more especially still when these are of one's own raising. Old favorites are no less welcome, those that have stood the test of time and won awards at trials and trophies at the carnation shows over many years. The growth habit of the plants is almost as interesting as their flowers; the color of the foliage, green or blue-gray, the height and strength of the stem, the type of calyx, the straight or curly leaves, the form of the flower and its coloring, and not least, the presence or absence of perfume. It is simply amazing how, after a sudden rainstorm, the flowers can be full of water yet still look beautiful, and then dry off in the sun and appear never to have been wet.

CUT FLOWERS FOR HOME DECORATION

Many gardeners are loath to pick flowers from their outdoor-grown plants because this would affect their flower display. A closely planted row or two of border carnations or pinks may be grown in the kitchen garden specially for cutting for the home. These could be surplus layers, cuttings, or plants grown from seeds. Some of the foliage could be useful as a foil to the blooms, whether at home or on the show table, and there is the added interest that some seedlings could turn out to be worthy of naming. The life of cut flowers is lengthened by the use of flower preservers like Bio Flowerlife or Chrysal, which are obtainable at flower shops and garden centers. I was very sceptical regarding the value of these products until I tried them for myself. The water in a vase containing a flower preserver does not need to be changed, only topped up. Vases or bowls of cut flowers should not be kept near fresh fruit because ethylene gas given off by the fruit makes the flowers "sleepy," making them old before their time.

Taking Cuttings of Pinks and Border Carnations

Cuttings from non-flowering sideshoots of pinks and border carnations should be made in summer, reducing them to five or six pairs of leaves and trimming square across below the joint bearing the lowest leaves. Use a very sharp knife or razor blade to ensure a clean cut. Remove the lowest pair of leaves and dip the base of the cutting into water, shake off the surplus water, and dip into a hormone rooting powder, preferably one incorporating a fungicide. For those who prefer to avoid the use of hormones or fungicides, dipping the cuttings in a solution of permanganate of potash helps to stimulate root formation and prevent fungal problems. Only a few crystals are required, sufficient to color the water a pale rosy pink. This was a well-known method before the advent of hormone powders. Insert the cuttings 4 cm (1.5 in) apart into a shallow tray containing a rooting medium consisting of equal parts peat and sharp sand, or peat and perlite. Alternatively, clean grit-sand alone may be used. Kept shaded and lightly sprayed over with water, the cuttings should root in three to four weeks. A propagator with bottom heat at 16 to 21°C (60 to 70°F) is required to root carnation cuttings successfully, and it is an advantage, though not a necessity, with cuttings of pinks, which can also be rooted in a shady spot in the garden, incorporating sharp sand with the garden soil to provide a good rooting medium.

Although most carnations can be increased by taking cuttings, it is my experience that border carnations do not respond to this method as well as other types of *Dianthus*. Border carnations seem to resent that three weeks' separation from the mother plant, which layered plants are not required to suffer. Border carnations are often mist-propagated professionally as well as by layering, but having tried this method for myself I am convinced that layering is still the better way.

Some northern England gardeners used to put border carnation cuttings into sandy soil in the open garden in autumn and replant into flowering positions when rooted in spring. I believe this worked well for a few old cultivars. In fact, I remember a very popular old carnation, one that seems to have been forgotten, that rooted very easily and was grown for cut flowers on allotments all over England; sometimes allotment growers who had surplus plants would advertise these for sale in the classified columns of such magazines as *Amateur Gardening*. This popular old cultivar was called 'Pillar Box Red', which may not have been its original name. I have never seen this name in any catalogue. The first named carnation plants I grew were bought at the Apple Market at Kingston-on-Thames, Surrey; these were in 9-cm (3.5-in) clay pots and cost nine old (pre-decimal) pence each. They were labelled 'Bella-Donna', 'Skirmisher', and 'Duchess of Wellington', the last-named being the lavender-gray self border carnation, not the perpetual-flowering carnation of the same name. All grew into large, strong plants in their second year, when several cuttings of each were taken and placed in the open ground under glass cloches in the autumn. One cultivar rooted very well, another poorly, and the third not at all.

Layering Border Carnations Outdoors

Before proceeding with this section on layering border carnations, I must repeat the following paragraph taken from my monograph on border carnations written three decades ago (J. Galbally 1966).

July is the month when all good gardening magazines, diaries and calendars remind us to layer our carnations. And so gardeners all over the country go down on their knees with penknives and wire pegs, pegging down everything resembling a sideshoot, disfiguring fine healthy plants in order to replace them with ten times as many baby plants. They could ensure more flowers for the following summer by just leaving their plants unlayered. A certain amount of propagation is necessary, of course, in order to keep up one's stock and to replace the older plants.

Plants may be propagated in two ways: sexually or asexually. Raising plants by sowing seeds is sexual propagation, and increasing plants by taking cuttings or layers is asexual propagation. When a desirable plant is raised from seed, to produce new plants identical to the original plant it must be propagated vegetatively (asexually) by taking cuttings or layers. New plants raised from seed taken from the original plant would be most unlikely to reproduce the original plant exactly. All plants produced vegetatively are extensions of the plant from which the propagating material was taken, and all such plants together form a clone (and have the same genetic make-up). That famous apple 'Cox's Orange Pippin' was raised from a pip, and since all 'Cox's Orange Pippin' trees all over the world were grown from buds or grafts they are extensions of that original tree, and together form a clone.

Although they can be increased by taking cuttings, border carnations are best increased by layering. Layering has always been favored by carnation experts, who believe this method to be much superior to that of taking cuttings. Layering is like taking cuttings except that the sideshoot is pressed into the compost and secured with a pin without being detached from the mother plant. By this method the shoot does not suffer any shock, but continues to grow on without check while starting to form roots. Some people find layering difficult, possibly because they do not do it properly. It really is very simple and certainly produces the best results, but you must have the right kind of knife for the job (see Making the Incision). Most people slit the stem upwards from the base of the shoot, because the knife they use is not suitable to cut it the proper way, which is downwards. Every professional I have known slits the stem downwards. Pictures showing stems being cut upwards always make the process appear so awkward and clumsy. Cutting upwards while holding the stem above the node to be slit means that the knife travels towards the fingers, rather like holding a piece of wood in one hand and pushing a chisel towards it with the other, which used to be rewarded by a cuff on the side of the head from the woodwork instructor.

Most people take cuttings of their pinks, although a few prefer to layer them. Some cultivars are better increased by layering, but most are not suitable because their growths are too slender for slitting with a knife. The procedure for layering pinks is exactly as described for border carnations.

PREPARING SOIL FOR LAYERING

Plants are ready for layering when they are in bloom in summer when the side growths ripen. Before this time they are too sappy and brittle and by autumn they are too hard. Plants in their first season of flowering are best for propagation, although two-year-old plants can be used. Loosen the soil about the plants to be layered to a depth of 8 cm (3 in) and stir in moist peat and sharp sand so that the mixture becomes one of equal parts peat, sand, and soil. The peat should first be wetted thoroughly and the moisture then squeezed out. Make the compost quite firm otherwise the shoots will not root well. Before starting you must decide how many shoots you wish to peg down; you may require a large number to increase your stocks considerably or just a few plants simply to replace older ones. Your choice will determine whether you layer every shoot on the plant or half of them, leaving the unlayered shoots to flower the following summer.

PREPARING SIDESHOOTS

When examining sideshoots to be layered you will notice that their internodal lengths, or distances between leaf joints, diminish as they approach the growing tips of the shoots. About four or five pairs of leaves down from the growing tip the internodal length will be rather shorter than those further down the stem. This joint is the one to choose for making the incision from which the new roots will emerge. There may be two or even three such joints to choose from, one of which may be more convenient for bending to soil level than the others. Remove all leaves below the chosen joint by holding each joint in turn between finger and thumb, and pulling sharply with the other hand. If a joint is not held firmly when its leaves are pulled the stem may snap at the joint and you will be left holding a broken-off shoot that was to have been layered. Strip all shoots intended for layering before proceeding further.

We always speak of pairs of leaves because every joint or node carries two leaves, one on each side. So any point on the stem is identified as, say, the fourth joint down or fourth node down, or as leaving four pairs of leaves.

MAKING THE INCISION

A small, really sharp, thin penknife with a fine point is the most suitable instrument for layering carnations. My own was bought from Woolworths long, long ago and has put down some half a million layers. It is so small that I can enclose it completely in the palm of my hand. I could not use a razor blade nor one of those scalpels with a detachable blade; the former is dangerous, also too small to allow for a firm grip, and the other is too long to be maneuverable. A knife completely enclosed in the hand is exactly right for the job. Before using the knife I wrap my thumb pad in a 1.25-cm (0.5-in) wide strip of thin adhesive plaster.

Push the point of the knife right through the middle of the stem immediately below the lowest joint with leaves, and bring the blade down through the stem, continuing through the next joint and bringing the blade out sideways immediately beneath that joint. Should the cut tip be too sharply pointed it must be trimmed square across (Figure 8-4). When the shoot is gently brought down to soil level the cut will open and the tongue thus formed must be pressed into the prepared compost (Figure 8-5). When pushing the shoot down to soil level, care must be taken not to snap the stem at a joint. Assistance may be given by pressing very hard into the stem with thumbnail and forefinger, which allows the stem to be manipulated without snapping it. This bruising of the stem must only be done between joints, otherwise the stem will snap. Deciding at which internode to pinch the stem to allow correct placing of the layer into the compost is quickly learned with practice; some longer stems may require more than one pinch. Push the shoot into the compost with one hand while also pressing down the stem, near the tongue, with the forefinger of the other hand, thereby ensuring the pressure does not snap the shoot.

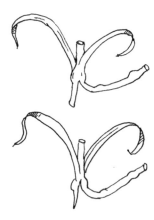

Figure 8-4. *Top:* correct cut in stem, tongue trimmed square across. *Lower:* incorrect cut, too sharply pointed at base.

While still holding the shoot down, push a layering pin into the compost at the spot vacated by the forefinger, about 1.25 cm (0.5 in) back from the tongue, and make the compost firm (Figure 8-6). Layering pins may be made from 16 swg galvanized-iron wire, cut into 15-cm (6-in) lengths with pliers and bent up to form miniature walking sticks. Do not use thinner wire or hairpins because these are not stout enough to hold down a strong layer. When such a layer lifts itself it leaves a cavity in the compost under its tip and, like a "hung" cutting, the layer fails to root. Peg the shoots down in succession around the main stem allowing not less than 5-cm (2-in) space between them. Spray or sprinkle water to settle the shoots in, and keep the compost moist by occasionally spraying as necessary.

Should my detailed description of layering make it seem impossibly difficult, may I mention that someone once said that it would take several pages to describe properly the process of shaving one's beard, yet the veriest beginner quickly learns to master the art.

LIFTING ROOTED LAYERS

After six weeks the layers will be sufficiently rooted to be separated from the mother plant. It has always been advised by growers of border carnations that the stem connecting the layer to the mother plant

Figure 8-5. Cutting tongue in layer; note sideshoot stripped of lower leaves.

should be cut after five to six weeks, but the layer itself not removed until a week later. The value of this procedure has been questioned, but it seems reasonable to me, and since it entails no extra work, I shall continue to cut my plants' umbilical cords a week before lifting. Should the soil be dry, water the layers before carefully lifting them with a trowel. Take care not to damage the new roots with the trowel or the layering pins.

Rooted layers may be planted directly into their flowering positions, or potted into 8- or 10-cm (3- or 4-in) pots according to size, and overwintered in a cold greenhouse or garden frame. These plants may be used as replacements for old or failed plants, or potted into larger pots when well rooted, and flowered in a greenhouse or even outdoors on a patio. I consider it a good plan to grow a few plants in pots specially for propagation, particularly if space can be found in a greenhouse or conservatory.

Figure 8-6. Kinked stem to facilitate layering; layering pin in correct position.

I grow border carnations in the garden borders, in pots in a greenhouse, and in pots outdoors. Now that I have only small greenhouses I take my pot-grown plants outdoors to layer them where it is cooler and there is more space for receptacles for new layering compost, old removed compost, canes, stripped-off leaves, and flower stalks. Layering pot-grown plants is much easier and more pleasant than squatting or kneeling to layer plants in the ground. The following section dealing with border carnations and pinks under glass discusses layering in pots in more detail.

Border Carnations and Pinks Under Glass

Pinks and carnations dislike hot conditions, therefore the greenhouse must have ample ventilation, including ideally a door at each end. Roof ventilators on both sides of the greenhouse are essential, and except in small greenhouses, there should also be ventilators in the side walls. Greenhouses that have side walls of brick or timber should have staging to ensure the plants have sufficient light. Green-houses with glass down to ground level need no staging but should have a concrete base for the pots to stand on to prevent ingress of worms and other undesirable creatures. Small grit or sharp sand, about 8 cm (3 in) deep, makes a good base on which to stand the pots, holding a reservoir of moisture to provide welcome humidity on hot days. It also saves well-rooted plants from drying out when their roots protrude through the pot drainage hole. Greenhouses are essential for border carnation and pinks trade specialists and for keen amateur exhibitors. Artificial heat is not used, except where forced blooms are required for a very early flower show such as the Royal Horticultural Society Chelsea Flower Show in May. Not only do greenhouse-grown plants have perfectly clean flowers, but their cultivation is not interrupted by bad weather conditions.

FIRST POTTING

In autumn, pot well-rooted cuttings of pinks and layers of border carnations into 10-cm (4-in) pots and those less well-rooted into 8-cm (3-in) pots, using JIP 1 or a soil-less or peat-free equivalent. My own preference is for clay pots, although plastic pots are becoming the more popular. It is not necessary to crock the pots (see Final Potting, below). Part-fill the pot with compost so that when potting is completed the lowest joint with leaves sits on the soil surface, which would finish about 1 cm (about 0.5 in) below the rim of the pot. Holding the plant in the pot with one hand, fill in with compost with the other. Pot fairly firmly with your fingers, but do not ram, and tap the base of the pot on the bench to level off the surface. When plants are to be final-potted two to a pot they should be first-potted two to a pot in 11-cm (4.5-in) pots of JIP 1 compost or a soil-less or peat-free equivalent. Press the two layers close together in the center of the pot and follow the same procedure as for potting layers singly. Water the pots gently to settle the plants in, and do not water again until the pots appear to be almost dry.

Watering Small Pots. Plants in small pots of soil-based compost should be watered only when they are becoming dry. Soil-less and peat-free composts must always be kept moist, otherwise they may refuse to absorb water. Should this happen, place the pot in a tray and water from below as well as from above. Some pots dry out more quickly than others; much depends on where they are placed in the greenhouse, the amount of ventilation, and how close they are to each other. Ideally they should be spaced so that their leaves do not touch each other, so as to allow a free flow of air about them. Except in very bad weather with storms or gales, the ventilators should always be open. This is where ventilators on both sides of the greenhouse are so useful; those on the sheltered side can be open while others are closed. Temperatures below freezing point do not harm the plants even when the compost in their pots is frozen. After a long spell of freezing weather, the pots may become extremely dry at the roots. Although normally they suffer no damage while they are frozen, during a thaw very dry plants will suffer unless watered sufficiently to damp the compost right through.

FINAL POTTING

There is no special time to repot because much depends on when plants were propagated and potted. The earliest propagated plants may be ready by late autumn, while late-propagated plants may not be ready until spring. A whisker of root showing through the bottom of the pot indicates that the plant may be ready and should be knocked out of its pot for inspection. Before doing so, water any pot that appears dry, otherwise plants may stick to the pot wall, causing their roots to be damaged or, worse still, the root-ball to collapse. Plants showing a fair amount of root, but still showing some bare soil, are just right for final potting. Plants showing little root are best left awhile; there is no point in putting such a plant into a large potful of compost.

Border carnations may be grown singly in 15-cm (6-in) pots, pairs in 19-cm (7.5-in) pots, and trios in 23-cm (9-in) pots. Pinks may be grown singly in 12-cm (5-in) pots, pairs in 17-cm (7-in) pots, and trios in 20-cm (8-in) pots. Use JIP 2 compost, or a soil-less or peat-free equivalent. During winter the smaller pots are easier to water, whereas the larger ones require more care; but in summer the smaller pots dry out quickly, so then the larger ones are easier to manage. With a small greenhouse the use of 15-cm (6-in) pots may seem an extravagant use of space; three plants to a 23-cm (9-in) pot allow more plants to be grown in a given space than the smaller-sized pots.

Free drainage of carnations and pinks in clay pots can be provided by the process of crocking the pots, which involves placing large pieces of broken pot over the drainage hole and covering this with a layer or two of smaller pieces; these pieces of broken clay pots used to be called potsherds. Small stones may be used as an alternative. Pot drainage may also be kept clear by the use of a perforated zinc pot-crock over the drainage hole. It may be that these metal pot-crocks cannot be purchased nowadays; if not, they can be cut out from a sheet of perforated zinc or metal gauze. The original zinc pot-crocks existed long before plastic pots arrived and so were made to one size only, to cover the clay pot's drainage hole. Plastic pots have holes all over their bases, so suitably sized pot-crocks can be cut to fit them. These can also be covered with a layer of small pieces of broken pot or small stones to ensure sharp drainage. Alternatively, the crocked pots can be placed on perforated zinc discs. These also prevent entry of worms, woodlice, and other undesirables.

After crocking, part-fill the pot with compost, estimating the amount required to allow the surface of the root-ball to finish about 2.5 cm (1 in) below the rim of the pot. Make the compost fairly firm, then place the plant or plants in the middle of the pot and fill in with compost up to, but not covering, the root-ball. The compost must be made firm but should not be rammed hard. Settle the plants in with a good watering and wait until the compost is almost dry before watering again. Do not stop the plants by pinching out the main stem; border carnations should not be stopped, but left to grow naturally. (See Stopping earlier in this chapter for the one exception to this rule.) Pinks stopped at the rooted cutting stage should develop into bushy plants, so should not be stopped again.

Some growers prefer to take their plants outdoors in early spring, standing them on concrete, or staging such as corrugated sheets, which is covered with grit or sharp sand to hold a moisture reserve. The pots are then returned to the greenhouse in early summer when buds are well formed, but before showing any color. This method keeps the plants sturdy, with strong stems, and also frees the greenhouse for housing those precious half-hardy bedding plants that need protection from late frosts.

Watering Large Pots. It is very difficult to tell for certain when a plant needs watering. The surface soil may appear dry, but halfway down the pot the soil could be very wet. A soil compost like the JIP composts shrinks when it is dry and so leaves a space between the compost and the wall of the pot. When a clay pot that needs watering is tapped with a stick it rings hollow, almost as though the pot were empty. When the soil is firm against the wall of the pot, the pot gives out a dull note indicating that the soil is wet enough. This method does not work with soil-less composts in clay pots, which sound hollow when tapped even when the compost is quite damp. The best idea is to use a moisture meter, an instrument that probes the compost and indicates on a visible scale whether it is dry, moist, or wet at any level in the compost. When watering almost-dry pots, fill them to the top with water to ensure they are wetted right through to the bottom. With correctly crocked pots the water should disappear from the surface in a minute or so. In summer the 15-cm (6-in) pots may require watering every day and the 23-cm (9-in) size every other day, but it all depends on the weather, the compost, ventilation, shading, and whether clay or plastic pots are used. Plastic pots hold water longer than clay pots and so require less watering. Soil-less and peat-free composts must always be kept moist, otherwise they may refuse to absorb water. Should this happen, place the pot in a tray and water from below as well as from above. My own maxim on watering is, when in doubt in summer, water; when in doubt in winter, don't water.

Some people collect rainwater in water butts or troughs; fresh rainwater is perfect, but not water that has been standing for a long time. Water from the tap is safer and it doesn't matter how cold it is. When I grew thousands of plants I used to water by hosepipe, straight from the tap throughout the year. When holding the hosepipe the decision to water or not water each pot needs to be made instantly, otherwise the greenhouse would soon become flooded. This caused some plants to be over-watered and others under-watered. Now that I grow no more plants than most amateurs, I use a small watering-can, dipping it into a 9-liter (2-gallon) bucket. I fill buckets with tap water and allow them to stand for an hour or so before watering, having read somewhere that this releases some of the chlorine from the water. Heavily chlorinated water is said to be harmful to carnations; an excess produces symptoms similar to that of potassium deficiency, scorched foliage with necrotic spots. Sensible watering is more easily learned from experience than taught.

VENTILATION AND SHADING

Greenhouses can become very hot in summer, especially amateur-type greenhouses. High temperatures can be reduced by increasing ventilation, spraying plants and pots with water, and shading the greenhouse glass. Spraying in hot weather promotes humidity, conducive to healthy vigorous growth. Spraying all over the plants, except the flowers, assists in checking red spider mite. Lightly shade the greenhouse glass—the object is to diffuse sunlight, not block it out. Good light is most important for good growth, so shade must be applied evenly and sparingly. Check that no weak spots in the shading would allow direct sunlight to scorch the flowers. It is most important to remove shading thoroughly in autumn, because carnations must have good light to grow well. The product, Coolglass, will withstand the heaviest rain and stay on, yet can be wiped off easily with a dry rag when no longer required. The small pack covers a greenhouse 1.8 m × 2.5 m (6 ft × 8 ft) and the large pack covers a greenhouse 4.5 m × 6 m (15 ft × 20 ft). It is recommended that a paint brush or sprayer be used to apply the material, but I always use an old soft nylon broom with a long handle. All doors and ventilators should be kept fully open in hot weather, day and night. Where birds and cats are troublesome, cover door openings with light wooden frames covered with plastic netting or chicken-wire. Fit netting over ventilator openings, making provision for the opening and closing of the ventilators. Very fine mesh plastic netting and old lace curtain material are useful for keeping out bees, moths, hover flies, and other such pests.

STAKING IN POTS

In spring the plants will develop sideshoots at the base of the plants and the stems elongate for bloom. For most border carnation plants 1–

m (3-ft) canes are long enough to support the stems, although some tall cultivars will need the 1.2-m (4-ft) size. Push canes through to the bottom of the pot and secure stems with sweet-pea rings at intervals along their length. Before inserting used canes it would be wise to stand their ends into a red spider mite insecticide for a short while.

It should not be necessary to stake pinks growing in pots, but since most exhibitors are naturally very tidy people, most of them like to keep their plants under control. Some use the circular galvanized-wire ring supports as used for perpetual-flowering carnations, while others prefer the simpler method using three 45-cm (18-in) split canes and garden twine to encompass the growing stem.

DISBUDDING

Pinks are not disbudded, but should be left to grow naturally with all their buds. Exhibitors disbud their carnation plants to obtain flowers of the maximum size possible. Many disbud drastically, leaving the crown bud only, but this does invite the specter of calyx splitting. A burst calyx is unsightly, but it is even worse for exhibitors because it warrants disqualification of the exhibit. To prevent calyx splitting, place elastic bands (No. 8 size) over the calyces as soon as the buds begin to show color (Figure 8-7).

Exhibitors grow new plants every year; some remove every bud except the crown bud, others leave two or three buds to flower. My own preferred method for plants grown for exhibition is to allow the crown bud plus one or two others to remain; this way seems to produce flowers of better exhibition quality than those disbudded to leave the crown bud only. Where grown for cut flowers or just greenhouse decoration I would advise leaving all buds to mature except the one that grows directly alongside the crown bud. When left on, this bud sometimes causes the crown flower to tilt its head at an odd angle to the stem. Whether disbudded or not, the crown bud flowers first, followed by the other buds down the stem in descending order. Occasionally the crown bud may appear to be defective in some way; when this happens remove the bud and promote another bud to the office of crown bud. The lower buds provide presentable buttonhole flowers, although in some cultivars where these have very good stems

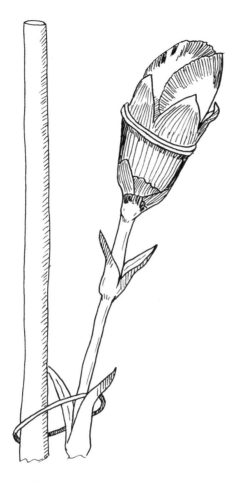

Figure 8-7. Calyx band.

they can be used as cut blooms for short vases. Some cultivars have beautiful flowers but lack scent, so since visitors invariably sniff flowers in a vase it would be wise to include a few blooms of clove-scented cultivars.

When disbudding, always wait until the buds are large enough to remove easily, otherwise the flower stem may become damaged in the process. To remove a bud, take the main stem between your thumb and forefinger, holding the node or joint from which the bud springs, and holding the stalk between the thumb and forefinger of your other hand give the stalk a sharp sideways pull (Figure 8-8). The bud should come out of the axil easily and quite cleanly.

While disbudding, look out for signs of insect damage. Greenfly can build up from only a few to an infestation very quickly, and it is at this time that thrips find their way into the growing buds to ruin the blooms even before they open. Spray with malathion or spray or dust with pirimiphos-methyl (Miracle Sybol), all of which also assist in controlling red spider mite. (See also Chapter 12.)

FEEDING POT PLANTS

Plants in soil-based composts should be fed when flower stems start to grow, and those in soil-less composts about six to eight weeks after final potting, according to vigor. Most modern compound fertilizers contain the three major elements, nitrogen (N), phosphorus (P), and potassium (K), as well as all the minor and trace elements required to grow plants well. The major and minor elements are usually expressed as percentages of the whole and the trace elements as ppm (parts per million). The minor and trace elements are particularly important with plants grown in a soil-less compost. Commence with a balanced feed, one having equal proportions of nitrogen, phosphorus, and potassium, such as Chempak Liquid Fertilizer No. 3 (20N 20P 20K), or Miracle Patio Formula (20N 20P 20K) for United States growers. Change to a fertilizer having a higher potassium ratio, such as Chempak No. 4 (15N 15P 30K) or Phostrogen (14N 10P 27K), when buds begin to form. Feed every seven to ten days according to the manufacturer's instructions and cease when buds begin to show color. Some growers prefer to feed plants with quarter-strength fertilizer at every watering instead of full-strength fertilizer at longer intervals. Lower-strength and more-frequent feeding should make for steadier growth.

New longer-lasting controlled-release fertilizers are available, the use of which would eliminate the need for regular feeding. In granule form, these have a special coating that, when in compost or soil, absorbs moisture; this unlocks the fertilizer inside the granules and the nutrients are released into the compost over a period of several months. Having successfully tried one of these products, with a balanced formula, during a month's absence on holiday, I would recommend this,

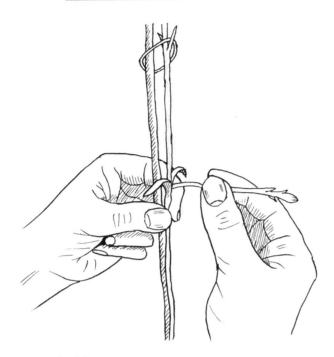

Figure 8-8. Disbudding.

particularly for those who are away from home all day. The granules are sprinkled around the surface of the pot, and a small amount of the fertilizer is released at every watering over the next four to six months. A check of the ingredients may reveal that trace elements are not included in this type of fertilizer. Where soil-less composts are used, the addition of a solution of both boron and magnesium when watering the plants would be advisable, given about once a month at the rates recommended in Chapter 12.

One or two high-potash liquid feeds may still be given when the stems have elongated and small buds have started to form, to improve stem quality and enhance flower color.

LAYERING IN POTS

When layering pot-grown carnations you need two stools or strong wooden boxes, one for the pot and the other for the propagator. The pot can be turned a little as each successive shoot is layered; so much easier than having to keep moving around a plant growing in the ground. About 2.5 cm (1 in) in from the rim of the pot, dig out a ring of soil about 5 to 8 cm (2 to 3 in) deep and replace with a layering compost made up of equal parts damp peat, sharp sand, and soil. Actually, I use John Innes seed compost plus peat and sand, which gives sterilized soil, and not garden soil, which could be infected with pests and diseases. Some growers use a half-and-half mix of peat and sand only. Fill the trench around the pot surface to soil level and make quite firm—firmness is important. (For details of the layering process, refer to instructions and diagrams earlier in this chapter.) Strip the shoot to be layered of all leaves except for the top four or five pairs. Press the cut shoot into the prepared compost fairly close to but not touching the pot wall, and peg down with a layering pin, ensuring that the cut slit opens to form a tongue (see Figure 8-4). Some shoots will need to be manipulated as previously described in order to confine them within the pot. This takes a little practice but one soon learns the knack. Make the layers firm and do not cram every shoot around the pot, because then most will not root well or will make skinny layers. Allow at least 5 cm (2 in) of space between layers, which will mean that some shoots remain unlayered (Figure 8-9). A strong plant may carry as many as a dozen sideshoots in three tiers of four shoots each. (They are not truly tiers; each sideshoot branches from the stem a little higher than the preceding sideshoot.) The lowest shoots are mostly rather hard and some of the higher shoots are undersized. The middle four make the best layers; the addition of the best two from the top and bottom tiers will give six shoots that should produce top-quality rooted layers.

After pegging them down, keep the layers well sprayed over for about three weeks, by which time they should have started rooting. After six weeks, snip through the stems connecting the layers to the mother plant, and a week later the rooted layers may be lifted and planted out or potted into 8- or 10-cm (3- or 4-in) pots as required. Take care not to damage roots when pulling out layering pins. Those mother plants from which layers were taken and which have a number of shoots remaining can be planted out in the open border to flower the following summer. Where there is space in greenhouse or conservatory such plants could be grown on in larger pots and produce

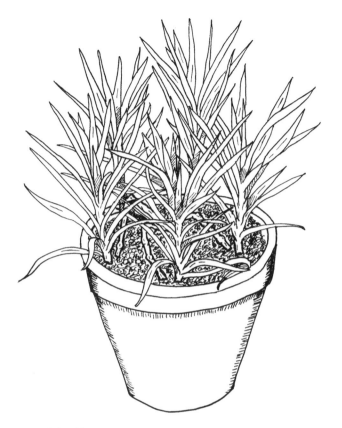

Figure 8-9. Potful of layers.

a good crop of fine flowers for cutting, or if fed generously even provide blooms fit for the show bench.

HOLIDAYS AND VACATIONS

Enthusiasts about to go on holiday or vacation become very concerned for the well-being of their plants during their absence. Watering the plants is their greatest concern. There are all kinds of ingenious methods of automated watering, including the use of battery-operated controllers to automate and control watering systems. There are mains drip kits for use with individual pots, or grobags and automatic capillary bench watering, using a small ball-valve tank. When I went away on holiday I left my plants in the tender care of my next-door neighbor, who cheerfully admits to knowing little about greenhouse plants so I knew my instructions on watering would be followed faithfully. Before leaving I pushed Phostrogen Plant Pins and Phos-Tabs into each pot, and when I returned six weeks later my plants were not even pleased to see me. They were all perfectly clean, well fed with no sign of aphids or red spider mites. Plant pins may be just the solution for those who dislike handling pesticides and therefore may be well worth the extra cost involved. Similar products to Plant Pins and Phos-Tabs are Keriguards and Kerispikes, although their active ingredients are different. Keriguards contain dimethoate and Plant Pins contain butoxycarboxim; Kerispikes and Phos-Tabs contain slow-release plant foods.

Plate 1. *Dianthus deltoides*, the maiden pink

Plate 2. *Dianthus deltoides*, the cultivar 'Microchip'

Plate 3. *Dianthus gratianopolitanus (D. caesius)*, the Cheddar pink (Gary Eichhorn)

Plate 4. *Dianthus microlepis* (Gary Eichhorn)

Plate 5. *Dianthus neglectus (D. pavonius)*

Plate 6. 'Becky Robinson', laced pink, around a rose bed

Plate 7. 'Ben Gascoigne', rock garden pink

Plate 8. 'Berry Burst', rock garden pink (Gary Eichhorn)

Plate 9. 'Bridal Veil', old-fashioned pink

Plate 10. 'Brympton Red', old-fashioned type pink

Plate 11. 'Chetwyn Doris', exhibition Allwoods pink

Plate 12. 'Constance Finnis', old-fashioned type pink

Plate 13. 'Coronation Ruby', laced pink

Plate 14. 'Dad's Favourite', old-fashioned pink

Plate 15. 'Devon Cream', garden pink (H. R. Whetman & Son)

Plate 16. 'Devon Maid', garden pink (H. R. Whetman & Son)

Plate 17. 'Devon Wizard', garden pink (H. R. Whetman & Son)

Plate 18. 'Doris', exhibition Allwoods pink, in a garden bed

Plate 19. 'Emil Paré', old-fashioned pink (Gary Eichhorn)

Plate 20. 'Gran's Favourite', laced pink

Plate 21. 'Helena Hitchcock', laced pink

Plate 22. Highland pink hybrids

Plate 23. 'Kesteven Kirkstead', exhibition pink

Plate 24. 'Little Ben', garden pink

Plate 25. 'Maureen Patricia', rock garden pink

Plate 26. 'Monica Wyatt', exhibition pink

Plate 27. 'Paisley Gem', old-fashioned pink

Plate 28. 'Queen of Henri', old-fashioned, painted lady pink (H. R. Whetman & Son)

Plate 29. 'Ursula le Grove', old-fashioned pink (Gary Eichhorn)

Plate 30. 'Whatfield Gem', rock garden pink (H. R. Whetman & Son)

Plate 31. 'Whatfield Joy', rock garden pink (H. R. Whetman & Son)

Plate 32. 'Alfriston', scarlet self

Plate 33. 'Bryony Lisa', white-ground fancy

Plate 34. 'David Saunders', white-ground fancy

Plate 35. 'Doris Galbally', apricot-ground fancy

Plate 36. 'Eileen Neal', heliotrope-gray fancy

Plate 37. 'Eileen O'Connor', apricot self

Plate 39. 'Golden Cross', yellow self

Plate 38. 'Eva Humphries', white-ground picotee

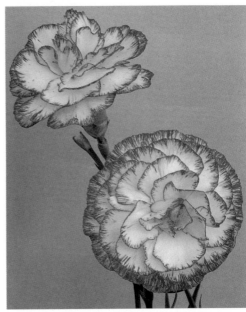

Plate 40. 'Grey Dove', gray self

Plate 41. 'Hannah Louise', yellow-ground picotee

Plate 42. 'Hazel Ruth', white-ground fancy

Plate 43. 'Howard Hitchcock', yellow-ground fancy

Plate 44. 'Maudie Hinds', yellow-ground fancy

Plate 45. 'Michael Saunders', heliotrope-gray fancy

Plate 46. 'Natalie Saunders', white-ground picotee

Plate 47. 'Peter Wood', light pink fancy

Plate 48. 'Sandra Neal', apricot-ground fancy

Plate 49. 'Sean Hitchcock', white-ground fancy

Plate 50. 'Uncle Teddy', white-ground fancy

Plate 51. Border carnations in the greenhouse

Plate 52. 'Ann Unitt', apricot-ground fancy

Plate 53. 'Audrey Robinson', white-ground fancy

Plate 54. 'Charlotte', white-ground picotee

Plate 55. 'Clara', yellow-ground fancy

Plate 56. 'Clara's Lass', white-ground fancy

Plate 57. 'Cream Sue', cream self

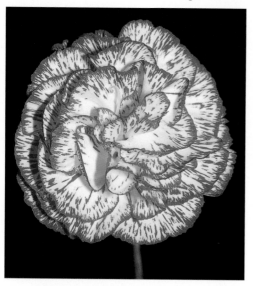

Plate 58. 'Crompton Classic', white-ground fancy

Plate 59. 'Dona', pink self

Plate 60. 'Dunkirk Spirit', apricot-ground fancy

Plate 61. 'Ivonne', yellow-ground picotee

Plate 62. 'Joanne', pink self

Plate 63. 'Joanne's Highlight', light pink self

Plate 64. 'Little Dianne', pale lilac fancy

Plate 65. 'Pierrot', lilac-pink fancy

Plate 66. 'Salamanca', yellow self

Plate 67. 'Scarlet Joanne', scarlet self

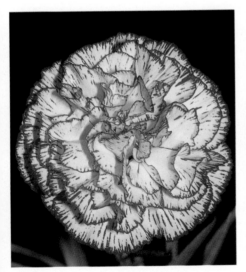

Plate 68. 'Tony Langford', lavender fancy

Plate 69. Malmaison carnation 'Duchess of Westminster'

Plate 70. Malmaison carnation 'Tayside Red'

Plate 71. Group of Malmaison carnations at Wisley gardens

Plate 72. Chabaud strain of annual carnation

Plate 73. 'Festival Cherry Picotee', annual dianthus

Plate 74. 'Raspberry Parfait', a dianthus for summer bedding

Plate 75. 'Rosemary Mixture', a dianthus for summer bedding

Chapter 9

Cultivation of Perpetual-Flowering Carnations

The best way to start with perpetual-flowering carnations is to obtain young plants in spring from a reputable specialist grower. The young plants should be pot-grown and "stopped and broken." This means that when the original rooted cutting was growing well it was stopped by having its growing tip pinched out, which induced its main stem to send out side growths from the remaining leaf axils. These branches are called breaks. The young plant, usually in or from a 8-cm (3-in) pot, should have four or five side growths. At this stage it is ready for potting into a 15- or 18-cm (6- or 7-in) pot.

Cultivation of Perpetual-Flowering Carnations

FINAL POTTING

As described for border carnations and pinks in the previous chapter, free drainage for clay-potted plants must be provided by crocking the pot. In addition to the placing of broken pieces of pot over the drainage hole, I use pot-crocks placed over the drainage hole and under the large crock. These are circular discs of perforated zinc that keep out worms, woodlice, and other pests, and the zinc is said to be lethal to slugs. They can be cut from sheets of perforated zinc, which were used for food safes before refrigerators became common. When I first grew carnations in a greenhouse I bought new pots, but when it came to potting my plants I had no crocks. The famous nursery of J. and E. Page was situated on the other side of my farthest garden fence, so I popped round and asked if I could help myself from the rubbish heap. Of course they grew their carnation plants in raised beds, but they also grew late chrysanthemums in pots outdoors for taking into the houses when their tomato crop was finished. (I thought their carnations were wonderful: 'Ashington Pink', 'Betty Lou', 'King Cardinal', 'Maytime', 'Topsy', and that massive white self 'George Allwood', the first carnation to be patented.) Growers who do not have crocks or nurseries at the bottom of their gardens can resort to using gravel covered with lumpy peat, which is also a good way to crock plastic pots.

Plants may be potted-on into JIP 2 or a soil-less or peat-free equivalent (see Chapter 10 on potting composts). Before use, the compost should be tested for condition by gently squeezing some in the palm of the hand; when the hand is opened the compost should stay in one piece, yet fall apart at a touch. If dry, it can be sprinkled with water sparingly until it feels right. Never use wet compost; spread it out thinly on large plastic bags in the garden and the sun and wind will soon dry it out. Also, before potting on, ensure that plants are not dry at the root. If dry, place in a bucket of water, remove when bubbles cease to rise, and allow the root-ball to dry off somewhat before potting on. After crocking, half-fill the pot with compost and make fairly firm. To remove the plant from its small pot, place one hand over the top of the pot with the plant's stem held between two fingers. Holding the base of the pot with the other hand, turn it upside-down and tap the pot sharply on the edge of the potting bench. The plant then should be placed so that the top of its root-ball rests about 2 cm (0.75 in) below the rim of the pot, this to allow for subsequent watering; fill in with more compost up to the top of the root-ball. Make soil-less composts fairly firm, soil-based composts rather firmer, but do not ram.

SUPPORTING PLANTS

Perpetual-flowering plants grown in pots can be supported with 1-m (3-ft) bamboo canes and plant support rings. Before inserting used canes it would be wise to stand their ends in a red spider mite insecticide for a short while. A new method of supporting carnation plants has been specially devised for those grown in plastic pots. Known as the Tri-port system, it consists of a triangular ribbed, strong plastic stake with a galvanized steel clip that is attached to the stake and grips the wall of the pot. The clip holds the stake erect and prevents any rocking movement. In conjunction with the system is a range of plant support rings, which are fixed to the stake as the plant grows. I find the system also useful for clay pots with a soil compost, although for these the steel stake clip is not absolutely necessary. The PVC stakes, which are claimed to be rot-proof, are in 45-cm (18-in) and 90-cm (36-in) lengths.

SECOND-STOPPING

About three weeks to a month after final potting, some of the plant growths will have grown eight to nine nodes or pairs of leaves. You now have to choose whether or not to "second-stop." If you intend to heat the greenhouse to obtain winter flowers, then second-stopping is necessary, otherwise all the plant's original sideshoots will run up to flower in late summer and early autumn. Most growers compromise and go for a "stop and a half"; this means you stop half the growths and allow the others to spindle for bloom. The most forward growth is stopped by snapping out the growing tip at a joint when the growth has eight or more nodes or pairs of leaves, leaving five to six pairs of leaves. With thumb and forefinger of one hand, hold the joint from which the tip is to be removed. With thumb and forefinger of the other hand, hold the stem just above the joint and, with a quick sideways pull, snap out the growing tip. This should come out cleanly provided the plant is held firmly in both hands. In a week or so after stopping, axillary growths will begin to appear and eventually each stopped growth will have five or six side growths of its own to produce a succession of flowers. The first of the second-stops will probably be made in early summer, the second at mid-summer, and the third in late summer. The unstopped growths will flower first in late summer and autumn, and the stopped growths throughout the winter and early spring. Unstopped growths produce earlier flowers, but stopped growths produce a greater total number of flowers. Note that the snapped-out growing tips should be discarded and not made into cuttings because such side growths never make up into vigorous plants. Note also that the spray-type carnations should be stopped once only; bought plants of spray carnations will have been previously stopped so no further stopping is required.

If you prefer to forgo early blooms in favor of producing a greater number, then you should stop all the sideshoots. These become ready for stopping at different times, according to their rates of growth, which ensures a succession of flowers over a long period in the winter. As a very rough guide, each stop should begin to produce flowers after about five or six months, but there are so many variables in cultivation that this should not be relied upon. Stalks from which flowers are picked during autumn produce new growths that may be taken as cuttings or left unstopped. These unstopped growths should produce a new crop of blooms throughout the following spring and summer. Ensure that growing stems are kept supported, adding further wire support rings as necessary.

WATERING PLANTS

In warm weather, newly potted plants may be sprayed over occasionally with a fine mist to prevent flagging. Water only when the compost begins to dry out and then fill the space at the top of the pot so as to wet the compost right through to the bottom. Watering is hard to learn, even harder to teach. Soil-grown plants must be watered carefully, more so than those in a soil-less compost. They should be allowed to become quite dry on top, with the knowledge that there is almost always moisture beneath the surface of the soil. Small plants can be knocked out of the pot, or their relative weight judged to act as a guide. Experienced growers can tell by the appearance of the foliage, but even the cleverest expert can be wrong sometimes. Most growers go by the appearance of the soil surface. Over- or under-watering is not critical in summer; carnation plants are extremely tolerant at that time. However, they should be examined every day at least to ensure that none dries out completely. I confess to over-watering small plants in spring and summer, but rarely lose one. Larger clay pots of soil may be tapped with a stick and those that ring hollow should be watered heavily; those that do not ring are not to be watered.

It is sometimes claimed that plants in soil-less composts cannot be over-watered, but I am rather sceptical of this. They should not be allowed to become as dry as soil plants sometimes are, however, because when really dry they may not be able to take up water. The surface appearance of most soil-less composts gives some indication of moisture content, and the plants can be watered accordingly, but I rarely flood a plastic pot containing soil-less compost as I would a clay pot containing soil. Clay pots are porous and absorb moisture from the compost, and therefore they dry out sooner than plastic pots, which retain moisture. The compost surface in a plastic pot can appear dry, yet the compost itself be quite wet halfway down the pot. Watering should always be finished early enough in the day to allow foliage to dry off before nightfall. Moisture on the plants in a still atmosphere predisposes them to attacks of mildew and botrytis.

Even the most experienced growers sometimes have difficulty deciding whether or not a plant needs watering. An ingenious device for measuring the moisture in a pot, called a moisture meter, has a probe, rather like a knitting needle, a scale, and an indicator that shows dry, moist, or wet. The clever part is that it indicates moisture conditions at any level from the top of the pot to the bottom, which is more than the best grower can do without knocking the plant out of its pot.

FEEDING

Plants cannot be fed all at once because they do not dry out uniformly and therefore require watering at different times. I resolve this problem by waiting until the majority are dry enough to require watering, feeding these, but not watering the remainder, which would then need watering and feeding a few days later. This should not be taken to extremes; do not wait until plants have dried out completely. Never feed a really dry plant; if in doubt, water with plain water first.

Also never feed an obviously sick plant; the most likely cause of its sick appearance is its sluggish root system. Water the plant carefully, keeping it on the dry side until a healthier appearance denotes its roots are growing again. Plants can be badly affected by too much fertilizer, which interferes with the normal function of the compost to conduct water and plant foods. To avoid this condition, water plants heavily with plain water about once a month during summer to leach out the chemical salts, then return to normal feeding and watering as before. Plants final-potted into a soil-based compost should not require feeding until flower stems start to grow, after which they should be fed as described for plants in soil-less composts.

Plants growing in a soil-less compost will require feeding from about a month after final potting. A balanced liquid fertilizer should be applied—that is, one having a chemical analysis with approximately equal percentages of nitrogen, phosphorus, and potassium—although it should be said that some exhibitors prefer to use a high-potassium fertilizer, such as Chempak No. 4 (15N 15P 30K) or Phostrogen (14N 10P 27K), when buds begin to form, which they claim strengthens the flower stems. The chemical analysis is given on the bottle or carton in percentages, always in the order of N, P, and K. Most liquid feeds are supplied in dry powder or crystal form, with instructions and dilution rates. Keep to the rates advised; as it says on the medicine bottle, "It is dangerous to exceed the stated dose."

In addition to the three major elements, plants require minor elements, usually expressed as percentages, and trace elements as ppm (parts per million). A commonly used product for feeding carnations is Chempak Liquid Fertilizer No. 3, described as an all-year-round feed for all carnation plants. This has a balanced formula (20N 20P 20K) and may be used as a root and foliar feed. It has all the necessary minor and trace elements included, most of them in chelated form to make them more easily assimilated. The instructions recommend mixing 2 level teaspoons (10 ml) in 4.5 liters (1 gallon) of water and feeding plants every seven to ten days during the growing season; but for best results mix one level teaspoonful in 10 liters (2 gallons) of water and apply at every watering. Growers who prefer weak feeding at every watering cannot see the sense of giving plants plain water when plant food could be given with it, which seems reasonable. They consider that small meals at short intervals maintain a steadier growth than big meals at longer intervals. Continue feeding until late autumn, finishing with a high-potassium feed.

Another popular product is Vitax soluble plant food (19N 19P 19K), a balanced fertilizer for general feeding. There are Vitax and Chempak fertilizers suitable for use with diluters. These contain nitrogen and potassium but not phosphorus, it being assumed that the potting compost contains sufficient phosphorus to last the life of the compost; phosphorus is rarely leached to any serious degree. Phosphatic fertilizers can block up narrow-bore tubes, which is one reason why a dye was introduced to indicate whether or not the fertilizer properly mixed with the water supply. The simple diluter I used was the Cameron diluter, which fitted between two lengths of hose-pipe and was designed with a narrow-bore tube to suck up fertilizer from the container to merge with the flow of tap water. When the small-bore tube became blocked the flow of fertilizer was interrupted and plain water only flowed through the hose-pipe, hence the need for a very strong dye that, even when greatly diluted, would still color the water sufficiently to act as an indicator. Diluters are most useful where a large number of plants are grown, and they are extremely time-saving. One small tip: always loosen the clamp after use in mid-winter; mine split open after a heavy frost and had to be welded.

Use of the new longer-lasting controlled-release granular fertilizers (see instructions on Feeding Pot Plants in Chapter 8) would eliminate the need for regular feeding. A balanced formula would take care of spring and/or summer feeding, whereas one having a much higher percentage of potash would be more acceptable for the late-autumn and winter months. Where a slow-release fertilizer has initially been incorporated in a homemade compost, however, supplementary liquid feeding would not be required for about five to six months, or even a year, after potting, depending on the type used. A check of the ingredients may disclose that trace elements are not included in this type of fertilizer. If soil-less composts are used, the addition of a solution of both boron and magnesium when watering the plants would be advisable, given about once a month at the rate recommended in Chapter 12.

Winter Feeding. Where the greenhouse is to be heated to around 13°C (55°F) for continuous flowering, the plants should be fed monthly during winter with a high-potassium fertilizer. Where the greenhouse is heated in winter to maintain a temperature of 4°C (40°F), the growth rate is slowed down considerably. Some flowers will be produced, but they are few and far between compared with those grown in the more usual higher temperature. The late-autumn high-potash feed is the last one of the year. Give another such feed early in the new year. With plants grown in an unheated greenhouse, give one feed of a high-potash fertilizer in mid-autumn. Water very carefully during winter and only when necessary to prevent plants from drying out completely. Provide plain water only with no fertilizer added.

Alternatively, a controlled-release granular fertilizer with a high potash content may be sprinkled around the pots in late autumn. This would be released slowly during the following months, as and when the plants are watered.

SUMMER AND AUTUMN CULTIVATION

Some growers prefer to stand their plants outdoors during the summer months, especially young plants, which will not flower until autumn. The pots should be stood on concrete or some sort of staging, such as corrugated sheets covered with sand or small grit. Red spider mite is less likely to be troublesome outdoors, and the plants should then be rehoused in early autumn, before night temperatures fall below 7°C (45°F).

In the greenhouse, watering becomes an everyday necessity in summer, and in hot weather the pots and paths must be lightly sprayed to keep them cool. Small grit or coarse sand beneath and between the pots may be well damped down and ventilators and doors kept open to maintain a movement of air among the plants. Wire-netting frames over the door spaces keep out cats and birds and enable doors to be kept open day and night when necessary. Warm conditions favor the breeding of insect pests. Greenfly will multiply very quickly unless checked as soon as seen. Spray with an insecticide such as pirimiphos-methyl (Miracle Sybol) or malathion, which will also check thrips and frog-hoppers (cuckoo-spit). Red spider mite can be checked by frequent spraying with clear water, and salt-water sprays are said to be effective, but only an insecticide specifically intended to deal with this pest will have any real control over it. All sorts of foliage and stem infections may manifest themselves; for treatment and remedies, see Chapter 12 on pests and diseases. For information on watering, feeding, and pest control during holiday or vacation absences, see Holidays and Vacations at the end of Chapter 8.

Some growers in Scotland and the north of England do not shade their greenhouse glass; in the warmer climate of southern England, shading in summer is an absolute necessity. It should be sufficient merely to diffuse the sunlight to prevent scorch, not to block out the light. The product Coolglass is very effective, easy to apply and, more important, easy to remove in autumn when no longer required. The plants' foliage may be sprayed over with a fine mist, but not so late in the evening that it would prevent the foliage from drying out before nightfall. In autumn, scarify the surface of the compost to remove algae. Plants grown in an unheated greenhouse should have all flower stems removed. Break them out at the fifth to seventh joint down from the bud to produce strong sideshoots and to provide flowers throughout the following summer. This operation should be done mid-autumn onwards and spread over a month.

DISBUDDING

Disbudding must be carried out methodically so as not to induce over-rapid growth, thereby causing calyces to split. Start with the lower part of the flower stem, removing the long thin stalks that would otherwise produce flower buds and eventually very small flowers. Allow a few days before removing the next stalk above, and so on until finally removing the small bud or buds close to the crown bud. These last buds must be removed only when large enough to handle easily. The crown bud is the topmost one, that which is to produce the bloom. Do not drop buds and stalks about, which could rot and cause mildew. Later, when the flower blooms, it is picked at about the seventh joint, or node, down from the calyx; when disbudding, remove axillary growths from all those joints, leaving a clear stem. With cultivars known to have a suspect calyx it is wise to use calyx bands. Most growers use the small elastic bands (see Figure 8-7), although I have seen wire bands used for this purpose. Some exhibitors even use twist-ties, while cut-flower growers resort to green artificial sepals, which are scarcely noticeable when tucked into a burst calyx.

Note that miniature or spray types of carnations are disbudded in a totally different way from the standard cultivars. With these types the crown bud is removed and all other buds left to bloom, thereby producing a spray of blooms rather than a single-specimen bloom.

WINTER CULTIVATION

Perpetual-flowering carnations will not stand up to a hard frost for any length of time. How you heat your greenhouse will dictate the quantity of winter flowers produced. A steady 4°C (40°F) may produce a few flowers, but 10°C (50°F) will produce many more, especially in periods of good light. Ensure that all traces of summer shading have been removed from the glass; winter sunshine is very welcome, stimulating growth. Also be sure to allow sufficient ventilation. Fresh air is always necessary but must be controlled so as to prevent cold air flow. Sun and air about the plants keep them dry, which is essential, but also increases their need for water. Keep a close watch on plants and only water the dry pots, ensuring the compost is wetted right through. Discontinue feeding in winter, except where higher temperatures are employed for increased winter flowering production. Aphids continue to be active throughout winter. Insecticidal smokes are most useful at this season when spraying should be avoided.

SECOND-YEAR PLANTS

Spring is the time to check up on one-year-old plants. Those well rooted in 15-cm (6-in) pots should be repotted into 20- or 23-cm (8- or 9-in) pots in JIP 3 or a soil-less or peat-free equivalent. Any that have not made good growth may remain in their original pots, which should have 1 tsp (5 ml) of ground limestone sprinkled over the surface, to be washed in by subsequent waterings. Those that have grown poorly should be discarded altogether as not worth greenhouse space.

One month after repotting, commence feeding with a balanced liquid fertilizer at fortnightly intervals, increasing to weekly in early summer. Alternatively, a controlled-release balanced fertilizer applied in spring would eliminate the need for regular liquid feeding. Warmer conditions favor the breeding of greenfly; spray with a suitable insecticide before they appear, and repeat weekly. Discontinue heating in late spring and keep the greenhouse atmosphere moist during hot weather. Admit full ventilation whenever conditions permit. On very fine days, spray the foliage, pots, and paths with a fine mist, but early enough in the day for plants to dry off before nightfall. Do not be deceived by daytime conditions; late-spring night frosts can check growth, so be prepared to reduce ventilation on clear nights.

CUT FLOWERS FOR HOME DECORATION

Although we call them cut flowers, they should not be cut but snapped out at a joint, at about the seventh joint down from the calyx, according to the vigor of the cultivar. Flowers may be cut at any stage after the petals have grown out of the calyx and have started to unfold, but usually they are left until the outer layer of petals is fully open. Ideally, flowers should be cut either in the early morning or the late evening, and they should be kept in deep water for several hours before being arranged in a vase. It is wise to take a tall container into the greenhouse to hold the flowers after the bases of the stems have been trimmed with a sharp knife. Remove the lowest joint, the knobbly bit, using a sloping cut, and the lower leaves, so that only the bare stems are placed into the vase. See the section on Cut Flowers for Home Decoration in Chapter 8 for information on preserving cut flowers.

Some flowers are naturally almost circular in outline, with their guard petals lying flat. I have noticed that a few of those cultivars that have flowers of good form have curly tips to the sepals. Since these sepal tips curl outwards the petals are allowed to lie back flat. When guard petals stick up it is because they are held up by the stiffness of the sepals. The pointed sepal tips can be curled outwards with small tweezers, the kind useful for removing splinters. This should improve the form of the flower and may also slightly increase its size.

PERPETUAL-FLOWERING CARNATIONS FROM SEED

Although, as with the border carnations, perpetual-flowering carnations are usually not grown from seed other than by breeders to obtain new cultivars, seed may be sown very early in the year in a temperature of about 15°C (60°F) in John Innes seed compost or soil-less or peat-free equivalent. They should be potted into 5-cm (2-in) pots in JIP 1 or soil-less or peat-free equivalent and gradually acclimated to the cooler atmosphere of the greenhouse. When ready they should be potted on into 9-cm (3.5-in) pots, and again when well rooted into 12-cm (5-in) pots in JIP 2 or soil-less or peat-free equivalent. The young plants must not be stopped but allowed to run up into bloom so that their value may be assessed, and the plants either can be grown on in the usual way or discarded outright. With plants to be retained, remove the flower with a short length of stem so as to induce the production of sideshoots for propagation.

Cuttings of Perpetual-Flowering Carnations

PROPAGATING EQUIPMENT

The first requirement for propagating cuttings of perpetual-flowering carnations is a suitable propagating frame or case, equipped with bottom heat. Professional establishments use mist-propagation on a large scale, and small-scale versions are available for amateurs. Carnation cuttings can be placed in a pot or tray of either sand, peat and sand, or peat and perlite, without heat, and many are rooted this way by amateur gardeners. However, to root them successfully at all seasons does require the assistance of bottom heat. When in the nursery business I used a large mist-propagating unit, but later I switched to a homemade wooden frame 2 m × 30 cm (6 ft × 1 ft) on legs tall enough to provide a convenient height for working. The bed is enclosed with heavy-duty polyethylene and filled to a depth of 5 cm (2 in) with builders' sand. A 6-m (20-ft) long electric soil-warming cable is laid on the level surface of the sand and evenly spread out in lines 8 cm (3 in) apart with loops at the ends in the form of a grille. An additional layer of sand about 5 cm (2 in) deep is placed upon the cable and made level. The cable uses 70 watts of electric power and heats the moist sand to about 26 to 32°C (80 to 90°F). Incidentally, I use a power-breaker socket for safety. Shallow trays of compost placed on the surface of the moist sand are warmed to a temperature around 18 to 24°C (65 to 75°F). The sand base must be kept moist to spread the heat evenly. This frame accommodates some 300 cuttings comfortably, which I keep misted over with a very ancient quart-sized brass pressure-sprayer. The sides of the frame are enclosed with polyethylene film and the top closed, when necessary, with a 2-m (6-ft) length of corrugated plastic roofing sheet. The frame is uncovered most of the time but closed at night. A simple, primitive affair, but very effective on an amateur basis.

A modest mist-propagating unit would be more useful for people who are away from home for much of the day, the fine mist controlled by an "electric leaf" that switches the water on and off at the right times. Even more simple for those who wish to root only a few cuttings is to insert them in a rooting medium in a flower pot, which should be placed in a polyethylene bag and kept closed with an elastic band or twist-tie. Improvements on the polyethylene-bag method are the propagating pots and trays with a tall cover that fits snugly over them to maintain the desirable close atmosphere. This close atmosphere obviates the necessity to spray over the cuttings frequently. However, cuttings do root better in a good light; in fact, with frequent misting they may enjoy bright sunshine right from the start up to the time they produce roots.

ROOTING MEDIUMS

Many rooting mediums are used for cuttings. The oldest, and still my own preference, is probably washed, sandy grit. Then came peat—I remember when it was called Sorbex and had to be obtained from Germany, and a similar product came from Denmark. Peat and sand mixtures became universally popular, although some growers favored vermiculite, a form of expanded mica. I never did well with vermiculite for cuttings; it was always too wet for my liking. Then came perlite, described as exfoliated volcanic rock. This product was widely used in the building trade for insulation purposes. The first time I acquired it I was obliged to write to the shippers at Hull Docks, who would send me a sackful, which although huge, was light enough for children to carry about. This is still the best medium, in my opinion; light, porous, and sterile, it can be mixed with peat both as a rooting medium and a soil-less potting compost. Peat-sand and peat-perlite mediums should be mixed to a half-and-half ratio and made damp, then allowed to drain off before cuttings are inserted. Plastic pots, half-pots, half-trays, and multi-pots may be used, although shallow containers are advisable, allowing the bases of the cuttings to be nearer the warmth. Rectangular trays are best because when placed close together on the propagating bed they conserve bottom heat. The medium must be made fairly firm, otherwise the cuttings may topple over when sprayed or watered.

I have tried out the new peat-free seed and cutting compost, in which coconut fibre replaces peat. Pink and carnation cuttings rooted very well in this medium and I found it a pleasure to work with, provided the compost was not allowed to become too dry.

TAKING CUTTINGS

Cuttings may be taken at any time of the year when strong healthy ones are available, but the most suitable time for amateurs to take a batch of cuttings is in very early spring, when they root easily and grow away well with the best season of the year before them. Never take cuttings from a dry plant; water plants the day before taking cuttings. Cuttings taken for propagation should look lively, healthy, and vigorous. Such cuttings never flag and seem able to root in about twenty days, but not all cultivars have cuttings like this. Cuttings may be made from growths produced on the stalks left behind when the flowers are picked. Don't take very stubby growths, nor very long shoots that are really flowering stems. Those shoots between these two extremes should be fairly short-jointed at the base, have about six pairs of developed leaves, and be 10 to 12 cm (4 to 5 in) long. Shoots should be snapped off at a joint, cut square across immediately below a joint, and the lowest pair of leaves removed. The cut must be made with a razor blade or very sharp knife. If you wish to ensure that cuttings are free of insect pests, immerse them completely for two to three seconds only in a diluted liquid malathion insecticide solution.

It is important that no time be lost between taking the cuttings and inserting them into the propagating bed; if cuttings have been removed but are not likely to be used immediately, they should be kept with their bases in water to keep them turgid. I am well aware of the advice that carnation stems should never be cut nor cuttings stood in water because these actions spread injury and disease. I have seen, however, thousands of unrooted cuttings standing in jars of liquid Hortomone A at a large commercial nursery, and I have always stood my own cuttings in water for 24 hours or more. Some border carna-

Figure 9-1. Correct and incorrect shoots for cuttings. *Left:* shoot too long-jointed; *right:* short-jointed shoot to make a good cutting.

tion cultivars have been layered, using the knife, for over sixty years, and some cultivars of garden pinks are considered to have survived with bits cut off them and pushed into sandy soil for hundreds of years. I am also aware that carnation cuttings have been "proved" by researchers to root without being trimmed off at the base, and to root satisfactorily even with the base "torn and mashed" before being inserted into the propagating medium. My own experience is that the bruised base of a perpetual-flowering carnation and the base of a border carnation layer that has struck a stone in the ground will certainly produce roots, but the bruise caused will slowly spread, as it does in a stored apple, apparently healthy until weeks later when the apple, or the base of the plant, is completely rotten. I agree that breaking out cuttings and flowers and not standing cuttings in water is good advice for a commercial business establishment where nothing should be left to chance, but it is a counsel of perfection as far as the amateur gardener is concerned, "not regarded as universally binding."

Always allow about 4 cm (1.5 in) of space between cuttings in pans or half-trays. Dip the end of the cutting in clean water, shake off the surplus, dip the base of the cutting into a hormone rooting powder, preferably one containing a fungicide, tap to remove surplus powder, and push the base of the cutting into the rooting compost. The lowest leaves should rest just above the compost surface. Place the container on the sand base of the propagator and spray over with a very fine mist. Successive trays of cuttings should be placed close together to prevent heat from escaping from the surface of the propagating bed. Spray cuttings with a fine mist whenever they appear dry; at times when this is not possible, keep the cuttings close by covering and enclosing them with a polyethylene sheet or a frame cover. The rooting medium must be watched carefully; when it appears dry on the surface it must be lightly watered sufficiently to reach the bottom of the tray. The sand bed upon which the trays of cuttings are placed must also be watched for signs of drying out. The sand must be kept moist to allow the heat to be distributed evenly. Always switch off the electric power before watering even when it is fitted with a power-breaker; I once had one of these that became faulty and had to be replaced by the distributors. After two weeks, when the cuttings appear perky, spraying may be reduced and the compost allowed to be less moist, thereby inducing roots to grow in search of moisture. By three weeks the cuttings should be ready for lifting, although some cultivars may take a little longer. Perpetual-flowering carnations are very easy to root well, so there is no reason why a 100 percent strike should not be achieved.

POTTING ROOTED CUTTINGS

When rooted, the cuttings may be potted into 8-cm (3-in) pots using JIP 1 or a soil-less or peat-free equivalent. The old-fashioned way with first potting was to pot the poorly rooted cuttings into thimbles (5-cm [2-in] pots), the medium-rooted into thumbs (6-cm [2.5-in] pots), and the well-rooted into sixties (8-cm [3-in] pots). This is very sensible advice; most amateurs seem to collect small pots of all sizes over the years so may as well put them to use. No crocking is necessary and potting should be fairly firm but not rammed. Ensure that the node with the lowest leaves rests just above the surface of the compost. Leave 1.5 cm (0.5 in) space above the surface of the soil to allow for watering. If space is scarce, the pots may be set down pot thick in the greenhouse—that is, touching one another. If a temporary lack of greenhouse space necessitates postponing the potting of rooted cuttings, they should be fed weekly with a high-potassium fertilizer such as Phostrogen or Chempak No. 4.

FIRST STOPPING

About three to four weeks after potting, when the plant has about eight or nine pairs of leaves, the growing tip must be snapped off at a node or joint, leaving five or six joints or pairs of leaves. This is called the first stop (Figure 9-2). With thumb and forefinger of one hand, hold the joint from which the tip is to be removed. With thumb and forefinger of the other hand, hold the stem just above the joint and, with a quick sideways pull, snap out the growing tip. This should come out cleanly, provided the plant is held firmly in both hands. Do not use the snapped-off tips for making into cuttings; these very rarely make up into good plants.

In a week or two after stopping, sideshoots will be observed growing out from every leaf axil; these are called breaks. About three to

Figure 9-2. First stop (perpetual-flowering carnations).

four weeks after stopping, when the young plants appear to be established, examine the bottom of each pot for the emergence of the tell-tale whisker of root, which usually indicates that the plants are ready for final potting. Knock the plants out of their pots to make sure they are sufficiently rooted. JIP 2 or a soil-less or peat-free equivalent and 15- or 18-cm (6- or 7-in) pots are used for final potting, and the plants should be potted as directed previously under Cultivation of Perpetual-Flowering Carnations at the beginning of this chapter.

Cultivation of Malmaison Carnations

POTTING MALMAISON CARNATIONS

Rooted cuttings of Malmaison carnations should be potted into 9-cm (3.5-in) pots in early spring using JIP 1 or a soil-less or peat-free equivalent. A zinc pot-crock over the drainage hole keeps out soil pests. Pot fairly firmly, fasten to a short thin stake, water in gently, and keep shaded for a few days. When well rooted, pot into 15-cm (6-in) pots with JIP 2 or a soil-less or peat-free equivalent. Use a zinc pot-crock plus small broken pieces of pot for drainage. Pot fairly firmly with the root-ball surface flush with the potting medium and about 2.5 cm (1 in) below the pot rim, and stake with a short cane. Feeding is similar to that for perpetual-flowering carnations. Disbudding may be light or severe according to the wish of the grower. A first-year plant may be disbudded to leave only the crown bud, or three to five buds. Obviously the more buds left on, the smaller the flowers they will produce; single-bloom plants produce flowers up to 15 cm (6 in) across. Strong two-year-old plants can sometimes have as many as twenty to thirty blooms in flower at once. Some old growers preferred young plants, while others grew their plants on until three or four years old. After flowering, repot for a second season into 20-cm (8-in) pots with JIP 3 or soil-less or peat-free equivalent, after having cleaned up the plants by removing all old stems and dead leaves. As new shoots appear, fasten them to short stakes to keep them looking neat and tidy. Pests and diseases are all as for perpetual-flowering carnations.

PROPAGATION OF MALMAISON CARNATIONS

Malmaison carnations were originally propagated by taking cuttings until layering became the vogue. The plants were layered in summer after they had flowered. A frame was made for the purpose with timber sides and closely covered with glass lights. The plants for layering can be of any age, knocked out of their pots and buried in the soil in the frame with the sideshoots spread out conveniently for layering. The flowering stems were removed, together with all old and unwanted leaves, and an 8-cm (3-in) layer of compost was spread all over the frame area. The shoots were then layered in the usual manner as for border carnations, discussed in Chapter 8. Malmaison shoots are very brittle, therefore layering was not easy. The layers were carefully watered in, the lights placed in position over them, and shaded. The soil was kept just moist and the shading kept on until the layers began to perk up and show signs of having rooted.

I feel sure that most enthusiasts would prefer to take cuttings of

Malmaisons rather than go through that procedure of layering, especially considering we now have propagating trays with bottom heat provided by soil-warming cables. Cuttings about 10 cm (4 in) long are ideal and may be taken in winter and treated exactly as cuttings of perpetual-flowering carnations, including stopping to induce a branching growth habit.

Chapter 10

Greenhouses and Potting Composts

Greenhouse Conditions and Site

Perpetual-flowering carnations are usually grown in a heated greenhouse; border carnations and pinks are grown in an unheated greenhouse by keen exhibitors for the show bench. Carnations themselves dictate the kind of greenhouse they require: good light, fresh air, and protection from the elements in winter. Good light is particularly important in winter and for this reason the greenhouse is best positioned with its length running east to west. Although this run is ideal it may not suit all gardens, and better light may be obtained by some other orientation; trees, buildings, and other structures have to be taken into consideration. Perpetual-flowering carnations can grow to a height of 2 m (6 ft), therefore greenhouse sides must allow for this. For sufficient ventilation, every alternate top pane of glass on both sides of the ridge could be an opening ventilator, except those at the greenhouse ends, thus a six-bay frame would have two ventilators on each side. Doors at both ends of the greenhouse are a necessity, also hinged or louvred ventilators in the sides. Greenhouses with a door at one end only should have an electric fan ventilator fitted fairly high up in the door-less gable end. A four-bay frame would have two ventilators in the roof, one on each side; with a door at each end there would be no need for ventilators in the side of the greenhouse. A three-bay frame would have only one roof ventilator.

People who are away from home most of the day do have a problem with greenhouse ventilation; a very cool morning can be followed by a very hot afternoon. The solution is to install automatic ventilator openers, of which the most commonly used are those of the Bayliss type. There are three models, to suit light, heavy, or side ventilators, which can be fitted to wooden or aluminum greenhouses. They are operated by a piston in a tube that is pushed out by the natural expansion by heat of the mineral wax within the tube. The piston is linked to the ventilator and causes it to open. When the air temperature falls the wax contracts, and the ventilator is then closed by means of a strong stainless-steel spring. A variable control knob can set the ventilator opening temperature between 13 and 24°C (55 and 75°F).

There is much controversy as to the efficacy of timber as against metal-framed structures. I have used both kinds; the timber frame is useful because one can knock nails into it to hang up various tools and pin up names, dates, compost recipes, dilution rates, and so forth on the rafters, and even temporarily board it up should a pane of glass be blown out by a gust of wind on a Saturday afternoon when glass merchants are closed. But I prefer the aluminum alloy frame, which allows more light into the greenhouse and requires no painting or oiling to preserve it. Insect pests cannot bore into an aluminum frame, nor does it rot away. The mass-produced small aluminum greenhouses are excellent value for the money and are deservedly popular. I do admit, however, that such a greenhouse would be out of place in the garden of an elegant home where one would expect to see a structure designed and erected by craftsmen. Cedarwood greenhouses are very attractive in appearance.

Dutch light structures are popular with those growers who require a larger greenhouse. These are made up of Dutch light frames, single panes of glass measuring 142 cm × 74 cm (56 in × 29 in), joined together. Although such large panes may suggest expensive replacement, some Dutch light greenhouses are claimed to withstand winds of 160 km (100 miles) per hour. I once had a very large Dutch light house in which the roof-panes merely rested in grooves in their frames and were not fixed in any way. The glass stood up to gale-force winds all right, but the noise of their rattling in the frames was terrifying. I am sure they are better-made nowadays. Handling such large panes is difficult at first, mainly due to trepidation, but it is surprising how quickly one adapts to it. Fitting panes into roof frames is rather tricky; with hands on the middle of the longer sides one lifts the pane and rests it on one knee. The pane is then lifted further so that the lower, shorter end rests across the chest and the opposite end points towards the eaves end of the roof frame. The glass end is then gently pushed into the ends of the grooves of the frames, gently because the glass bends alarmingly in the middle. The glass pane is then fed slowly into the grooves, straightening the bend in the glass as it goes in.

I once found my own Dutch light greenhouse leaning ominously and was obliged to remove a hundred panes of glass before I could deal with the weakened framework. I had the glass all back again the same day without mishap, which is how I came to learn to handle Dutch light glass. When erecting a Dutch light house always check that frames are fixed truly square because rectangular glass won't fit into a rhomboid frame.

I learned a lot more about greenhouses when I bought a commercial-type greenhouse at an auction sale on a nursery sold for residential development. I dismantled it, carted it some sixty miles (96 km) to my own nursery where I re-erected it, complete with ventilator winding gear for roof and sides. The ventilators had counter-weights that afforded effortless operation, to the delight of young children who would turn the handle round and watch all the ventilators opening or closing at the same time. When I retired to a seaside-town bungalow my garden boasted one small aluminum greenhouse. These words are written on the anniversary of the great hurricane of October 1987, which blew my greenhouse right through the garden wall. I erected a new greenhouse, same make and size, and with some of the non-twisted metal salvaged from the wreck, plus a similar amount salvaged from a neighbor's wreck, I put up a second greenhouse on a brick base, the bricks salvaged from the wrecked wall. The two half-greenhouses were not of the same make, but their separate parts seem to get on all right together.

Greenhouses for carnations must afford the plants maximum possible light in winter and summer, therefore glass must extend to the base of the house or nearly so. Where there are walls that would obstruct light from the plants, then some form of staging must be employed to raise the pots. My own greenhouses have glass to ground level except for one course of bricks all round on the concrete base and on one row each side of the central concrete path. The two areas surrounded by bricks are filled with small stones right to the top of the bricks. This conserves moisture in summer, helping to keep the greenhouse cool, and also acts as a safety measure against plants completely drying out when short of water.

GREENHOUSE HEATING

Perpetual-flowering carnations are not completely hardy like border carnations and pinks and must be protected from frost. A wide choice of heating appliances are available using paraffin (kerosene), gas, and electricity. Eltex paraffin heaters are very well known and useful for small greenhouses; they provide a bonus for the plants with the carbon dioxide (CO_2) they generate. Electric fan heaters are useful in that their fans can be employed for cooling in summer as well as circulating heat in winter. There are two-kilowatt and three-kilowatt sizes, with a thermostatic control to maintain a selected temperature. Gas heaters are available with a four-kilowatt output and thermostatic control. The foregoing appliances are intended for the average-sized amateur greenhouse, up to 3.5 m × 3 m (12 ft × 10 ft). Electric tubular heaters are more expensive, but they are more permanent in that they are fastened to the greenhouse walls with fixing brackets. Greenhouses larger than the popular garden types may be heated by hot-water pipes, employing a boiler fuelled by coal, oil, gas, or electricity. Another commonly used method is to attach a perforated polyethylene duct to an electric fan heater, the duct running the length of the greenhouse to disperse warm air to all parts of it. Cool air can be blown through in summer, providing the movement of air so desirable in hot weather.

Lining the greenhouse roof and walls with polyethylene to conserve heat in winter is widely advised, and this can now be made considerably more effective because the new bubble and double-bubble polyethylene provide a kind of double-glazing effect. Some growers, however, find the loss of light, and the condensation thus caused, to be detrimental to plant health, the condensation causing botrytis. To obviate the condensation problem the polyethylene can be fastened to the outside of the greenhouse instead of inside it, fitted up to eaves level and attached with nylon string. Except for very small greenhouses, the roof can be insulated by fixing a number of wires across the width of the greenhouse, with polyethylene resting on it; the polyethylene may be pulled along to give protection at night or during extremely cold weather, and pulled back during the day to allow in more light. The doors and ends of the greenhouse must also be insulated; greenhouses with outside-sliding doors obviously must have their ends insulated on the inside.

To keep perpetual-flowering carnations in flower during winter the greenhouse temperature should be maintained at 10°C (50°F); some growers prefer 13°C (55°F), others 7°C (45°F). Plants will survive temperatures down to freezing point, but they will not produce many flowers under such conditions. They can be grown in an unheated greenhouse—many are—but there is always the danger that a very severe frost could destroy one's whole stock. The commercial Sim-type cut-flower carnations are less hardy than the exhibition types, which have more border carnation in their breeding. Some enthusiasts grow the exhibition type for showing only, without heat, and do not attempt to obtain flowers during winter.

Flower Pots and Potting Composts

Every grower must make a choice between clay pots and plastic pots, and between traditional soil composts and soil-less composts. Generally, soil-grown plants are potted-on into soil and plants grown in soil-less compost are potted-on into a similar compost. Soil-grown plants grow better in clay pots, while those in soil-less compost may be grown equally well in plastic pots or clay pots. Newly bought clay pots should be immersed in water and allowed to soak and dry out before being used, otherwise they will absorb moisture from the potting compost.

JOHN INNES COMPOSTS

John Innes loam-based composts are the outcome of long research into the subject by W. J. C. Lawrence, Head of Garden Research Department, and J. Newell, Curator, both of the John Innes Horticultural Institution, Hertford, England. They are the standard composts used by English gardeners.

JIP composts are made from good quality sterilized loam, spaghnum peat, and sharp sand in the ratio of seven parts loam, three parts granulated peat, and two parts sand by volume. To 36 liters (8 gallons) of this mixture is added 110 g (4 oz) John Innes base fertilizer and 20 g (0.75oz) ground chalk or ground limestone. John Innes base fertilizer is two parts hoof and horn, two parts superphosphate of lime, and one part sulphate of potash, all parts by weight; this mixture can be bought ready-made. The compost made by mixing the foregoing ingredients is called the standard compost or JIP 1; this compost is suitable for plants in 8-cm (3-in) pots. When potted-on, the plants go into JIP 2 or JIP 3 according to pot size. John Innes potting compost No. 2 is the recognized medium for final potting into 15-cm (6-in) pots. JIP 2 is similar to JIP 1 except that it contains twice as much base fertilizer and chalk, and JIP 3 contains three times as much of these components as JIP 1.

Although JI composts are regarded as standard, it must be said that they never can be that. There are many manufacturers of JI composts, all working to the same formula, but the basic ingredients loam, peat, and sand can and do vary greatly from one manufacturer to another. Many products bear the seal of approval of their manufacturers' association, but this cannot guarantee good results. Lawrence and Newell, originators of the JI composts, stated that these should not be stored for more than one month and never longer than two months or they would become too acidic. Bags of compost can lie about in wholesale depots, large stores, and small shops for longer periods of time, deteriorating, and some garden centers and large retail establishments keep such goods stacked outdoors where heavy rains find their way into the plastic sacks, leaving the contents sodden and unfit for use. Even when obtained in good condition, composts differ so much in texture from bag to bag that they must be regarded as anything but standard.

One virtually buys a pig in a poke and is obliged to trust to luck as to how well the precious plants will perform. However, it must be admitted that fortunately most plants do survive and some grow well, but there are always doubts when they grow poorly or not at all. I would suggest that if the John Innes Compost Manufacturers' Association sincerely cares about the gardeners who buy their composts they should have their bags printed with a "sell-by" date. Not only do food products bear such dates, but photographic films and most medications also bear a "do not use after" date. Insecticides and fungicides should also be date-labelled; I once mentioned to a knowledgeable acquaintance that a certain insecticide did not control pests as claimed and was told some products have a relatively short shelf-life. Some gardeners have bottles of this and that for many years, trusting these will do the job when called upon.

COMPOSTS FOR AMERICAN GARDENERS

Although a number of proprietary brands of compost are marketed for specific plants in the United States, some gardeners may prefer to experiment. The American Dianthus Society recommends any one of the following mixes for seed-sowing: (1) one-third commercial cactus-growing mix, two-thirds commercial sterile seed-starting mix; (2) half each of sterile seed-sowing mix and coarse washed builders' sand; or (3) half each finely milled peat moss and vermiculite. If available, I would personally recommend perlite in place of vermiculite. The mixture should be moistened slightly before use and squeezed out until just damp.

HOMEMADE COMPOSTS

Some exhibitors who grow a large number of plants find that mixing their own compost is economical compared with buying proprietary composts. There was a time when nurseries and carnation enthusiasts would stack grass turfs for several months and then use them as a base for making their potting composts. One also could buy top-spit loam; Kettering and Cranleigh loams were very popular and the Douglas firm of carnation growers used to sell their Bookham loam. I well remember seeing those neat and tidy turf stacks at Great Bookham. Amateur gardeners used to mix their own composts adding well-rotted animal manure, sharp sand or grit, bonemeal, wood ashes, and old mortar rubble in the following proportions: six parts loam, one part manure, half-part each sand and mortar-rubble, plus two 12-cm (5-in) potfuls of wood ashes and one 12-cm (5-in) potful of bonemeal per barrowload of the mixture. Very few growers considered sterilizing the loam; even if they did, the manure could well be suspect. This is probably the reason why so many gardeners lost so many plants to stem-rot and similar fungal diseases. The following advice was given by a nursery grower about 150 years ago:

> in order that the soil may be perfectly clear, or to make assurance doubly sure, I insert pieces of carrot and slices of potatoes, to entrap any grubs or insects which may have before escaped. But a more certain way than this has lately been adopted by an old friend of mine; he puts about two pecks of soil at a time into his side oven, and, after subjecting it to a heat destructive to vitality, whether in the shape of worms or eggs, he removes it, and subjects another parcel to the same process, till he has sufficient for his use; and, in this part of the country where side ovens constitute the principal feature in the cottager's fire-grate, and where of course, there is a constant and abundant heat, a great deal can be effectually cleaned with no other expense than the trouble. All this may to some growers appear needless, and a trouble which the difference will not repay; but it is punctuality and care in small matters, attending to the minutiae of the thing, which very often enables the grower of 50 pairs to beat the careless cultivator of 500, and at the same time prevent the loss and mortification of seeing layer after layer of some favorite sort to go in rapid succession. If this can be prevented, I think it would be acknowledged that no trouble is too great that will accomplish it. (*The Gardener and Practical Florist*, London, 1844)

Some growers now favor using a half-and-half mix of John Innes and soil-less composts. For the benefit of those who mix their own ingredients, this could be translated per bushel (4 × 2 gallon buckets) into one bucket of sterilized soil and one and a half buckets each of peat and sharp sand. For those who wish to reduce the weight of their pots of compost, I would suggest using instead one bucket of sand and half a bucket of perlite. Incorporating a slow-release fertilizer would avoid the need for the early supplementary feeding that is recommended with most brands of soil-less compost. The most suitable type for final potting of pot-grown carnations would seem to be one with a balanced formula, plus minor and trace elements, and that lasts about five to six months, used according to the manufacturer's instructions

SOIL-LESS AND PEAT-FREE COMPOSTS

Many brands of soil-less composts are available, mostly based on peat with the addition of fine sharp sand and plant foods. Having tried several, I cannot say I am impressed by all of them for growing carnations. I sometimes mix my own, using a proprietary brand of soil-less compost base fertilizer, as do many keen exhibitors who all seem to have their own favorite method. Most consider that the proprietary brands of soil-less composts are not sufficiently porous for carnations, which prefer a very open and gritty medium, that the ratio of peat to sand is too great, and that the sand itself is of too fine a grade. The sand for homemade composts should be washed grit-sand, 0.5 cm (0.2 in) down to fine sand in size, evenly proportioned. Spaghnum moss peat is generally favored, broken down finely and soaked and squeezed out before mixing. Some enthusiasts favor a one-to-one ratio of peat to sand, others two parts peat to one part sand, and a few prefer three parts peat to one part sand. All these ratios are by volume, and not by weight. Some growers also mix in perlite, others use perlite in place of sand. Perlite is made from volcanic rock, expanded by intensive heat treatment that gives it a microscopic internal cell structure. It is extremely light in weight, which makes the handling of pot plants much easier. Charcoal, at a ratio of one part charcoal to ten parts compost, is often added to keep the compost sweet and to prevent acidity. All methods seem to grow plants well enough, which proves that carnations are tolerant of a very wide range of cultivations.

Base fertilizers for making soil-less composts are obtainable from shops and garden centers and include Vitax Q4, Bio Bases, and Chempak products. Chempak also has a special compost base for carnations that contains more lime than their general base fertilizer. Where not obtainable locally it may be obtained by mail-order. Chempak also supplies a non-ionic wetting agent for adding to homemade composts, which assures a uniform water distribution and improves the water holding capacity. I learn that "non-ionic" is a technical term and that a non-ionic wetting agent will not carry an electrical charge—I am assured that non-ionic wetting agents are far superior to ionic ones for horticultural purposes.

Soil-less cultivation became the vogue because of the scare that good quality loam was becoming very scarce, and therefore the quality of commercial loam-based composts would suffer. Now, because of the concern that the continued use of peat may damage the environment and harm bird life, we have composts in which coconut fibre is used instead of peat. Some expert growers are not at all impressed by the results of the use of coconut fibre potting compost, saying more research needs to be done to produce a satisfactory product. I happened to pick up a brochure disseminated by commercial peat producers and I must say their arguments and facts are very convincing. At the present time John Innes loam-based composts, which, of course, include a proportion of peat, and peat-based soil-less composts are still available. Granulated peat is also available. So we all have a free choice to do as our conscience directs.

I remember the time when trade growers of carnations would meet at Horticultural Research Station open days to discuss cultivation techniques. They would also meet at carnation shows to learn from one another. One day when lunching with Steven Bailey and Charles Fielder, both well-known carnation specialists, Charlie asked Steve whether he used sterilized loam for his pot plants. Steve and I were surprised to learn that Charlie did not. "What about the weeds?" we asked. Charlie said it took him and his staff 11 days to go through the pots to clean them up. My point is that we enthusiasts are a bit stubborn, and prefer to make up our own minds, and when we have a satisfactory technique we like to stick with it.

SOIL-LESS CULTIVATION

Soil-less culture of plants, hydroponics, was first devised by W. F. Gericke, an American. In Chapter 2 I mention R. J. Morton's method of feeding carnations grown by soil-less culture. It was always advised that sand had to be lime-free and the water supply low in chlorine, neither of which was true of Morton's sand and water at Sunbury-on-Thames. I knew because my own nursery was only a mile away. Our sand came from the local quarry, Thames Sand and Gravel Co. His plants were grown in sand in 15-cm (6-in) and 20-cm (8-in) pots and in beds with asbestos-cement walls 18 cm (7 in) deep, and fed with his SSS fertilizer. Plants grown in pots and beds require a 1-cm (0.5-in) bottom layer of small stones or gravel, and filling in with sharp sand. The best sand grade is an even mixture of 0.5-cm (0.2-in) grit down to fine sand. To discourage the growth of algae the sand is covered with fine grit. Fertilizer is spread over the surface weekly and watered in, except in winter when it is used every two weeks. Some growers use an equal-parts mixture of sand and vermiculite, or sand and perlite. The Chempak Exhibition Carnation Fertilizer is said to be an updated version of Morton's formula.

Another interesting, but now rarely used, method using liquid fertilizer fits a waterproof trough about 30 cm (12 in) wide and 8 cm (3 in) deep along the bottom and in the middle of the growing bench. Wire mesh is placed in the trough and covered with glass wool saturated with the nutrient solution. The bench is filled with a mixture of vermiculite and sand to a depth of 18 cm (7 in) covering the trough. The trough is filled with liquid fertilizer, which is conveyed to the growing medium by capillary attraction via the glass wool. Not only are carnations grown well by this method, but also lettuce, tomatoes, melons, cucumbers, and strawberries.

GROWING BORDER CARNATIONS IN SAND

I was so impressed by Morton's sand cultivation of perpetual-flowering carnations that in the mid-1950s I decided to try the same method for growing border carnations. The habit of growth of border carnations is very different from that of perpetual-flowering carnations, however, and commercially it would have been very easy to go wrong. I had no one else's experience from which to benefit. Perpetual-flowering carnations continue growing throughout the year, whereas border carnations have a resting period during the winter.

Growth does not cease completely, but it does slow down very considerably. Over-feeding border carnations after flowering time would excite the sideshoots into growth just when they should be settling down to rest. This would cause them to spindle and to produce winter buds. Were such sideshoots to be layered, the resulting young plants would be unsaleable both in autumn and the following spring. This pitfall may be avoided in pot cultivation by reducing feeding to half strength by flowering time and to quarter strength by the autumn. Plain tap water only is used during winter, and only just sufficient to keep the plants alive.

When buying sand for potting, ensure it is "sharp washed" sand or grit; never use the soft sand used for making mortar. When final potting, cover the surface of the sand with small stones, the size normally used for gravel paths, which will prevent the growth of algae. Feed plants weekly, except in winter. Layering sand-grown plants calls for a departure from sand cultivation, but is still soil-less cultivation. Mix a layering compost of two parts granulated peat and one part sand and fill in to replace a 8-cm (3-in) deep channel of sand removed from all around the pot wall, having first taken off the layer of stones. I should mention that even though fertilizers used for sand cultivation contain the necessary trace elements, plants do sometimes show symptoms of boron and/or magnesium deficiency. These can be corrected as explained in Chapter 12.

I grew my plants three to a 23-cm (9-in) pot and took them to a Royal Horticultural Society show in a furniture van. It was very hard work, carefully carting and arranging the heavy sand-filled pots on the exhibition stand. I did it all once again at the Royal Windsor show a week later, but decided I would thereafter return to more normal methods of exhibiting. After nearly twenty years of sand cultivation I realized I was not cut out to be a weight-lifter, so I changed my ways and grew my carnations in a mixture of peat and sand, using twice as much peat as sand. In my retirement years, however, I sometimes use ready-mixed commercial compost.

Chapter 11

Commercial Carnation Production

In growing carnations for the cut-flowers, although there is a great difference between the amateur's cultivation and that of the market grower, the broad principles are the same: the plant's need of fresh air, good light, and a hygienic environment. Commercial growers' greenhouses are large, very light and airy with an abundance of ventilation—I remember an establishment that had a greenhouse called "The Cathedral." Most professional growers do not propagate their own plants but obtain them from specialist propagators; I used to import rooted perpetual-flowering carnation cuttings from a Danish company and was amazed to learn how many tons of carnation cuttings they exported to various parts of the world.

Plants for commercial use are usually grown in long raised beds of sterilized soil, about 1.2 m (4 ft) wide with narrow paths in between. The beds have low walls to retain the soil, which is about 15 to 23 cm (6 to 9 in) deep. The beds, made of concrete, are raised above ground level to isolate the soil from the ground below. These and other similar types of beds all serve the same purpose: to prevent infection of the soil in the growing beds by soil-borne wilt diseases from the soil beneath them. Set in rows about 20 cm (8 in) apart, the plants are spaced about 20 cm (8 in) apart in the rows. Horizontal bars and posts at the ends of the beds support networks of wire and string that in turn support the plants. Tiers of such netting are fixed at 15-cm (6-in) high intervals to support the plants as they grow. I should mention that 20 cm × 20 cm (8 × 8 in) is a very generous spacing; some establishments prefer to grow two to three times as many plants in the same space.

The beds are planted up with rooted cuttings and immediately watered lightly with a fine rose spray to settle the soil about the roots. A close atmosphere is maintained with temperatures between 15°C and 26°C (60°F and 80°F) and the young plants sprayed frequently for a week or more to prevent flagging. When the plants are established the night temperature is allowed to fall to 13°C (55°F) and day temperature regulated by ventilation to between 15°C and 21°C (60°F and 70°F). The first stop is applied in about three to four weeks after planting, not when individual plants require stopping but when almost all of the plants in the bed are ready, thereby economizing on labor costs. Planting is done at all seasons of the year, and stopping is regulated to reduce flower production at glut seasons. Flowers are picked with stems having six or seven pairs of leaves, including the very small leaves just below the calyx. They are then placed in water for at least 24 hours, then graded and packed. I can remember when they used to be packed in returnable wooden crates: Extra-Specials 24 to a box in rows of three blooms, Specials 36 to a box in rows of four blooms, and Seconds 48 to a box in rows of four blooms. The best grades had perfect calyces, the middle grade a small number of split calyces, and the lowest grade was allowed the use of artificial calyx supports. These standards were more or less over-ruled in the early 1960s when the British Flower Industry Association formulated new requirements. The Extra-Specials, Specials, and Seconds became Gold, Silver, and White grades, with specific standards for size of bloom, quality of stem and calyx, and packed in non-returnable cardboard boxes.

In recent years almost the whole of the output of Great Britain was bought by florists for making up into bouquets, floral tributes, and floral arrangements for functions. Only the low prices of the summer glut period induced street traders to take an interest. Nowadays every corner greengrocer sells carnations all the year round imported from various countries, particularly Holland, Israel, and South American countries, with the spray carnations the most popular of all for home decoration and bouquets.

American breeders of commercial carnations dominated all others from the end of the nineteenth century up to recent times. Spray carnations originated in the United States in 1952 with the cultivar 'Exquisite', pink ground and edged lavender, which was followed by its sport 'Elegance', pink ground edged white, in 1958. I grew them myself when they were first introduced and remember them particularly for their very distinct, spicy, almost medicinal perfume.

Spray carnations are now extensively grown for cut-flower purposes in many parts of the world, often as outdoor crops, and new attractive cultivars in various combinations of colors constantly appear. The flowers are larger than those of the garden pink but smaller than standard perpetual-flowering carnations. Most of these modern cultivars are highly productive and extremely resistant to fusarium wilt.

The American breeder Dr. Leonard Carrier, previously of the University of California, pioneered the breeding of perpetual-flowering carnations resistant to fusarium wilt disease, *Fusarium oxysporum*, because of the great loss of money to growers caused by the disease. Dr. Carrier raised new plants from seed, of which only 2 percent survived. He bred from these survivors through several generations to obtain resistant strains, following which he began breeding and selecting for flower quality. Some of his cultivars included 'Lucy Carrier', lavender-pink, 'Melody', lavender-rose with frosted edges, and 'White Melody', all very highly resistant to fusarium wilt. He then turned his thoughts to breeding fragrance into carnations by using *Dianthus sylvestris* as the seed parent. I wrote to Dr. Carrier about his work and he said modestly that he had introduced several cultivars with some success but not world-shaking. He told me that he had resolved to develop fusarium-resistant carnations and felt gratified that he was able to do so.

Dr. Carrier also told me that Dr. Harry Kohl had been working on carnations with no side buds and had done well with them. These were described in the American Carnation Society newsletter of 1969, which stated that a new type of carnation, one without lateral buds, had been developed but was not at that time in commercial production.

The Japanese Seed Company, T. Sakata and Co. of Yokohama, introduced dwarf carnations around 1970, plants of which were grown in demonstration gardens of Colorado State University. At that time the University was experimenting with dwarf pot-plant carnations under the direction of Dr. Ken Goldsberry. It was decided the plants should be grown singly in 10-cm (4-in) azalea pots, also with three plants in 15-cm (6-in) pots. The criteria for breeding and selection were that the plants should develop rapidly from cuttings, make strong breaks soon after potting, produce 2.5- to 3.5-cm (1- to 1.5-in) flowers three months after stopping, be 23 to 25 cm (9 to 10 in) tall, flower for three to four weeks in the home, have a clove scent and a variety of colors, require no disbudding, and have attractive curly blue-gray foliage. These were designed to be as attractive to purchasers as all-year-round chrysanthemums were, without being treated with growth retardants. The plants were said to be virtually disease-free and not affected by normal carnation diseases because of their short growing life. They are, however, susceptible to thrips, aphids, and red spider mite. During production they require the normal conditions of carnation growing in the greenhouse and require shading in summer. Over the 12-year testing period the plants were grown in a compost of two parts sphagnum peat, one part perlite, and one part soil.

Very popular for commercial growing nowadays, and available in nurseries and garden centers, are the group of dwarf pot carnations known as the Adorables series, discovered by accident by the California Florida Plant Company of Salinas, California. During their cut-flower carnation breeding program they noticed some seedlings that were very compact and short-growing. They continued to research and stabilize the cultivars, testing them in field trials. The inspiration for the trademark name "Adorables" came when one of their research team exclaimed, "How adorable" on first seeing these dwarf plants. A series named Socialite, 15 cm (6 in) tall, was also introduced, and cultivars of both series have been patented. Named plants in the 10-cm (4-in) tall Adorables series are currently available in almost all of the self colors, including the yellow 'CFPC Nugget', the mauve-pink 'CFPC Debutante', and 'CFPC Noel', white with red picotee edge, popular for Christmas and Valentine's Day sales. 'CFPC Sugarplum', an attractive purple-flush color, is the most fragrant of this series.

American breeders intercrossed many well-known species of *Dianthus* in order to discover their potential traits, also using *Dianthus sylvestris* for its scent. I am aware that some breeders have also used Malmaison carnations for this same purpose. The breeding initiative of the commercial cut-flower carnation that was born in continental Europe, and developed in the United States, has now passed back to France, Germany, Holland, Italy, and Israel.

That world-famous Italian breeder Dr. Giacomo Nobbio most kindly gave me the following information and permission to quote it:

At the present time there are a number of good carnation breeders in our country. The most important are Agostino and Nicoletta Baratta, Flavio Sapia and Ezio Brea. However, there are also carnation breeders in Holland, Germany and France.

The most developed type is now the Mediterranean which is cultivated almost exclusively by professional growers for the production of cut flowers. Besides the Mediterranean, spray carnations have a great diffusion. During the last few years many different types of carnations have been obtained through interspecific crosses (Eolo, Pulcino, Alfa, Chinesini, Unesco, etc. . . .). Lately pot carnations, usually not higher than 6 inches [15 cm] are becoming popular for house and garden use. In Italy the Chabaud type and the English Border type are not grown by amateurs. . . . The largest part of the breeding programmes are oriented towards cultivars which are more productive, have a longer vase life and are of a better quality. Special attention is being paid to the raising of cultivars which are resistant to the different strains of *Fusarium oxysporum*.

For your information I annually make about 5000 crosses between September and the middle of October; from those I obtain about 25,000 seeds and after the germination a little less than 25,000 seedlings. By means of selection during the first year I choose about 60 to 70 of the most promising plants. In the following year I check the characters of these cultivars and keep about 10 cultivars for the third year selection. After the third year I put three to four cultivars on the market for the first commercial trials. At this point the market indicates one or two cultivars. Every five years or so an exceptionally good cultivar like 'Alice', 'Raggio di Sole', 'Manon' etc., turns up.

In the early 1990s the great firm of P. Kooij and Zonen of Aals-meer, Holland, offered a complete range of the American Sim-type cultivars, which at that time still played an important part in the car-nation industry. Their other "standard" cultivars, including many new introductions from Dr. Nobbio and other breeders mentioned in his letter, were described as hybrids, having a positive influence on prof-its and a reduction in costs compared with the Sim cultivars. Kooij and Zonen based their claims of higher returns on a higher production of best quality blooms, less or no split calyx, improved prices, a reduc-tion of loss by vascular diseases due to high fusarium-wilt resistance, considerably less disbudding, and faster processing of the cut blooms. Many of these modern cultivars are available to amateur gardeners in Britain and are listed and described in Chapter 6. The Sims have now disappeared altogether from their catalogues.

New cultivars are now widely available in a considerably increased range of colors, and color combinations reminiscent of border carna-tions, many even incorporating their smooth-edged petals. The firm Van Staaveren, also of Aalsmeer, markets its perpetual-flowering and spray carnations under the title "New Generation Carnations" in a stunning color brochure. This also features an innovative new range of plants, developed as a result of intensive market research into the re-quirements of the present-day cut-flower industry, introduced in 1989 and registered as the Gipsy series. The cluster-headed five-petalled fimbriated flowers are reminiscent of sweet william in flower and fo-liage. They are sweetly scented and at present come mainly in shades of pink and white. They are very popular with florists. The plant is quite different from the traditional carnation, with narrow bright green foliage and long narrow pointed buds. 'Giant Gipsy' is bright cerise, 'Brilliant Gipsy' is a very attractive bicolor, dark pink with a deep cen-tral zone of red, and 'Smiling Gipsy' is light purple with a small eye and pale picotee edging to the petals. They can be grown under glass or outdoors.

The Dutch growers M. Lek and Zonen, in addition to their ex-cellent standard and spray cut-flower types, also include the dwarf pot-grown type in their catalogues, naming their cultivars after famous painters: 'Lek's Vermeer', single, deep pink with light crimson central zone and fringed petals; 'Michelangelo', bright red; and 'Da Vinci', rich pink with double, almost smooth-edged flowers. All are borne on short sturdy stems rising above thick broad green foliage. These make attractive pot plants and can also be planted as an outdoor crop.

I have also recently learned of some very interesting Japanese *Dianthus*, called Ise dianthus, in which the fimbriation has been extremely developed so that the flowers appear to have been extensively shredded. I understand they were developed from *Dianthus chinensis* and a native Japanese species during the Edo period of Japanese history. This dates from the 1590s when the Tokugawa Shogunate was established and the capital of Japan moved to what is now Tokyo (Edo). After the Meiji restoration in 1868 when the Emperor regained supreme control from the feudal samurai, the growing of the plant was restricted to the Royal Court, which presumably has led to its current rarity. It is currently grown in the Mie region of Honshu. The plants are self-fertile and are easily raised from seed, and they also root easily from cuttings.

It is clear from the above that commercial carnation production is still a very buoyant industry in many parts of the world and that experiments in hybridization continue to flourish.

Chapter 12

Pests, Diseases, and Disorders

I should begin this chapter by emphasizing that this book is written at one point in time based on my personal experience as a nurseryman in Great Britain. All of the chemical measures mentioned in the following pages are approved for amateur gardeners in my country, but I cannot speak for gardeners elsewhere. Most of the treatments below are probably expedient in other countries, but may be found under different trade names. Keep in mind, too, that pesticide regulations change constantly in any country; formulations that are legal one year may be discouraged in the next. Readers in any country are advised to check with their local horticultural extension office or pesticide authority before using any chemical with which they are unfamiliar.

Since pests can become resistant to some chemicals it is advisable to alternate use of these. It is for this reason that more than one chemical is recommended wherever possible, followed by the trade name or names of such products. Chemical preparations are given, but for those readers who prefer natural or organic methods, some alternatives are suggested. Biological pest control is also fully discussed under Alternative Measures for Eradicating Pests, later in the chapter.

The most important thing about pests and diseases is the care that must be taken in treating them. Many modern chemical formulations can be extremely dangerous to human beings and animals when used carelessly; always observe the manufacturers' instructions. Lock pesticides and measuring spoons away when not in use and never leave any residues lying around in cans or buckets. Always keep pesticides in their original containers and do not put small quantities in different bottles for convenience of handling. If you use weed-killing preparations, keep these well away from pesticides and use a distinctly different sprayer or watering-can; bright red might be an appropriate color for the weed-killer. Never use for any other purpose a vessel that has contained weed-killer, however well washed out. Some gardeners' "unaccountable losses" of favorite plants have been traced to carelessness or thoughtlessness concerning weed-killers.

Pests

GREENFLY AND OTHER APHIDS

Greenfly and aphids are a common nuisance but are easily controlled, which is fortunate because they transmit viral diseases from infected plants to healthy ones by sucking the sap, just as mosquitoes infect people with malaria by sucking blood. Punctures in the foliage and loss of sap weaken the plants, and the honeydew deposited by the aphids debilitates them even further. The yellowish spots on the foliage resulting from infection caused by the aphid punctures is sometimes referred to as bacteriosis or stigmanose. This condition is aggravated by cool, damp conditions. Greenfly multiply at an alarming rate because they reproduce viviparously, i.e. they give birth to young female aphids without laying eggs. They are normally wingless and only develop wings when food stocks become depleted and conditions inhospitable. These winged female aphids do lay eggs and can start new colonies of their own. Systemic insecticides containing malathion, heptenophos/permethrin (Murphy Tumblebug), or dimethoate (Doff Systemic Insecticide) are most effective against aphids and also control thrips and frog-hopper or cuckoo-spit. Pirimicarb (Miracle Rapid), one of the environmentally friendly products, controls aphids only, without harming bees and ladybirds.

Another type of aphid attacks by feeding on the roots of the plants. These are small and of bluish gray color, and can cause poor, stunted growth, particularly of pot plants in a hot dry summer, when plants may already be suffering from a shortage of water. Watering with a spray-strength mixture of systemic insecticide may assist in controlling and preventing a buildup of this pest. Small plants could have their roots washed in the insecticide and then be repotted into fresh compost.

ANTS

Ants arrive just when the plants start to bloom; they climb up and down the stems into the open blooms to feed on the nectar. Tapping the flower or stem does not dislodge them and they are most adept at hiding between the petals when disturbed. Ants also eat the central tips of the petals, causing the petals to fall out and the flower to shatter. There are several remedies including bendiocarb, pirimiphos-methyl, and pyrethrum, most available as dusts.

EARWIGS

I find earwigs less of a nuisance than ants, because I seem to have less of them, but they do as much damage chewing buds and petals. HCH (lindane) (Murphy Gamma-BHC Dust) should keep them down. The old method of trapping them in flower pots lined with straw, grass, or crumpled paper certainly reduces their numbers considerably.

SLUGS AND SNAILS

Slugs and snails do not cause serious damage to carnations, possibly because *Dianthus* stems and foliage are rather tough. The small black keel slug is the worst offender, especially on young plants in the greenhouse. These can usually be found under the pots hiding in the crock hole. Long ago when we had plenty of greenhouse space, enough to store odd piles of boxes and stacks of pots, we used to have a few toads that preyed upon the slugs. But now that greenhouses are kept clinically clean we are denied their assistance. Both slugs and snails may be removed by hand, but where particularly troublesome may be controlled with methiocarb slug pellets (Bio Slug Gard). These contain a special blue dye, which makes them unattractive to birds. The safe way to use these is to place a few pellets in short pieces of broken drainpipe, or on flattish stones or broken pot, covered with curved pieces of pot. Even safer is setting out shallow saucers of stale beer; the slugs are attracted by the fermenting liquid and will drown. Some organic gardeners may still prefer the friendly toad.

THRIPS

There are several species of thrips. The one that damages carnations, the onion thrip *(Thrips tabaci)*, breeds outdoors in summer and in greenhouses throughout the winter. They appear black in color in winter, light yellow in summer. Adult female thrips have two pairs of wings and are about 0.8 mm (0.03 in) long (Figure 12-1). Since the males have not been seen in greenhouses it must be assumed that thrips breed by parthenogenetic reproduction, a kind of immaculate conception. Those thrips that swarm from hayfields and cornfields in summer, sometimes called thunder flies, are of a different species altogether. Onion thrips damage the foliage of many different kinds of plants, but the flowers of only a few greenhouse plants, notably *Arum*, chrysanthemum, *Cyclamen*, and *Dianthus*. Some cultivars of carnations seem to be immune to attack, while others nearby suffer serious damage. Thrips lay their eggs on the calyx, at the points of the sepals, before the flowers begin to open. When hatched, the nymphs feed on the tiny petals inside the bud, sucking the pigment from the petals as they grow, so that when the flower is fully open its petals reveal unsightly pale blotches devoid of the flower's natural color. This disfiguration shows up most on the darker red and crimson flowers. Systemic insecticides containing malathion or pirimiphos-methyl (Miracle Sybol) are the most effective and also control aphids.

WIREWORMS

Wireworms are grubs of the click beetle (Figure 12-2). The beetle itself is harmless, but its grubs do great damage. These soil pests eat the roots of all plants and also burrow right up into the stems causing

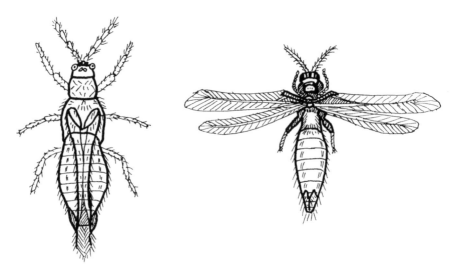

Figure 12-1. *Left:* thrips larva; *right:* adult thrips.

their death. As wireworms they live in the soil about three to five years, mostly in grassland where there is an abundance of plant roots. They are about 2.5 cm (1 in) long and shiny orange-yellow in color. They are very hard-skinned and so are difficult to squash, even difficult to pull apart, hence their name. They often were found in potting composts before the days of sterilized loam. In fact, the best way to clear wireworms used to be to allow chickens to pick them out of the loam; they are so brightly colored that the chickens had no difficulty finding them. I can remember seeing short sticks protruding from commercial carnation beds. These were baited with potatoes or carrots and when lifted out of the bed would be found to be spiked with wireworms. Now that potting composts have sterilized soil, or no soil at all, there is no problem. Plants in the ground, however, are sometimes attacked, the wireworms leaving the lawn edges for a change of diet. HCH (lindane) (Murphy Gamma-BHC Dust) raked into the surface is also effective and controls wireworms, chafer grubs, leatherjackets, woodlice, and cutworms.

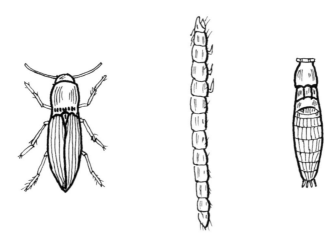

Figure 12-2. *Left:* click beetle; *center:* wireworm; *right:* beetle larva.

EELWORM AND MUSHROOM FLY MAGGOTS

Eelworm is rarely encountered as a problem of *Dianthus*, but should the base of a carnation stem become grossly swollen and growth of the plant come to a standstill, then eelworm may be suspected. Large white or gray patches at the base of the leaves confirm the diagnosis and cause of the trouble, and the microscopic eelworms may be found in the infested parts of the leaves together with the eggs and larvae. There is also a rootstem eelworm. There is no cure for these troubles other than burning the plants and disposal of the surrounding soil.

Eelworm should not be confused with the almost transparent, wormlike creatures sometimes found in potting composts. These are the maggots of fungus gnats or sciarid flies sometimes called mushroom flies. These black flies are up to 5 mm (0.2 in) long and fly slowly about the plants, especially carnation seedlings. Most are harmless, but some species can attack young plants, cuttings, and seedlings. Their maggots, less than 1 mm (0.05 in) in diameter and up to 7 mm (0.4 in) long, normally feed on decaying plant material. When a plant is knocked out of its pot the maggots may be seen around the outer surface of the root-ball. I have never known them to cause damage, but where there are too many in a pot they may feed on healthy roots when their normal food supply becomes exhausted. To control maggots, water in permethrin (Bio Sprayday or Miracle Picket), HCH (lindane), or pirimiphos-methyl (Miracle Sybol) at normal spray strength.

LEAF-MINING CARNATION FLY

Border carnations and perpetual-flowering carnations seem each to have their own leaf-mining fly (Figure 12-3), although they appear to cause exactly the same sort of damage. The border carnation fly *(Hylemia nigrescens)* is similar to, but smaller than, the ordinary house fly. The fly deposits its egg, sometimes two, between the upper and lower skins of the leaf, and the resulting creamy white maggot burrows its way between the leaves towards the center of the plant, in order to burrow into the central stem. When the maggot succeeds, the plant takes on a soft grayish appearance, like that of a lettuce whose stem has been eaten through by a cutworm. Where the plant is a precious one, such as a seedling of promise, one should winkle out the maggot in the hope that sideshoots will eventually appear and the plant be rescued. Sometimes the leaf-mining tracks can be clearly seen on the leaf, which may be cut off before the maggot proceeds further. When left undisturbed, the fully grown maggot drops to the soil, where it pupates, and about one month later at mid-summer it becomes a fly, just in time for the layering season. The fly prefers to lay its eggs on very young seedling plants and can destroy whole trayfuls. Its second choice is new layers of border carnations, especially those placed or grown outdoors. It may be attracted by the smell of the cut stem.

The carnation fly rarely enters greenhouses, one reason why specialist growers of border carnations keep their stocks under glass. Outdoor plants need regular checking, and hand-picking to remove mined leaves or tunnelled plants is useful. Spraying with pirimiphos-methyl (Miracle Sybol) or one of the malathion-based sprays can also help if the infestation is spotted before serious damage has occurred. As discussed further under Environment-Friendly Pesticides, the planting of garlic alongside carnation plants seems to be an effective organic deterrent to the carnation fly.

The other carnation fly *(Delia brunnescens)*, found on perpetual-flowering carnations, is not a common pest and is said to be found

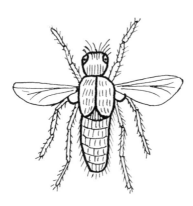

Figure 12-3. Carnation fly.

outdoors more often than in greenhouses. The carnation fly is some-times referred to as *Delia cardui*.

TORTRIX MOTH CATERPILLAR

The carnation tortrix moth inhabited the Mediterranean coast from Spain to Italy and Corsica and Sicily in 1859. It was found in the Channel Isles in 1898, and one single specimen was recorded by R. Adkin at Eastbourne in 1905, one of the earliest British records. In 1925 Adkin found tortrix moth to be abundant in gardens of *Coronilla*, and that it did much damage to plants under glass at the Royal Botanic Gardens at Kew. Apart from this, no other authentic record of the insect occurring in greenhouses was found except in the Hampton district of Middlesex. I started my first nursery in the Hampton district, where I remember the tortrix moth was a serious pest. I retired to Eastbourne where it was first recorded in this country and where, growing on a wall in the garden, was a splendid specimen of *Coronilla glauca*, its favorite host plant.

The moth is small, about the size of your smallest fingernail, and bright orange in color (Figure 12-4). It may be seen on fine summer evenings at dusk, flitting about the garden. Its caterpillars grow to a length of 2 cm (0.75 in) and are olive-green with brown heads (Figure 12-5). They spin and roll the plants' growing tips with a fine web, beneath which they protect themselves against insecticidal sprays and other dangers. Ensconced in the carnation's growing tips, they eat their way through the foliage until fully grown, then cover themselves in a tight web to pupate. After only two or three weeks they emerge as tortrix moths.

Caterpillars can be controlled by the following sprays: bifenthrin (Monsanto Polysect), heptenophos/permethrin (Murphy Tumble-bug), and pirimiphos-methyl (Miracle Sybol).

OTHER CATERPILLARS

Although almost free of tortrix moth here on the south coast of England, I find I have merely exchanged one moth for another. The caterpillar of my new unfriend lives inside the calyces of carnations and pinks, both in the garden and under glass, and it feeds on the flowers whether open or tight in the bud. It eats the entire contents of the calyx, including the ovule and seeds whether unfertilized, immature, or even ripe. Fortunately many of the caterpillars arrive too late to damage many flowers, but they greatly reduce the crop of carnation seeds in the greenhouse and pinks seed in the garden. They must be about in good numbers, yet for all the caterpillars I have found I had

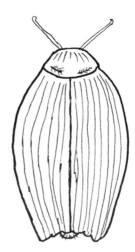

Figure 12-4. Tortrix moth.

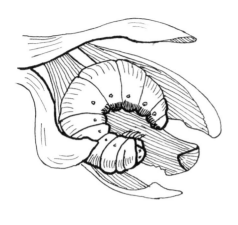

Figure 12-5. *Left:* calyx eaten out by caterpillar; *right:* tortrix caterpillar.

never set eyes on their parents. So I put a few live caterpillars in a stout envelope and posted them to the RHS entomologist, Andrew Halstead, who very politely requested I send a few more specimens since my first consignment was squashed by a modern post-office sorting machine. The second batch was packed in a plastic film carton and I was rewarded when Mr. Halstead identified my caterpillars as the larvae of the lychnis moth. As its name suggests, it feeds on *Lychnis* plants as well as on plants of the campion *(Silene)* and dianthus family. Later Mr. Halstead informed me he had bred out the moth from my caterpillar and confirmed that it was *Hadena bicruris*, the lychnis moth. On my next visit to Wisley I called in at the Entomology Department and was given permission to photograph our moth. I was surprised at its size; I had expected a much larger creature. I still have not seen a live one, so suppose it must only fly at dead of night. The lychnis moth should not be confused with the Silver Y moth. While studying a bed of *Clarkia* I noticed that it was visited by bees all morning and Silver Y moths all afternoon.

I did find, however, a different, larger moth in my conservatory. This conservatory is on the side of the house—a glorified porch, really—with a door facing the front garden and another facing the back garden. It serves as a breakfast room for two in summer, doubling as a photographic studio, there being just enough room to swing a tripod. I photographed my moth, then took it out into the back garden to release it. Having watched it fly upwards around the house, I returned to the porch/conservatory via the back door and met my moth coming in the open front door. I often wondered, had I taken it out through the front door, whether it would have returned by the back door. It stayed a few days, having an occasional flutter round before deciding whether to leave by the front door or the back.

RED SPIDER MITE

The red spider mite was once known as *Tetranychus telarius*, but that name seems to have gone out of fashion. In 1939 the experimental research scientists E. R. Speyer and W. Read of the Cheshunt Research Station, Hertfordshire, wrote a study of red spider mite, which they referred to as *Tetranychus telarius*, and they classed it as a "Spinning Mite," with a spinning salivary gland. When a carnation plant is depleted of moisture by the sucking mites, the mites climb to the top of the plant and congregate on buds and flowers, where they commence to spin webs. A single strand of webbing is about one thirty-thousandth of an inch in diameter and what would appear to be a single strand is actually many strands spun together. A whole mass of mites hangs from the top of the plant by the rope, suspended as from a crane, and as with a crane the load swings to and fro like a pendulum. The mass of mites swings from the depleted plant to a nearby healthy plant, the mites' only means of transport since they cannot fly.

The scientists of the Cheshunt Research Station mentioned a problem in connection with the breeding of red spider mite on carnations, which they described as very obscure. In all stages, eggs included, the mite's color is of a deeper reddish tint on carnations than those living on most other plants. The scientists also observed that the mites on carnations do not hide away in crevices of the greenhouse as do mites living in tomato *(Lycopersicon)* and cucumber *(Cucumis)* houses. Instead they continue to breed very slowly throughout the winter, when they cause little injury to the plant. Their numbers are also greatly reduced due to natural mortality. The adult female mites in carnation houses do not assume the bright red color of the hibernating form of spider mite on most other greenhouse plants. Although Speyer and Read discovered that the carnation red spider mite is very different from other greenhouse spider mites, they regarded it only as being a different form of the same species, *Tetranychus telarius*.

The mite known as *Tetranychus telarius* was a serious pest of a great many greenhouse subjects and was called the two-spot mite by American growers because it had two blotches that showed through its almost transparent greenish yellow skin. It was a serious pest on carnations, which meant that both the red and the greenish yellow forms would feed on carnations. There came a time when the species name *telarius* was dropped and the species became known as *T. urticae*, referring to the greenish yellow two-spot mite, and then as the glasshouse spider mite. The red form originally observed by Speyer and Read became known as the carmine red spider mite, *T. cinnabarinus*, and as the carnation red spider mite. The main differences between *T. urticae* and *T. cinnabarinus* are that *T. urticae* eggs are whitish green, whereas *T. cinnabarinus* eggs are pinkish orange, and that *T. urticae* female mites hibernate in autumn and winter when they change color to become bright red. In spring they return to the plants to begin a new egg-laying season; except for the winter season they breed throughout the year. *Tetranychus cinnabarinus* neither hibernates nor changes color.

Adult female mites are about 0.5 mm (0.02 in) long (Figure 12-6). The mites are the most damaging pest of carnations and are difficult to control. They puncture the leaf surfaces to feed on the contents, and when in large numbers do serious damage. They congregate on the undersides of the leaves, usually beneath the top of the leaf curl. Bleached patches upon the upper leaf surfaces are usually the first indication of the mite's presence. Unless dealt with promptly, a severe infestation can develop, the plant's leaves turning yellow like straw, culminating in its death. Adult female mites can each lay up to 120 eggs during a span of three weeks. Their rate of reproduction is greatly affected by greenhouse temperatures; in a warm summer they breed four to five times faster than in spring.

In hot dry weather the plants, pots, staging, and surrounding areas should be sprayed over with a fine mist to check the pest. Shading the greenhouse glass also assists in reducing the temperature. Badly infested plants should be destroyed and any dead leaves, stalks, and other rubbish cleared out. If possible, plants also should be taken out in autumn

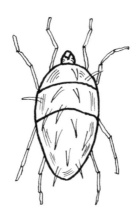

Figure 12-6. Red spider mite.

and the greenhouse washed down thoroughly with a solution of Jeyes fluid or Lysol disinfectant. Choose a fine day so that plants can be re-housed without delay. Insecticidal sprays should be used about every six days to catch young mites hatched out immediately after the previous spraying. Before spraying, ensure that the plants' roots are not dry and that their leaves are not wet. The following insecticides help to reduce the mite population: bifenthrin (Monsanto Polysect), malathion, pirimiphos-methyl (Miracle Sybol), and rotenone (Liquid Derris), a natural plant extract insecticide. Many amateur gardeners have found, however, that once red spider mite gets a hold they have no certain cure. Montagu Allwood's remedy for red spider mite was to mix one ounce common salt in one gallon of water (28 g in 4.5 liter) and early in the morning use a very fine spray reaching every part of the plant, and hose or syringe after a few hours to wash off the mites. Professional growers use more potent acaricides, which in the past have found their way into the hands of keen amateurs. Although use of such materials by amateurs is now illegal, one cannot imagine a grower who has built up a fine collection, some cultivars of his own breeding, standing idly by watching the plague-stricken collection annihilated, when a couple of spoonfuls of some concoction would effect a magical cure.

Tetranychus urticae, which should not be confused with the fruit-tree spider mite, is known to damage outdoor-grown strawberry *(Fragaria)* plants, ornamental garden plants, and hops.

BIRDS, RABBITS, HARES, MICE

Progressing from mites and insects to animals, we have birds, rabbits, hares, and mice. The field-grown carnations in the Royal Horticultural Society Wisley trials are chewed down by birds every spring, yet almost miraculously they recover to flower profusely by the following mid-summer. I have never bothered to tie black cotton over my own plants, but it is probably worthwhile where only a few plants are grown.

The carnation plants at Wisley are protected from rabbits by a boundary of wire netting. Rabbits may also be deterred by sprinkling powdered rock phosphate on the leaves. Mice can be very troublesome in winter, when their usual kinds of food are covered with snow, and can do much damage to young plants in the greenhouse, chewing them right down to the stump at soil level. Ratak pellets are an effective remedy, as is D-Con, available in the United States. However, the good old-fashioned mouse trap is still available, and safer.

Alternative Measures for Eradicating Pests

SMOKE CONES

Insecticidal smokes are useful against a large number of pests, including aphids and red spider mite, but for these to work effectively all gaps in the greenhouse must be sealed. The smoke cones burn for less than thirty seconds, so having ignited the touch paper, vacate the greenhouse at once and close the door tightly. Leave the greenhouse closed for about four hours and do not enter before it has been opened for at least one hour. A follow-up smoke should be employed within five to six days.

ENVIRONMENT-FRIENDLY PESTICIDES

A great many people are concerned nowadays about the environment, which is, after all, our home. We practice "green" gardening and use "friendly" products to kill those other inhabitants that in their innocence feed upon our cultivated plants and which probably inhabited our environment before we did. A large number of friendly products are now available, and one firm of suppliers (Pan Britannica Industries Ltd.) expresses the following view:

> Many gardeners are quite happy to use the products of modern research, but there is an equal number who want to use products which contain only natural and organic materials. There is no point in arguing who is right or who is wrong. People have a right to choose. We devote this new and exciting range of products for those people who wish to use organic remedies, natural feeds and non-chemical methods. (Hessayon 1990)

This is a very fair view; I regret I cannot personally recommend any particular product at present, because so far I have only used the traditional carnation feeds and remedies. But I shall certainly experiment with some of the environmentally friendly products in my own garden. In the meantime I am sure I speak for all carnation enthusiasts when I say that the first pesticide to exterminate all red spider mites will be the friendliest of them all.

For those gardeners who wish to avoid using chemical dusts against such soil pests as leatherjackets, cutworms, and others, a natural biological product for the control of these is now available. It is marketed as Biosafe Soil Insect Control, the active ingredient being a beneficial nematode, *Steinernema carpocapsae*. It may be used in gardens, greenhouses, pots, and containers. There is also a biological control for slugs and snails.

A Canadian friend in British Columbia experimented with growing garlic *(Allium sativum)* among his outdoor-planted *Dianthus*, planting one clove of garlic near each *Dianthus* plant with a view to deterring cats and rabbits from the area, and subsequently found it also acted as a pest deterrent. The garlic smell has been found to deter the carnation fly in the same way that onions *(Alliumcepa)* grown side-by-side with carrots *(Daucus carota)* in the vegetable garden deter the carrot fly. Fresh pieces of chopped garlic leaves sprinkled around newly layered carnation plants might well have the same effect, masking the smell of the cut stems. A mite repellent that contains only garlic oil and water has also been recommended. It is diluted and sprayed onto plants before insect and mite pests appear, and repeated at intervals throughout the season. The product is claimed to repel spider mites, leafhoppers, ants, aphids, and thrips, among other pests, and is safe and non-toxic.

There is not room in this book to adequately cover the whole subject of organic gardening and pest control, but three comprehensive books on this subject are listed in the bibliography. The organic-gardening approach also emphasizes the necessity of building up a healthy soil full of nutrients and teeming with beneficial bacteria, which in turn encourages healthy plants, more able to withstand pest attacks.

BIOLOGICAL CONTROL OF CATERPILLARS

My younger daughter, who lives in Victoria, British Columbia, writes "friendly gardening" articles. In a recent letter she suggested I include a section on organic pesticides. She wrote,

Tell them I grind up bugs with water in a blender, strain them through a sieve and spray the liquid back onto the affected plants. It is a well-known organic method which actually works, although not for all insect families. It is based on the chance that one of those bugs usually has a disease which will affect all the others which subsequently eat the sprayed leaves. Don't laugh! It is not as silly as it sounds; BT *(Bacillus thuringiensis)* is based on the same premise, and is widely used here for effective control of the caterpillar family. Scientists are now isolating other bacteria, fungi and viruses which have the same destructive effect on particular species of insects, while having no harmful effect on friendly insects, animals or humans. This is very "respectable" over here, and is being researched for commercial use on crops. Maybe you could check out the trade name in England and suggest your readers give it a try; they can always keep their old poisons at the ready until they prove to themselves that it works! At the moment I believe it is only marketed for the caterpillar family, but you should keep your eyes peeled for future developments because the race is on to discover less toxic (for the good guys anyway!) pesticides, and your old favorites are disappearing fast from the shelves as one after another are discovered to be more lethal than we thought.

I checked out the trade names as instructed, and English Woodland Biocontrol of West Sussex sent me some very helpful literature. Dipel is a wettable powder containing spores of the bacterium *Bacillus thuringiensis* that is made up into a solution and sprayed over the plants very thoroughly to effect complete coverage. When eaten, the bacterium paralyzes the caterpillars so that they stop feeding and die within a few days. Plants in greenhouses are sprayed at intervals of three weeks. This product is harmless to beneficial insects. It is compatible with most formulations but incompatible with a few others that include dimethoate and Bordeaux Mixture. Always check instructions for details.

BIOLOGICAL CONTROL OF RED SPIDER MITE

The predatory mite *Phytoseiulus persimilis* is bright red in color, slightly larger than its prey and moves much faster. It is widely used to control red spider mite on tomato *(Lycopersicon)* and cucumber *(Cucumis)* crops but not to a great extent on carnation crops. The predatory mite will control the glasshouse spider mite *Tetranychus urticae* by feeding on all its stages of growth including eggs, but it will not control the carnation red spider mite (also known as the carmine red spider mite), *T. cinnabarinus*. My own experience is that the predators will starve to death rather than feed on *T. cinnabarinus*. Where used to control *T. urticae* on carnations it must be realized that since the predators cannot fly from plant to plant one must transfer leaves containing a few predators to other plants that appear to have none.

Late April onwards is the best time to introduce the predators, the earlier the better to allow the predators time to breed and multiply, thereby continuously improving their effectiveness in mopping up the red spider mite population. Although they will survive at temperatures as low as 13°C (55°F), daytime temperatures of at least 21°C (70°F) are necessary to enable the predators to thrive and breed rapidly. They should not be put into a greenhouse that does not have active red spider mites, because they would die of starvation. Red spider mites like hot dry conditions, but the predatory mites prefer cooler moist conditions, which means that pests could congregate at the tops of plants while the predators stay below. Spraying plants with clear water twice a day during hot weather assists the predators in their work. Aphids and thrips must also be kept in check and so will need to be sprayed, and since some insecticides can damage the predators, it would be safer to use pirimicarb formulations, such as Miracle Rapid, which do not seriously harm them. Should it be necessary to use an insecticide against some other pest, such as thrips, a short-persistence product such as derris or pyrethrum should be used. To be on the safe side, a few plants accommodating the predatory mites should be taken out of the greenhouse when spraying is contemplated, and returned about a week later.

Some suppliers provide predators on bean leaves, which should be cut up into five or six pieces and distributed over the plants. It is important to place the leaf pieces the right way up so that predator eggs on the underside will be protected from bright sunlight. Adults leave the bean leaves within a few hours and eggs on the leaves hatch out over the next three or four days. The newly hatched mites move on to the plants in search of their food. There is no need to keep the greenhouse doors and ventilators closed, the predators will not run off while there are red spider mites about for them to feed on.

I wish to reiterate that there are two spider mite species that feed on carnations, and the predator will control one species but not the other. Within a few days of the introduction of the predators the red spider mite population should have decreased considerably. If after two weeks there is no reduction, then the attempt must be written off as a failure.

At an RHS committee meeting I attended in connection with trials of perpetual-flowering carnations, it was stated, "The Wisley Entomologist has recommended that biological control measures be taken in the event of an infestation of two-spotted (red spider) mite." However, I understand that fresh supplies have to be reintroduced from time to time throughout the season, so the cost could prove inhibitive to the small amateur grower.

Research is going on into the use of a predatory midge whose larvae feed on red spider mites. If successful, this could be a considerable improvement: a flying predator. It is said to fly into greenhouses in summer and is claimed to be highly effective. The predatory midge *Therodiplosis persicae* will probably be marketed as cocoons to be placed on plants, where they will hatch out and mate and lay eggs among red spider mite colonies. When I read this news in a gardening magazine

I became quite elated, but the euphoria was short-lived. A little research revealed that this midge had been noted in tomato houses some 65 years ago. It is light red in color and is active between July and October. The bright red fly-grubs, which eat the mites and their eggs, prefer to live on the undersides of carnation leaves. That the grubs remain nine days in the pupal stage, long enough for a whole new spider mite generation to be completed, and that it was improbable that the predator could be bred in such quantities as to satisfy commercial growers, were considered drawbacks.

Diseases and Disorders

Before you read about all the diseases carnations are heir to, I should assure you that it is quite likely you may never see the majority of them on outdoor plants. Providing good growing conditions is the best preventative in the greenhouse, with abundant fresh air, avoidance of high temperatures wherever possible, and keeping a watchful eye open for early symptoms. Should you see anything really nasty-looking on one of your plants, then dispose of the plant without delay, along with the soil or compost immediately about it. The simple disorders can be dealt with simply; the complex disorders are so complex that most experts do not completely understand them and research into them is continuous. Reading research papers can be interesting, but I find some quite baffling; researchers do not always agree with each others' findings. Their studies are made for the benefit of the cut-flower industry, although some of the remedies used professionally do eventually come to benefit amateur growers when taken up by gardening product retailers.

Great care must be taken in the use of fungicidal preparations, especially in their storage and disposal, and the same precautions apply as outlined for the use of pesticides at the beginning of this chapter.

CURLY TIP

Curly tip usually is seen between late winter and early spring and is associated with poor light. Plants begin to grow again early in the year, even outdoor plants, but the quality of light is not good enough to support the early growth. The leaf tips bind together—that is, they fail to separate. A high-nitrogen feed may improve the situation and cleaning the greenhouse glass could also help, but the main ingredient for a return to normal growth is a spell of good weather with brighter light. Where not too hooked-up, the bound-together leaf tips can be gently freed using the end of a pencil.

WHEATEAR

Wheatear is not only the name of a small bird, it is also the name of a physiological disorder. Instead of axillary bud stalks, the flower stems produce side growths with numerous small, closely packed bracts along their whole length, causing them to resemble ears of wheat (Figure 12-7). This peculiar habit seems to cause no harm and does not appear in plants propagated from affected plants. It goes away as mysteriously as it comes, and most people may never see it at all.

SPLIT CALYX

Cultivars that are more prone to split the calyx than others should be discarded. There are so many causes of calyx splitting that when it happens it can be difficult to decide the actual cause; the physical cause can happen several weeks before the calyx splits. Also it is usually a combination of causes that does the damage. Sharp variations in temperature can cause a stop-go effect upon growth, as can sudden changes in the moisture content of the growing medium due to erratic watering methods. Incorrect feeding can also cause surges in growth, followed by inactivity. A cold flow of air can upset steady growth, leading to checks followed by spurts in warmer conditions. It may be, however, that calyx splitting is not immediately dependent on any of the foregoing conditions, but on changes in the number of petals in the flower. A normal commercial cut-flower carnation has from fifty to seventy petals, but it can increase to one hundred petals and so cause calyx splitting. Extra growth centers with more whorls of petals in the calyx are induced by sudden falls in temperature that occur about a month or so before the bloom matures, and when the bud measures

Figure 12-7. Wheatear.

about 0.5 cm (0.25 in) across. Sudden large rises in temperature one to two weeks before flowers mature can also cause calyx splitting; therefore, the answer is to try to avoid wide temperature fluctuations. Spring and autumn can be difficult times, especially for growers away from home all day who cannot open and close ventilators as and when necessary. Such people could install automatic ventilating appliances; otherwise pin their faith in calyx bands. Sometimes another calyx with petals forms within the flower. Biologically the carnation is a heterozygote, an unstable hybrid containing hidden characters of its parents that are capable of being transmitted. There are three types of carnation flower: the single, the double, and the bullhead. The perpetual-flowering carnation is the heterozygous result of crossing the single and the bullhead. It is believed that the bullhead character is inherited in some crosses, thereby causing an increased number of petals in the flower and causing the calyx to split. With perpetual-flowering and border carnations only the double-flowered types are cultivated. Singles and bullheads do appear among seedling plants in breeding plantations, but they are discarded and only the double forms retained for consideration.

RUST

I remember when carnation rust was a matter of serious concern; even plants straight from a nursery would arrive complete with blisters and cocoa-like spores (Figure 12-9). I haven't seen rust for a great many years, either on plants in the ground or in pots. The other bugbear was stem rot; carnation society members would bring horribly diseased specimens to the flower show for experts' diagnoses. Overwatering was invariably proclaimed to be the cause, but that was just

Figure 12-8. Split calyx.

an easy way out. I believe the true cause was the compost the plants were grown in. Chopped-up turf laced with animal manure or leaf-mold, mortar rubble, road-grit, etc., were the usual ingredients, and the plants usually were fed with water from a barrel into which a gunny bag of sheep manure was suspended. And of course the compost would be rammed hard in the pots, thereby eliminating porosity and ruining any possibility of normal drainage. I believe also that the old cultivars were more susceptible to rusts, leaf spots, and stem rots than are the modern ones. Abundant ventilation is the best preventative. Should you ever find split, raised blisters exuding cocoa-like spores on your plants' leaves, remove badly affected leaves. If necessary, spray with bupirimate with triforine (Miracle Nimrod-T) or mancozeb (Bio Dithane 945).

FAIRY RING SPOT

When a plant is infected with fairy ring spot, light brown spots appear on leaves, calyces, and stems, with darker concentric rings, the fruiting spores, in the center (Figure 12-9). High greenhouse temper-

Figure 12-9. *Left:* fairy ring spot; *right:* rust disease.

atures and overdamp conditions favor the spread of the disease. The copper compound spray Bordeaux Mixture may be useful, or spray with mancozeb.

DAMPING-OFF

Damping-off can occur on seedlings and cuttings, causing stems to collapse and rot off at soil level. It usually occurs when the plants are crowded, the soil is wet, and the temperature high. When seedlings and cuttings are spaced sufficiently far apart, air circulation helps moisture evaporate. As a preventative measure, seed and cutting composts could be watered with a solution of copper sulphate/ammonium carbonate (Bio Cheshunt Compound) or copper oxychloride (Murphy Traditional Copper Fungicide) before and after sowing seeds or taking and transplanting cuttings.

LEAF SPOT

Leaf spot, or *Alternaria dianthi*, is seen as small purple spots with yellow margins that develop black powdery spores. The spots spread and join together to become large areas affecting whole leaves that eventually drop off. *Septoria dianthi* leaf spot has brown spots with purple margins on leaves and stems and is encouraged by warm damp conditions. Drenching with Bordeaux Mixture or spraying with mancozeb (Bio Dithane 945) should prove effective against both leaf spot diseases.

POWDERY MILDEW

Mildew in the form of a white powdery covering on leaves and flowers is usually found when plants are overcrowded, thereby deprived of proper ventilation, and especially in summer when the roots lack water. Abundant fresh air is the best preventative.

BOTRYTIS

Botrytis is a fungal disease in which a gray powdery mold appears on the flowers. It is brought on by warm damp conditions. Moldy flowers must be removed, taking great care because the spores can be dispersed at the slightest touch, thereby spreading the disease further. Carbendazim sprays (Bio Supercarb or Doff Plant Disease Control) should help with both botrytis and powdery mildew.

FUSARIUM STEM ROT

Fusarium roseum is a soil-borne disease that penetrates wounds caused during potting or planting. Spores can be splashed up from infected soil during watering. The disease causes stems to rot at the base of the plant. Picking flowers and taking cuttings, whether snapped out or cut out, leave stubs that can become infected. The fungus spreads down the stub to infect the branch, which can cause the whole plant to die. Most losses occur with young plants, but mature plants can become infected and do not recover. Symptoms are a reddish brown discoloration at the base of the stem with clusters of pink spores. Infected plants and the surrounding soil should be destroyed.

RHIZOCTONIA STEM ROT

Rhizoctonia solani is also soil-borne. It thrives on rotting vegetation in warm moist conditions and is a very common fungal disease. Infected plants usually rot at soil level, with the plant tops wilting and turning brown before the death of the plant. Symptoms are very similar to those of fusarium stem rot except that there are no clusters of pink spores. This stem rot is common with cuttings grown in an unsterilized medium. Destroy infected plants and cuttings and the medium immediately about them. A lower greenhouse temperature is said to assist in control, but the most important factor is the use of a sterilized medium.

ANTHER SMUT

Anther smut is a fungal disease first recorded in 1907 on *Dianthus deltoides*. It renders carnation flowers unsightly, and so commercially unsaleable, by the appearance of a sootlike dust. This dust is formed inside the bud, and when the flower opens the anthers are covered with the violet-black dust, which is spread over the flower. This dust is the spores, or smuts, of a parasitic fungus, the individual spores being about the same size as pollen grains. The disease is spread by wild and cultivated plants of the family Caryophyllaceae, which includes *Cerastium, Lychnis, Saponaria,* and *Silene.* Severe outbreaks of the disease in carnations have been traced to infection by wild flowers. The fungus is systemic and can invade the whole plant. More importantly, it persists near the growing points, eventually to infect the anthers, where it replaces pollen with smut spores. The disease does not injure the plant; apart from the smutting of the flowers the only significant difference is the excessive production of apparently healthy sideshoots that would seem to be ideal for making cuttings. Plants produced from such cuttings grow well and themselves have precocious axillary shoots, although their flowering times are not affected. However, when a large batch of cuttings known to be infected was grown on to the flowering stage, every flower on every plant was infected with anther smut. Some species of the disease-host *Lychnis* have separate male and female plants. Since reproduction of the disease spores depends on the male plants, which produce pollen, one would presume the spores to be wasted on the female plants. But the disease has another extraordinary trick up its sleeve. It causes the development of male sex organs in the female plants, and these too produce smut spores instead of pollen. There is no cure other than the removal and burning of all carnation plants seen to be infected, taking care in the selection of cuttings, and keeping surroundings clear of caryophyllaceous weeds.

WILT DISEASES

Wilt diseases mainly affect perpetual-flowering carnation plants grown in greenhouse beds, and they are to be feared more than any other disease—there is no cure for them. Most new cultivars, however, have been bred to be highly disease-resistant. Wilts travel rapidly, so to minimize the spread of the disease, infected plants must be removed and burned as quickly as possible, and the soil about them sterilized. Plants grown in pots, together with the soil, should be disposed of safely and the pots and crocks sterilized before reuse. The whole idea of raised beds for carnations is to isolate the growing medium from the soil about it; I have seen carnation plants grown in Grobags (bags of potting medium with planting slits), also on straw bales, to prevent contact with the soil.

Bacterial Wilt. Bacterial wilt causes plants to wilt suddenly with the stem brownish and slimy. Stem wounds allow bacteria to enter initially, therefore newly planted cuttings are particularly vulnerable.

Fusarium Wilt. Fusarium wilt is a fungal disease in which one side of the plant becomes stunted and discolored. When broken, the stems are discolored but not slimy. Wounds allow the fungus access to the plant tissue. Cuttings taken from apparently healthy (symptomless) plants can carry the diseases.

Verticillium Wilt. *Verticillium cinerescens*, which U.S. authorities call *Phialophora cinerescens*, is a fungal disease that causes sideshoots to twist and leaves to turn the color of straw. Broken stems show a dark brown discoloration.

CARNATION VIRUSES

Almost all carnation plants carry viral diseases to some degree. Some cultivars show symptoms, others do not. The most common method of transmission of viruses is sap-sucking by peach aphids. Using a knife to cut flowers and make cuttings is also said to be a cause. Healthy looking plants without symptoms act as carriers, as do plants obviously infected with virus. Those showing severely mottled or streaked foliage should be destroyed, as should those that bear flowers of broken color or are otherwise uncharacteristic of the cultivar. Plants that crop poorly should also be suspected. The mosaic virus of sweet william *(Dianthus barbatus)*, also found in carnations and pinks, now has the name of vein mottle virus, due to its mottling of the leaves and particularly of the calyx. Etched ring virus, which is very common, is identified by its chlorotic spots and rings, and carnation ring spot virus by its green rings. Carnation mottle virus, said to be present in the vast majority of commercial cultivars, has only slight mottling; carnation streak has purple, red, or yellow streaks and spots. Many growers may never notice any of these symptoms, except perhaps for slight mottling in some plants.

Commercial cut-flower growers obtain rooted cuttings from specialist propagators whose own stock plants are grown under ideally hygienic conditions in order to protect them from fungal and viral diseases and vascular wilts. Scientists found that with diseased plants the pathogen was always a little way behind the growing tip, which means that the minute growing-tip is disease-free. It was also found that a high temperature slows down the advance of viral diseases within the plant. Thus when plants from which cuttings are to be taken are subjected to a temperature of 38°C (100°F) for about two months, the tip growth is encouraged while the chasing pathogen is discouraged.

In a process commonly known as meristem or tissue culture or micropropagation, about 0.5 to 1 mm (about 0.2 to 0.4 in) removed from the growing tip, called a meristem, can be placed into a nutrient solution, where it forms roots after about three weeks. After two to three months it is potted into a sterile medium and fed just like any other young plant. From the initial taking of the tiny meristem to the flowering plant takes seven to nine months of careful cultivation under laboratory conditions. These new plants are grown to form a nucleus of disease-free stock plants for the production of cuttings, not flowers. Cuttings taken from stock plants are superior to those taken from flowering plants; they root quicker and are less likely to carry wilt disease. But the disease-free stock plant does not stay disease-free forever; it is recommended that given proper pest and disease control, the stock plant should be kept for about 15 months only.

A few years ago my wife and I were privileged to inspect the experimental meristem propagation unit set up in Kelowna, in the Okanagan Valley fruit-growing area of British Columbia, Canada, by Dr. David Dunstan, a product of Wye College and a friend of our family. We saw rows and rows of shelves containing glass honey jars, no larger than tea cups, each containing some thirty or so tiny plants of what were destined to become apple trees and giant timber trees for reforestation.

MINERAL DEFICIENCIES AND EXCESSES

In order to maintain balanced growth, plants require certain chemical elements in correct proportions. The plant's roots collect water and minerals that the stem conducts to the leaves, which absorb carbon dioxide from the atmosphere. These materials form starch, sugar, cellulose, and protein. Nitrogen, phosphorus, and potassium are some of the major elements taken up in water by the roots. Nitrogen promotes growth of stems and leaves, phosphorus produces a strong root system, and potassium promotes healthy foliage and perfect flowers. The minor element calcium assists root growth.

There was a time when much attention was given to the plant's diet, its uptake of nutrients in correct quantities measured in parts per million. This was very necessary on commercial holdings with the crops grown in beds of soil, especially when these soils had been used for successive crops over many years and straight fertilizers were used to bring the basic plant foods up to the optimum levels for healthy growth. It was assumed that the minor and trace elements occurred as impurities in the straight fertilizers and in the water supply. To some extent they did, but soils and water supplies vary, and many growers found their plants affected by poor growth and peculiar symptoms. Commercial growers now have their soils analyzed at intervals and make the necessary corrections. Amateurs can buy modern ready-made composts, which should include the correct ingredients, whereas those who make up their own composts use modern fertilizer packs specially designed for the purpose and which include the basic ingredients and the necessary minor and trace elements. Symptoms of mineral deficiencies should therefore be a thing of the past, but if they do appear, an application of a liquid fertilizer with the appropriate chemical analysis should correct the deficiency. It should be realized that where a complete fertilizer is used regularly, one having minor and trace elements included, these deficiencies should not arise. Watering pot plants heavily with clear water once a month during summer should prevent a build-up of chemical salts in the compost. Carnation plants' leaves live for about a year and are best removed from the base of the plant when they become dry and yellowed. They should be detached carefully to avoid wounding the stems.

Nitrogen Deficiency and Excess. Nitrogen deficiency causes the leaves to turn yellowish green, thin, narrow, and without curl. Older leaves may have red and purple tints. Bud initiation is delayed, and hard growth with calyx splitting is evident. Nitrogen is the most commonly leached-out plant food, but the problem is easily corrected. A teaspoonful of dried blood can be sprinkled around each plant. Excess nitrogen causes thin, pale foliage, weak stems, and flowers lacking substance.

Phosphorus Deficiency and Excess. Phosphorus deficiency is not common, but a very alkaline (high pH) soil can render phosphorus unavailable to the plant. Growth is very restricted, with leaves narrow and reduced in size, and lower leaves dying off. A sprinkling of superphosphate watered into the soil can correct this, but over-feeding renders calcium insoluble and therefore unavailable to the plant. The dried blood recommended for nitrogen deficiency also supplies some phosphorus.

Potassium Deficiency and Excess. Potassium is the second most important plant food after nitrogen. A low potassium level causes scorching of leaf tips and margins and die-back of shoots. Flower stems are thin and weak and lower foliage has necrotic spots. Flower quality is reduced and leaves on flower stems show scorch with necrotic spots. For outdoor plants, an application of sulphate of potash, or if available, a top-dressing of fresh wood ashes, watered-in if the soil is dry, may be applied. Excess potassium causes premature loss of leaves at the base of the plant and brittle stems.

Boron Deficiency and Excess. Boron is the trace element most likely to be in short supply, particularly with plants growing in a soil-less compost. Deficiency causes excessive axillary branching of the flower stems and chlorotic leaf tips with red-purple discoloration. Flowers become deformed and calyx splitting is common. Reduced hormone levels at the buds can cause death of the flower buds. The plant's boron requirement is related to light, so deficiency is more likely to be seen between spring and autumn. A slight deficiency may be remedied by adding a trace of boron when watering. On a small scale, a stock solution may be made up by dissolving 3 milliliters (0.5 teaspoon) of Borax in 0.5 liter (1 pint) of hot water (it will not dissolve in cold water). For watering plants, dilute the stock solution at 18 ml (1 tablespoon) of stock per 4.5 liters (1 gallon) of water. However, since serious damage can be done by overdosing, it would be advisable to use a complete fertilizer that contains boron, and so prevent a deficiency arising rather than having to correct one. Excess boron causes browning of the plant's leaf tips.

Calcium Deficiency and Excess. Calcium deficiency is rare in plants where garden lime is used, but not uncommon in soil-less potting composts, acid soils in greenhouses, and soils heavily fed with phosphates. Tip-burn on young leaves is typical in calcium-deficient plants and flowers do not open properly. A calcium deficiency can be corrected by sprinkling 1 teaspoon (5 ml) of ground chalk or limestone on the surface of the compost, to be washed down by subsequent waterings. Too much calcium resulting from over-liming can produce a boron deficiency.

Magnesium Deficiency. Magnesium is a constituent of the green coloring matter chlorophyll. Symptoms of magnesium deficiency are yellowing of foliage, with veins remaining green. When serious, most of the foliage turns yellow and older leaves die off. Magnesium is easily leached following heavy applications of potassium and can also be locked up by over-liming. This condition can be corrected by watering with a solution of magnesium sulphate (Epsom salts) at 0.5 tsp (3 ml) of crystals to 4.5 liters (1 gallon) of water. Dissolve the crystals in a little hot water before mixing. Magnesium deficiency should not arise where the fertilizers used contain minor and trace elements.

Chapter 13

Breeding New Cultivars

The history of border carnations is a continuing saga of enthusiasts' patient dedication to improving the flower over four or five centuries. The perpetual-flowering carnations of the past 150 years never quite rivalled border carnations for variation of color combinations, but the perpetual-flowering types were more fortunate in that outstanding cultivars, and especially those derived from 'William Sim', produced desirable sports in many colors. Such cultivars might never have rewarded the patient breeder's careful cross-pollination efforts, yet can appear as free gifts to anyone growing the plants. It must be said, however, that the wider variation in color combinations is now being bred into the modern perpetual-flowering carnation.

Perpetual-flowering carnations were never an easy commercial crop until the mid-twentieth century when the cultivar 'William Sim' arrived, followed by its hundreds of sports. A further stroke of good fortune, the evolution of meristem (tip-culture) propagation, kept the Sims in cultivation when they might have succumbed to wilt and viral diseases. New cut-flower cultivars, said to be unrelated to Sims—which seems hardly possible—are now being bred in continental Europe and taken up by some flower growers in Great Britain, where commercial breeding appears to be almost non-existent. (See also Chapter 11 on commercial carnation production.)

There is no such apathy in England concerning the exhibition-type perpetual-flowering carnations, for new cultivars arrive in a steady stream, including some fine sports from amateur growers as well as professionals. I should say that plant breeding of various genera by amateurs is now carried out on a very large scale, particularly in Great Britain and the United States. Professional interest in breeding border carnations has just about died out, but keen amateurs are producing new cultivars in good numbers. The basic principles of cross-pollination are simple enough and some amateurs find success without a deep knowledge of plant genetics. The simplest form of raising new cultivars is to take a few specks of pollen dust, the male seed, and place them upon the receptive stigma of a flower whose pod is to bear the seeds. The seeds ripen in the autumn and may be sown in winter, given warmth, or in spring when heat is not necessary. One can plan all sorts of crosses and even the veriest novice can strike lucky. Those enthusiasts who wish to go into the matter more deeply might prefer to obtain books on plant breeding before proceeding further. Many raisers feel that a study of genetics is useful, but the breeder's judgement is even more so. This has been described as a "guiding sense," the ability to select that which has potential and discard everything else. The reward for raising an outstanding new cultivar is its acceptance as such by those who have the knowledge and experience to appreciate its true value.

The usual advice to would-be breeders is to cross selfs with selfs, white-ground fancies with white-ground fancies, and so on; in other words, like with like. But this does not guarantee any measure of success, as breeders have found out all too often. James Douglas, the greatest breeder of border carnations, said that although a gardener may cross the finest cultivars, he should not expect that the seedlings will be as good as the parents, or even resemble them. Of his own raising he said he would be well content to obtain 5 percent worth growing on. There is great variation among plants obtained from a single pod and having the same parents. One such pod, obtained by pollinating the white perpetual-flowering carnation 'Fragrant Ann' with pollen from the same cultivar, contained 15 seeds that produced 13 pink cultivars, 1 yellow, and 1 white with deep pink stripes. It is obvious that all seeds in a pod have but one female parent; what is not generally understood is that a flower can be pollinated by several male parents. There can be as many as a hundred ovules in the ovary waiting to be fertilized; a few specks of pollen from one flower can only fertilize a few ovules. This explains why some seed pods contain only one or two ripe seeds while others may have up to a hundred. A number of different crosses can be made using pollen from different cultivars to fertilize one flower. This operation must be completed in the space of one day because flowers sometimes close up within a few hours of fertilization. E. Frank Palmer, who raised the famous *Gladiolus* 'Picardy', said of pollinating: "Get there first with the most."

James Douglas once raised 500 seedlings of a cross between two light-edged white-ground picotees and obtained only one light-edged picotee worth growing again. He also found large numbers of purple selfs among the seedlings, but not a single white self. In the 1892 National Carnation and Picotee Society *Carnation Manual*, James Douglas wrote,

> I have raised thousands of seedlings, and could write much on the curious variations of color observable in seedlings from white-ground carnations and picotees, as they are endless and unaccountable; but as I can lay down no methods by which they can be regulated, and suggest no processes by which they can be affected, I must leave amateurs to gain their own experience in this field of Flora's fair domain.

From a very large batch of seedlings from yellow-ground picotees Douglas found many with a white-ground, also pink, red, maroon, and scarlet selfs. He also mentioned a bed of 300 seedlings from a yellow self cultivar of which only one came up yellow, and that one was worthless.

Curiously enough, in 1969, I crossed the two white-ground picotees 'Eva Humphries' and 'Ganymede', and I did produce a white self. It is very free-flowering, with clove-scented flowers of perfect form and a short stiff stem. Named 'Whitesmith' after the Sussex hamlet, it received First Class Certificate (FCC) at the Royal Horticultural Society Wisley trials in 1975 and has grown well there every year since; in 1992 it received the RHS Award of Garden Merit (AGM[H4]). It has also been judged Premier Bloom at carnation shows. In 1968 I raised a pure white-ground picotee from 'Eva Humphries', which I described in my "stud-book" (notebook for keeping records of crosses, new seedlings, etc.) as

> seedling 6843, a white-ground picotee, wire-edged deep rose. The flowers are as large and full as any border carnation, yet are of excellent form for exhibition. The stems are short and stiff and the habit of growth is that of a normal border carnation rather than of a picotee.

I named it 'Pevensey' and it did well on the show bench and occasionally even beat 'Eva Humphries' to take Premier Bloom Certificate. I discarded it after a while because its margin faded in the garden in bright weather and it required heavy shading to keep its edge color in the greenhouse.

The second James Douglas stated that he had never seen such complete and exhaustive records of cross-fertilization and pedigree as those kept by his father, James Douglas, and Martin Ridley Smith. He said he had heard both men state that no hard-and-fast law could be laid down for selection for color production in selfs, picotees, or fancies. The second James Douglas gave as an example his 2000 fine seedlings obtained from crossing the yellow selfs 'Germania' and 'Daffodil', which produced plants of almost every carnation color except yellow. He observed that the gift of clove scent was even more elusive than color; from a bed of some 3500 seedlings bred from two of his best clove-scented carnations, only five plants possessed a clove scent. Referring to the advice that the use of a closely related parent should be guarded against, the second James Douglas stated,

> If I am qualified by opportunity of observation to speak of the border carnation in this connection, I should say unhesitatingly that all or practically all modern cultivars are consanguineous, and that consanguinity in no way compromises the beauty, strength or usefulness of the race. (Douglas 1946)

Some people say that carnation breeders have bred the scent out of the flower. In fact, carnation breeders of the twentieth century put the scent into the carnation. James Douglas the second, referring to carnations of a hundred years ago, mentioned an almost total absence of scent, saying those with any pretensions to a clove scent could be counted on the fingers of one hand. He himself had raised very many fine cloves in every carnation color except yellow and he said he had never yet seen a yellow carnation that possessed a clove scent, even in a faint degree. Curiously, again in 1969, in the same bed as the seedling that became 'Whitesmith', I found a yellow self that also obtained FCC at the Wisley trials, and on the same day in 1975 that 'Whitesmith' received the same award. More curious still, the Royal Horticultural Society described the flower as having a strong clove scent. I must say that definitions of scent vary from person to person; with carnation enthusiasts the clove scent is really strong and smells like the taste of the strong clove humbugs usually eaten in winter because they are thought to keep one warm. The sweet perfume of carnations we refer to as a carnation scent but not a clove scent. We say this because carnation shows have classes for clove carnations, where it is important to ensure that those exhibited are truly clove cultivars. I would not class 'Golden Cross' as a clove for exhibition, and I do not consider 'Whitesmith' to be a true clove, even though it is listed by the British National Carnation Society as a clove cultivar for exhibition purposes. In 1979 I raised another yellow self, which my notes described as "795, large flower, short stiff stem, bright yellow, nice scent." I named this seedling 'Eppie' after the little golden-haired girl in George Elliot's *Silas Marner*. I listed it in my catalogue but deleted it after a few years because it is so similar to 'Golden Cross', even to the "nice scent." It does still exist, however, because I know it is exhibited at carnation shows in Scotland.

When I first grew carnations from seeds I would obtain the seeds from carnation specialists; although they produced many plants with pleasing flowers, these did not approach the standard of the existing named cultivars. It was only when I produced my own carnation seeds, choosing my own parent plants, that I began to obtain some good cultivars. A Canadian enthusiast wrote to me for seeds because he had found the commercial English border carnation seeds to be no better than those of the Chabaud strain, and the perpetual-flowering carnation seeds to be of the Marguerite strain. V. M. Gerard, an American from Seattle, Washington, wrote in the 1950 British National Carnation Society *Year Book*,

I received the catalogue from one of our largest mail-order houses in which were advertised "Hardy Border Carnations," so I ordered two dozen. They came in the spring of 1948 and bloomed in the summer but they proved to be Marguerite carnations. The following spring the same firm sent me another plant list and asked me how I had fared with the plants previously supplied. I replied, pointing out that they were selling plants under a false name, and after some correspondence, they were gracious enough to express their readiness to make the necessary corrections and adjustments and to see to it that in future catalogues the hardy border carnations should be properly described and distinguished from other dianthus species. There is no use in letting the Border Carnation get a bad name by having an annual carnation masquerading as the real thing.

During my early years of growing carnations I was also very interested in auriculas and came across a book by Rowland Biffen, *The Auricula*, published in 1949. Sir Rowland Biffen was a famous breeder of new wheat cultivars who, while at Cambridge, was one of the pioneers of the Mendelian experimentation. In the foreword to Biffen's book, F. T. Brooks, Emeritus Professor of Botany at University of Cambridge, said of Biffen that he had

> a remarkable flair for plant breeding in general; in his private garden, and constantly assisted by his wife, new kinds of peas, strawberries, delphiniums, gladioli, sweet peas and other ornamental plants were produced, but above all, auriculas were his chief and most constant love.

I learned from Biffen's book that early in the nineteenth century it was realized that seed production was the result of a sexual process. Auricula hybridizers, instead of merely accepting whatever seeds the bees caused to be produced, set out those particular plants selected as parents in a position away from other auriculas in order to reduce the number of unwanted crosses. Crossing like with like was advocated, even though pollination was still left to the bees. Crossing plants soon graduated to pollinating by hand, a considerable improvement. There then followed those strange beliefs that the male parent determined the coloring of the flowers and the female their shape and general form. Biffen wrote, "It is hardly necessary to say that the system was not infallible." The same old wives' tales persist with some carnation enthusiasts. It was Gregor Mendel's paper *Experiments in Plant Hybridization* that changed the whole outlook on plant breeding. The essential discovery was that the various characters of a plant—color, stem, foliage, etc.—are either dominant or recessive, so that when two unrelated plants are crossed their progeny exhibit the dominant characters, but when that progeny (siblings) are self-pollinated or crossed with each other, their progeny exhibit dominant and recessive characters in fixed proportions. Rowland Biffen experimented with his auriculas in great detail in order to ascertain which characters were dominant and which recessive, something that has never been done for border carnations. I am sure that parents with flowers of excellent form and sound calyx reproduce these qualities in their offspring, and that the habit of growth, such as compact or lanky, is also passed on.

NEW ZEALAND AND THE UNITED STATES

The British National Carnation Society *Year Book* of 1985 carried an article by Dr. Keith Hammett, former plant pathologist and now full-time plant breeder of *Dianthus*, *Dahlia*, and sweet peas *(Lathyrus odoratus)*. The article, "British Border Carnations and Pinks Re-established in New Zealand," tells how by 1976 no border carnations were available in New Zealand. He named nine English cultivars he had managed to collect, but these were badly infected by a number of viruses and so were destroyed. Since the business of importing carnations into New Zealand was a "hassle for all concerned," Hammett chose to import seeds. His account of his progress followed:

> Seed was obtained from John Galbally of Sussex, long time border carnation specialist, and from two carnation nurseries who offered seeds as well as plants. Seeds arrived in September—our spring. . . . Germination was good, and strong plants were raised and planted during April—our autumn. From the onset the Galbally plants could be seen to be distinct from the other material. The leaves were broader and more glaucous. All the plants performed well and flowered from November till January/February of the following year. It was when the plants flowered that the differences were most obvious. The Galbally plants were classical bor-

der carnations with smooth-edged petals and with fine form. In contrast, the others were much closer in type to the annual Chabaud strains obtainable from any seed-house and presumably came from a common source. They may well have been suitable for growing in a border, but they were certainly not what I know as a border carnation, and were soon discarded. A remarkably high proportion of the Galbally plants were of good quality and offered an excellent range of colors and color combinations. Cuttings were taken and plants of each selection were trialed for a number of subsequent seasons. In 1980 I tried my hand at exhibiting the best of the selections. They acquitted themselves well, though it must be admitted that competition at carnation shows in New Zealand is not currently comparable in strength to that found at dahlia and rose shows. A demand arose for these cultivars and as a result a nursery has been licensed to propagate and distribute them within New Zealand. A year ago seven cultivars were released throughout New Zealand. . . . These cultivars have started to appear at shows throughout the country and 'Filigree' and 'Topline Supreme' did well at the main Auckland show in 1984. . . . Since the first importation of John Galbally's seeds in 1976, five further importations of seeds have been made. These have given me a very good genetic base on which to make further developments and to maintain the diversity of colorings found in the border carnation. Currently I have a good quantity of seedlings at various stages of development resulting from my own crosses. John Galbally has not only provided me with seeds, he has freely answered my questions and given me much advice and encouragement. It must be a source of satisfaction to him to realize that his work over many years is now giving pleasure to many people on the other side of the world. Let us hope that the re-establishment of the border carnation in New Zealand will prove to be a link in the continuing survival of this historic plant.

And, I may add, also the re-establishment of the border carnation in the United States, because cultivars raised by Keith Hammett from my seeds have been launched by the American nursery Jackson and Perkins of Medford, Oregon, as "old-fashioned, double-flowered border dianthus created from English origins." 'Filigree', a white-ground picotee edged crimson, was announced as "the premier 1990 Award-Winner." The newest introductions include 'Driven Snow', pure white self, and

'Apricot Dream', apricot self. The catalogue describes these cultivars as border dianthus rather than border carnations, which may explain why American friends tell me border carnations are not grown in the States. I remember nearly forty years ago some of my Canadian customers included orders for American friends in with their own.

Dr. Hammett informs me that a woman at Auckland University recently completed a Master of Science thesis based on a study of chromosomes and breeding barriers using material originally obtained from my seeds. He is now cross-breeding border carnations with other *Dianthus* in an effort to produce a hardy plant with a flower and colors like a border carnation, but with the compact habit of the pink and repeat-flowering.

I would advise those contemplating breeding carnations or pinks to grow named cultivars and produce their own seeds. At least they would know they have seeds of the type they desire and not of some totally different unknown type.

Basic Principles of Breeding

To understand the basic principles of breeding, a little knowledge of Mendel's laws of inheritance is desirable. Gregor Mendel was an Austrian monk who studied the generation-to-generation inheritance of the many characters of plants. He published his findings in 1866, although his work was not fully understood by the botanists of the day. Mendel died in 1884, but his papers were discovered in 1900 by the scientists C. Correns, E. von Tschermak, and H. de Vries, who verified his findings, and from that time plant breeding acquired a scientific basis.

With the breeding of some genera it is important to know their chromosome counts. Fortunately for breeders of carnations and pinks, almost all the *Dianthus* species and cultivars are compatible. In fact, they have even been described as "hopelessly amoral." The immortal bard, William Shakespeare, wrote,

> The fairest flowers o' the season
> Are our carnations and streak'd Gillyvors,
> Which some call nature's bastards.

For *Dianthus* the basic haploid chromosome number is 15; most carnations are diploid and have 30 chromosomes per cell, 15 from each parent. Some carnations are triploid and others tetraploid, with 45 and 60 chromosomes per cell, respectively. Some natural *Dianthus* hybrids may be triploid or tetraploid. Tetraploids crossed with diploids result in triploids, which are usually sterile. Diploids combine easily with diploids, diploids and tetraploids may combine on occasion, and tetraploids can combine with tetraploids. The chromosomes carry the plants' genes, the units of heredity, which determine the new plants' characters, height, size, flower color, scent, habit of growth, etc. Some genes are said to be dominant, others recessive, and when plants with different characters are crossed, the dominant genes influence the first-generation (F_1) seedlings, and the second generation (F_2), obtained by self-pollinating or intercrossing the F_1 seedlings, produce dominant characters in three out of four plants, the remainder showing recessive characters.

Dominance and recessiveness are not always so conveniently clear-cut, however, because with some plants the dominance is incomplete. When a plant with red flowers not completely dominant is crossed with a recessive white-flowered plant, the progeny all have pink flowers. When these F_1 seedlings are self-pollinated, the second-generation (F_2) plants follow Mendel's laws of inheritance: 25 percent of them having red flowers, 50 percent with pink flowers, and the remaining 25 percent white flowers. Since some desirable characters, scent for example, are recessive traits, they do not appear in first-generation crosses but are obtained in second-generation crosses. The qualities of the parents can be further exploited by third- and fourth-generation crosses, also by crossing the F_1 seedlings with either or both their parents (back-crossing).

CHOOSING PARENTS

It is important to make a note of the parents of each cross you make, or at least the female seed-bearing cultivar, for this provides a valuable list of good parent cultivars for future use. Novice growers who grow very few plants have little choice but to cross those cultivars they have. Those with a large number of cultivars may be spoiled for choice and become bewildered. Where there are choices some simple guidelines may be useful. The flower's form is no accident of nature; flowers of perfect form should breed flowers of similar form, and those of imperfect form are most unlikely to produce blooms of good form. There are several kinds of calyx: the fat dumpy calyx, the long thin calyx, and the in-between type that contains the petals without bursting. Stem and foliage also vary considerably. The stem does not need to be stout but must support the flower without arching too much. The foliage that is blue-gray is more pleasing than the greenish kind, and curly foliage is infinitely more attractive than straight leaves. These assets can all be taken into account when choosing parents for seed production. In the days when I grew many seedlings I would take a single pod of known parentage containing about thirty seeds, sow the seeds into one box and then plant them in a greenhouse bed all close together. When the seedlings bloomed I would discard the singles, bursters, weak-stemmed, and poorly formed, leaving about five or six plants. I would cross-pollinate each plant with every other plant in the group, and also perform the reverse crosses, giving me up to thirty pods. These thirty pods would normally all have the same two grandparents—my method of exploiting the F_2 generation system. As mentioned earlier, it was the second James Douglas who said that consanguinity in no way compromised the vigor and constitution of the border carnation.

To aspiring raisers of border carnations who are puzzled about how to start breeding, may I suggest they try raising picotees. I say this because picotees are slipping out of cultivation; there used to be hundreds of cultivars, but now only a handful are left. There is also a fair chance of success; when I crossed picotees I did obtain a reasonable proportion of picotees among the seedlings. Existing picotees are very good, but they are so few in number that any new cultivar should evoke interest. Some good white-ground picotees are seen, but few yellow-ground cultivars. It can be done—my own yellow 'Hannah Louise', raised in 1974, was a seedling from William Thorburn's 'Dot Clark', one of whose parents was 'Margaret Lennox', raised by James Douglas in 1909. 'Hannah Louise' was awarded FCC in 1987 after trial at Wisley, and AGM(H4) in 1995. It was considered by the late Jack Humphries, raiser of the peerless 'Eva Humphries', to be the best yellow-ground picotee he had ever seen. Some thirty years ago I produced a pink-ground picotee that had large perfectly formed flowers with a wire edge of deep ruby-red. The ground color was a lovely shade of pink, much pleasanter than that seen in the few pink picotees in circulation at the present time. I grew the original seedling plant outdoors in the border, and while it was in bloom a carnation-enthusiast friend, who was very clever with cuttings, came almost every day to admire it. I am ashamed to admit that I began to nurse fears for the safety of my new creation; after all, no one had ever raised a pink picotee, and in fact it was later nicknamed "Galbally's pink picotee." So I covered it with a large cloche, and even went so far as to count its sideshoots. I am reminded of a certain old florist who wrote around 1828,

> In general amateurs do not admit every body into their gardens; they have a particular horror of certain descriptions of persons, whom they call flower clippers and stealers. Bribery, wall-scaling, false keys, abuse of confidence have nothing in them to deter certain persons, when intent on procuring a graft, or a bud of a rose tree, which they possess not themselves.

To the "graft, or bud of a rose tree" he could have added "or shoot of a new carnation." Named 'Catherine Ramsden', my new picotee cultivar was submitted to the Royal Horticultural Society Joint Committee in 1968 and obtained Preliminary Commendation. After a while, however, some of the flowers sported large ticks on the petals and eventually some plants carried picotee and fancy flowers on the same stem. When it became quite unpredictable I gave it up altogether.

OBTAINING AND TRANSFERRING POLLEN

Even when it is easy to work out which cultivars you would like to cross, however, it is quite likely that you will find no pollen on the parents of your choice. It is wise to collect pollen from those desirable cultivars that have some, and then decide upon your crosses. I record the parentage of most of my own-bred cultivars, and when pollen is scarce I use it on cultivars to which the pollen donor is already related, thereby promoting use of the plants' recessive traits. Plants grown for breeding should not be disbudded in the usual way, because the larg-

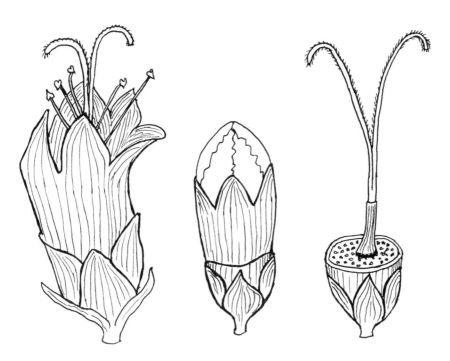

Figure 13-1. Preparing for pollination. *Left:* filaments and styles (petals omitted); *center:* bud stage for emasculation; *right:* styles ready for pollinating.

est bloom is sometimes devoid of pollen while the secondary blooms may have it in abundance. Some suggest that removing the crown bud induces an increase in pollen production on the remaining secondary flowers. Filaments, usually ten in number, grow between the petals and are topped by pollen sacs, called anthers. When the male seed, pollen, is ripe and like golden dust, it is ready for use. The pistil comprises the female parts of the flower: ovary, styles, and stigmas. The styles, usually two or three in number, rise from the ovary, which houses the unfertilized seeds, called ovules. When the tips of the styles, the stigmas, curl over and their upper surfaces become viscid and slightly feathered, they are ready to receive the dry pollen. Pollen is usually found on very fresh flowers and is best taken in the middle of a warm dry day.

With border carnations, the golden pollen may sometimes be seen spilled upon the petals of scarlet, crimson, or heliotrope flowers, where it can be easily collected, but with perpetual-flowering carnations the anthers have to be searched for among the petals. Some petals have to be removed; in fact, many growers prefer to remove all the petals, or to leave just enough to be able to tell when consummation has occurred. Those gardeners who dabble at plant breeding for enjoyment are happy just to find a little pollen on a favorite cultivar, use it to pollinate another favorite, and wait for results. They obtain great pleasure from this and sometimes produce good cultivars. But serious breeders do not risk having their plans endangered by the risk of self-pollination, and so they emasculate their breeding plants before pollinating them. Emasculation is performed by cutting through and all round the calyx at about the top of the basal bracts, thereby removing sepals, petals, and anthers and leaving only the ovary and styles. Some breeders crown their efforts with muslin bags against insect interference, but many believe that this causes mildew and rotting of the seedpods.

Pollen can be transferred by means of a fine paint brush, a feather, the edge of torn blotting paper, and so on. I have used soft furry pods of *Lupinus*, which seem to have been made for the purpose; one does not need to sterilize them for reuse, just use a fresh one each time. Another alternative is using tweezers to remove the anther completely and convey the pollen to the stigma. A day or so after the union is consummated the petals close together. The cross should be recorded in a notebook—it is common practice to put the female parent first—and some indication fixed to the plant for future identification. The petals will dry out and should be removed as soon as possible, but only when they come away easily. The sepals must be gently split down their length and removed altogether to prevent retention of moisture about the seedpod. The pod swells and in about a month to six weeks its tip starts to turn brown.

COLLECTING SEEDPODS

The seedpod must be watched carefully for signs of splitting at the tip; when this happens the pods must be collected immediately, otherwise some seeds may be lost. Store the pods in paper bags or used envelopes, not in airtight jars or tins, remembering to note their parentage.

For detailed information on growing border carnations and perpetual-flowering carnations from seeds, see Chapters 8 and 9.

Sports

Another way of obtaining new cultivars is by "finding" bud-mutants, sometimes called bud-sports or just sports. A sport results when some chemical change occurs within a plant and it ceases to grow normally, and some external change is seen. A sport may be considered fixed when plants propagated from the sporting plant themselves produce plants all of whose flowers are similar to those of the sport. When fixed, the plant becomes a new cultivar and is given a name, usually one bearing some relation to the original name, but this is not compulsory. (I am sure any amateur who produced but one cultivar in his life would want to name it after his wife, mother, father, child, or even himself.) A modern example is 'Scarlet Joanne', a scarlet sport of the cerise-pink self 'Joanne'. The most famous of all sportive carnations is the scarlet cultivar 'William Sim', which presented cut-flower producers with literally hundreds of sports in almost every known carnation color, such as 'White William Sim'. Perpetual-flowering carnations are particularly sportive, the changes usually affecting only the colors of the flowers. Some sports are not particularly desirable, but those that are should be fixed to become new cultivars with their own names. When, in addition to its normal flower, a perpetual-flowering carnation plant throws a flower that could be considered a desirable sport, the mutant character may be reproduced by taking cuttings from the branch carrying the sport. This is also true of border carnations, except in the case of young plants in their first year of flowering when all the sideshoots should be layered, so that when in flower the following summer the plants of the sports can be distinguished from those of the original cultivar.

RUN FLOWERS

Perpetual-flowering carnations are more sportive than border carnations, although the latter do sometimes throw "run" flowers. Very few run flowers are desirable; in fact, they have been an abomination to exhibitors for hundreds of years. With fancy cultivars of border carnations, those with contrasting flakes or stripes upon a lighter-colored ground, the deeper coloring floods the ground color, sometimes so widely that the ground color is completely superimposed and the flower is no longer a fancy, but a self. Those run flowers that are desirable may be regarded as sports and can, when fixed, be given names. It is quite common for fancies with flakes of scarlet, crimson, or purple on a gray or pink ground color to throw self-colored flowers, but their colors, although originally attractive as contrasting colors, are usually rather less so as self colors. Fancy cultivars bought from nurseries sometimes throw self-colored flowers. The stock reply to complaints used to be that the plant would, in all probability, revert to its normal fancy-colored flowers the following summer. This is not strictly true; in my experience a plant of a fancy cultivar that throws all self-colored flowers never reverts to the original fancy. Proof of this is simple: named self cultivars obtained as sports from fancy cultivars never throw fancy flowers. When a nurseryman propagates a fancy plant that has produced self flowers and sells the plants as the original fancy, he is just asking for complaints. When in business, I would discard sportive fancy plants as unfit for propagation, thereby reducing considerably the possibility of disappointing a few customers.

Naming New Cultivars

A new cultivar raised from seed is termed a "seedling" until such time as it is given a name. Having bred a new cultivar of merit the raiser will wish to give it a name. The earliest breeders used to name their flowers after kings and queens, princes and princesses, dukes and duchesses, and other royalty as well as admirals, generals, and famous beauties of the day. Most amateurs produce only a few new cultivars, so usually they wish to name them after a member of their own family or people they know and admire. Some growers name their new plants after places of which they have nostalgic memories, holidays, honeymoons, or adventures, as some people name their houses. I named some of my cultivars after members of my family, and some after places. 'Golden Cross' and 'Whitesmith' are hamlets close to Hailsham, where I had my nursery. 'Alfriston' is named after the tourist-attraction village quite close to Upper Dicker, where I lived before retiring to Eastbourne.

INTERNATIONAL DIANTHUS REGISTER

It is important to ascertain whether the name you choose is not the same as a carnation or pink currently in cultivation, nor one that has been used in the past. The *International Dianthus Register* lists all known names of carnations, pinks, sweet williams, and other kinds of *Dianthus* that are, or have been, in use. In choosing a name, attention should also be given to the rules and recommendations in the *International Code of Nomenclature for Cultivated Plants*. Publications and application forms for registration of new cultivars are obtainable from The Secretary, Royal Horticultural Society Garden, Wisley, Woking, Surrey GU23 6QB, U.K. The RHS is the International Registration Authority for the genus *Dianthus*. The second edition of the *International Dianthus Register* (1983) lists some 27,000 names of pinks and carnations, and annual supplementary lists follow. Names are given in strict alphabetical order and preceded by an abbreviation of the type classification, for example b = border carnation, pf = perpetual-flowering carnation, m = Malmaison carnations, p = pinks, p.a. = annuals. The p.a. classification now includes all "annual" carnations as well as annual pinks or dianthus; all *Dianthus barbatus* and *D. chinensis* cultivars are placed in this class.

The cultivar name is followed by the name of the raiser, date of raising, brief color description, and date of any Royal Horticultural Society award. The second edition of the *International Dianthus Register* also lists some 3000 raisers' names and addresses, with the names of new raisers included in each of the supplementary lists. The Register is compiled by Dr. Alan Leslie, who generously acknowledges the assistance given by many people, and particularly Syd Wilson and Audrey Robinson, historians of the British National Carnation Society.

Many of the cultivar names registered are purely academic, having been searched out from very old books, some nearly 400 years old. Also, many of the modern names are those of cultivars raised by amateur gardeners that never become generally available. Originally it was a prerequisite for inclusion of a name in the Register that it had been validly published in a list, catalogue, article, or show report, but I believe many of the names included in recent supplements have never been so published. The introduction to the Register states,

> It is of obvious value to all those interested in *Dianthus* that their nomenclature should be as stable and free from duplication as possible. *Dianthus* are exported and exchanged throughout the world, so any Register must be maintained on a world-wide basis, and it is only through the co-operation of all concerned that this objective can be achieved.

I have a catalogue dated 1990 that contains a short revised list of perpetual-flowering carnations. One of the cultivar names included appears in the Register 5 times, another 6 times, another 8 times, another 21 times, and yet another 23 times. Checking through the 1983 Register and its supplements, it is obvious that these latest cultivars to acquire their much-used names have not been registered. Clearly the desired co-operation to avoid duplication of names is not forthcoming.

Following a suggestion by the Royal Horticultural Society that a register of border carnations be prepared, Eileen produced the 1955 *Register of Hardy Border Carnations*, which named, classified, and described all the 800 cultivars then available from carnation specialists. Names of raisers and introducers with dates of raising and awards were included, together with relative flowering times and heights. Clove-scented cultivars and those useful for exhibition were also indicated. This register was well-received and warmly commended.

PLANT BREEDERS' RIGHTS

Another register of plant cultivars is published in the U.K. by the Plant Variety Rights Office, which was set up under the Plant Varieties and Seeds Act 1964, but this register should not be confused with the *International Dianthus Register*. The Plant Breeders' Rights Regulations give the holder the exclusive right to sell plants of the protected cultivar and to reproduce that cultivar for the purpose of selling it. Such protected cultivars appear in specialists' catalogues with a small sign, ®, against the cultivar name. Catalogues also will state that the cultivar is protected by Plant Breeders' Rights and that the purchaser may not propagate for sale plants of that cultivar except under license from the holder of the rights. I understand that an amateur grower may give away a plant so registered, as long as that gift cannot be construed as a sale. In the United Kingdom, any breeder considering applying for Plant Breeders' Rights should apply to the Plant Variety Rights Office, White House Lane, Huntingdon Road, Cambridge CB3 0LF, U.K. I think amateur breeders would probably find the scheme far too complicated and expensive.

Long before this scheme was instituted, Montagu Allwood took out an American patent on his pure white, strongly clove-scented perpetual-flowering carnation 'George Allwood', named after his brother, the first and only carnation to be so patented. A photograph of the document, bearing the official seal and dated 10 June 1948, appeared in the 1949 British National Carnation Society *Year Book*.

Royal Horticultural Society Awards and Trials

AWARDS TO CARNATIONS AND PINKS

New cultivars may be submitted to one of two committees of the Royal Horticultural Society for award, the Border Carnation and Pinks committee and the Perpetual-flowering Carnation committee. These are joint committees, comprised of equal numbers of members representing the Royal Horticultural Society and the British National Carnation Society. The committees usually meet at the Chelsea Flower Show in May and at the Royal Horticultural Society hall at Westminster on the dates of the British National Carnation Society shows in June, July, and October. The requisite form requesting information about the new cultivar must be completed and handed in to the RHS official before the time of the meeting, together with a vase of flowers for the committee to examine.

Border carnations and pinks may be entered as plants for the garden or for exhibition or both. The committee may select the cultivar for trial at the Royal Horticultural Society Wisley garden in Surrey. It may also award Certificate of Preliminary Commendation (PC) and, where the plant is entered as an exhibition cultivar, recommend Award of Merit (AM) for exhibition. Cultivars that have received AM for exhibition may be submitted again, though not in the same year, for consideration for First Class Certificate (FCC) for exhibition.

There is an important difference between awards for exhibition given previously to 1992 and those given after, however. The earlier awards for exhibition were all given to cultivars eminently suitable for competition on the show bench. The Royal Horticultural Society now dictates that with the new awards the citation "for exhibition" does not necessarily imply "for competition," and that an award for exhibition need not imply that the plant possesses all the attributes currently favored in that group on the competition show bench. Both the joint Border Carnation and Pinks and the Perpetual-flowering Carnation committees, however, still insist on desirable exhibition qualities when making exhibition awards. Since all the exhibition awards to border carnations mentioned in this book are pre-1992, it may be accepted that the cultivars concerned are all suitable for showing in competitive classes.

Perpetual-flowering carnations may be entered as useful for exhibition or garden decoration (in the open or under glass) or both. When seen for the first time the cultivar may be awarded PC, after which it becomes eligible for AM. To obtain this award the cultivar must be seen at three different seasons of the year within a period of two years. FCC may only be awarded to cultivars that have previously received AM. An Award of Garden Merit (AGM), with a hardiness rating, may be given after a period of further assessment. See under Border Carnation and Pinks Trials, below.

Perpetual-flowering carnations have not in the past had trials as such, but a few cultivars have recently been grown at Wisley to compare the winter-flowering properties of some of the newer cultivars with those of the older cut-flower type. Reports have been favorable, and the trials are now conducted to include assessment for the Award of Garden Merit.

BORDER CARNATION AND PINKS TRIALS

When a cultivar has been selected for trial, rooted plants of it are sent, usually by the raiser, to the Royal Horticultural Society Wisley garden in September. The trials are known as "on-going trials," meaning they continue from year to year, although a new trial with fresh plants is planted every year. Therefore, when a cultivar has been grown in the trial, the RHS writes asking the sender to supply plants in the autumn for inclusion in the following year's trial. A cultivar may be included in the trial for as long as the sender wishes to supply it, or until it is deleted from the trial. When a cultivar deteriorates markedly the committee may vote on its deletion from the trial; not only does this improve the appearance of the trial bed, but it saves the sender the trouble of supplying plants that have no chance of obtaining an award. When all the trial plants have been received they are planted out in the trials field, usually in October. The only protection given them is a low wire-mesh fence surrounding the trial area to prevent their being demolished by rabbits. When seen in early spring the damage done by birds often seems irreparable, yet by flowering time in July the plants are all in rude health and full of bloom. Each set of plants has its label with details of name, raiser, sender, and dates of previous trial awards. The plants are inspected by the committee who, before the year 1992, could recommend one of the following awards: C (Commended), HC (Highly Commended), AM (Award of Merit), or FCC (First Class Certificate). A plant that received C or HC in a previous year would have that information on its label and the committee could upgrade this to AM. Only cultivars that received AM in a previous year were eligible to be considered for the highest award, the FCC. Cultivars that were awarded FCC could not improve on this, but they were included in the trial to act as standards for comparison, provided the senders wished to continue supplying them. Some FCC plants were standards for comparison for so many years that they were jokingly and affectionately referred to as being worthy of "FCC and Bar."

Since 1992 the Commended, Highly Commended, Award of Merit, and First Class Certificate awards are no longer given to hardy border carnations and pinks after trial at Wisley, although all awards previously given are to stand for historic purposes. A completely new single award, AGM (Award of Garden Merit), replaces the four previous categories. It is given to plants of outstanding excellence for garden decoration or garden use whether for the open garden or under glass. This award may only be given following a period of assessment, and plants with this award are subject to periodic review. The title AGM is now accompanied by a hardiness rating:

> H4 for plants hardy throughout the British Isles
> H3 for plants hardy outside in some regions
> H2 for plants requiring an unheated greenhouse
> H1 for plants requiring a heated greenhouse

This new Award of Garden Merit is not to be confused with the original award of the same name that was instituted in 1921 and which has now been rescinded. The previous AGM was given to plants grown in the open garden that were of good constitution and excellent for ordinary garden decoration. Plants recommended for the award were judged by an Award of Garden Merit Committee and voting carried out in the same manner as for awarding the original First Class Certificate.

Chapter 14

Exhibiting Carnations and Pinks

Visitors to carnation shows are sometimes puzzled and consider a show to be "just a lot of lovely flowers." All sports, games, and competitions are so much more interesting when one knows a bit about it. Before even considering entering flowers for competition it is essential to obtain the relevant schedule and show regulations, also to visit a carnation show to get some idea of what goes on there. I often receive letters from aspiring exhibitors asking for advice and clarification of rules, some requiring quite simple points explained in detail. One visit to a show should put all fears at rest, but do ask questions of the show stewards who are there to assist you. It really is all so simple you will wonder why you were ever concerned. The show schedule must be studied carefully to be clearly understood; most shows have classes for novice growers, and the definition of a novice is usually made clear. The British National Carnation Society publishes the booklet *Rules for Judging, Standards and Classifications*, which sets out the standards of excellence for judging, including rules and regulations relating to exhibiting pinks and border and perpetual-flowering carnations.

Carnation shows (which include pinks) are held around mid-summer in the south of England, about a week later in the Midlands, and during early August in northern England and Scotland. Shows also are

Figure 14-1. My trade exhibit at the Royal Horticultural Society hall at Westminster, 1958. (Photo by Reginald Malby)

held in early autumn for perpetual-flowering carnations, where a few classes for repeat-flowering pinks are often included. Intending exhibitors are usually required to complete an entry form denoting the classes in which they wish to compete. At some shows this can be done on the show day, but with large shows entry forms have to be posted some days in advance.

Timing Flowers for Shows

We all have fine flowers at various times of the year, but to become a successful exhibitor one needs to be able to pick one's best flowers at the right time, a day or two before the show dates. Timing flowers for show dates is the hardest part of cultivation for exhibition, and it is made difficult mostly by capricious weather conditions, not just around the show dates but all through the growing season. The good news is that with perpetual-flowering carnations there are almost always other buds, slightly more forward or backward, to fill the breach. It is surprising how often the blooms we have been so carefully nursing mature just a day or so too early and we are obliged to fall back on unconsidered and overlooked specimens. These often turn out better because being fresher than fully mature blooms they are more likely to catch the judge's eye.

Every greenhouse is a law unto itself, and the exhibitor comes to learn how he or she can manipulate his or her plants and greenhouse to produce the best flowers at just the right time for the flower shows. Because weather conditions affect timing to a great extent, the exhibitor must learn to adjust cultivation accordingly. In a normal season it takes about two weeks from buds showing color to flowering time. Depending on the weather this period can vary from a few days shorter to one week longer. It is not difficult to encourage plants to flower earlier than they normally would. Ventilation can be reduced to raise the greenhouse temperature, and the shading thinned somewhat to allow the sun to assist a little more than it otherwise would. During dull weather the doors can be closed, and especially during breezy spells. To hold plants back is more difficult. Maximum ventilation day and night and spraying foliage and pots with a fine spray assist in reducing temperature. Do not allow pots to become too dry; lack of moisture hastens flowering.

Many experienced exhibitors have their own methods of cultivation learned from experience as to what suits their own particular circumstances. There are exposed and sheltered gardens, large and small greenhouses, town, country, and seaside environments, high and low altitudes, wet and dry districts, and so on, all of which affect cultivation and particularly timing. Some exhibitors have an open-air plant shelter of frames with glass, or polyethylene, covering the plants—like a greenhouse without sides—and take plants into it from the greenhouse to cool down and so retard flowering. Exhibitors whose flowers invariably bloom too soon should consider increasing greenhouse ventilation; some side-panes of glass could be replaced by louvred ventilators. There are early and late cultivars of both carnations and pinks, and since greenhouses usually have warm and cool sides, the exhibitor can exploit the differences and swap plants' positions as necessary.

An interesting suggestion in a book written at the beginning of the century called *Carnations and Pinks*, with contributions from T. H. Cook, James Douglas, and J. F. McLeod, recommends the use of superphosphate at a rate of a quarter of an ounce to each plant on benches, or dissolved in water for pot plants, to induce or hasten flowering. I have not yet tried this, but a conversation with a gardener tending the potted plants inside Canada's Vancouver Airport revealed that growers there are favoring the use of a fertilizer with a much higher phosphate content than is normally used in Britain for potted plants. The liquid fertilizer called Miracle-Gro contains an analysis of 15-30-15 and is claimed to promote fast, strong, beautiful growth. Exhibitors wishing to hasten their blooms for an early show might like to experiment with this "old carnationist's tale."

A week or two before the show date is the time for checking the state of the greenhouse shading; patches worn thin could cause blooms to be scorched by summer sunshine. Do not allow plants to become dry at the root, otherwise stems will suffer and lose stiffness, also calyces become liable to split. Slip calyx bands carefully onto carnation buds, and use two bands on suspect cultivars. Stem support rings must be adjusted to allow for fast growth and new ones added as necessary. When flower petals are square to the calyx, slip on thin cardboard or stiff paper collars to prevent the petals reflexing. These can be made about 8 to 11 cm (3 to 4.3 in) in diameter with a 1.3-cm (0.5-in) diameter hole in the center and about eight radial slits, one of which cuts through the edge of the card. One small finger pushed through the hole prepares the card to be placed under the flower right up to the petals, thereby supporting the flower and providing it with the desirable flat back. Apart from losing quality in a show bloom, the reflexed petals actually reduce its size. Try placing a collar under a reflexed bloom to see the difference it makes. Special clips can be obtained to hold the collars, thereby supporting the flowers, which are fastened to the cane.

Flower shows often coincide with a heat-wave. Where it is feared that flowers may mature too quickly, they can be held back a little by picking them a day or two earlier than planned and keeping them in a cool shaded place and up to their necks in water. Where possible, pick flowers with about eight pairs of leaves on the stems; this may not be possible with some modern cultivars. Specific requirements for minimum and maximum lengths of the stems for both carnations and pinks are set out in the British National Carnation Society rules booklet. Normally flowers should be picked a day or two before they are to be staged, and then placed in a deep container. Flower preservatives like Chrysal and Bio Flowerlife are very useful in that they not only make flowers last longer but induce them to continue growing in the vase.

When to take cuttings of perpetual-flowering carnations for exhibiting purposes, and how to stop plants, is learned from experience. What is most important is the quality of the stock. When a really good cultivar fails to work for you, try obtaining it from a different source. Select cuttings only from plants that produce fine flowers; your aim should be to try to improve your plants. Take only good quality cuttings, clean, healthy, and not long-jointed nor too stubby. Take good cuttings whenever they present themselves, so you will not need to cling to second-quality plants to keep your numbers up.

To produce blooms of perpetual-flowering carnations for summer shows, once-stopped plants from small pots should be potted into their flowering pots between early new year and early spring. Similar plants potted during spring should produce autumn flowers, whereas plants potted in winter should bloom in late spring and early summer. This means that the times for inserting cuttings should be winter for summer flowers, spring for autumn flowers, and autumn for spring to early summer flowers. Second-year perpetual-flowering carnation plants are more likely to produce blooms for early summer shows than first-year plants, which usually start flowering in autumn.

How and when to cut flowers is described in detail in Chapter 9. For exhibiting purposes, the flowers preferably should be cut and stood in water for 24 hours before the show. A tip from five-time winner of the perpetual-flowering carnation Gold Cup, Desmond Donaldson, is that for autumn shows, when not enough flowers are ready a week before the show, all flowers with buds only half out of the calyx should be brought indoors, placed in small bottles of lemonade, and opened in heat, say around 21°C (70°F). He tells me that in this way the flowers can be opened within a couple of days.

Exhibiting and Judging

Most towns and villages in Britain hold a flower show in summer and most have classes for carnations and pinks. But the judges often find in border carnation classes exhibits that contain perpetual-flowering carnations and the Chabaud and Grenadin strains of annual carnations. When the judges are no more knowledgeable than the exhibitors, then all is well and everyone is happy. But pity the poor exhibitor who does exhibit true border carnations but does not win a prize; he claims that he is the only one in step and that all the other exhibits should be disqualified as NAS (not according to schedule). Show officials and sometimes even judges then argue that the exhibits are according to schedule because they were grown in the border and therefore are border carnations. Plants described as border carnations can be purchased that, although able to be grown in the border, are not the type the border carnation trade specialists grow and sell and exhibit at carnation shows. There are also perpetual-flowering carnation plants offered for sale that are not the type the carnation specialists grow and that are seen at carnation shows. Some experts consider the offering of inferior plants to be a form of cheating, but I doubt anything could be done about it because the trade descriptions of these plants could not be proved to be false. As I have said, the inferior garden carnation plants can be grown in the border and the cheaper types of perpetual-flowering carnations are as perpetual-flowering as any other type. When judging at a village show and confronted with the situation where most of the exhibitors are obviously not knowledgeable about *Dianthus*, generally I explain the position to the show officials. I ask how they wish the classes to be judged: strictly, and therefore disqualify most of the exhibits, or with compassion and treat the class as calling for carnations generally, not specifically. They have always preferred the easier latter option—after all, they do have to continue to live with the local exhibitors. However the classes are judged, well-grown exhibits of true, named border carnations should always take the top prizes against other types of garden carnations.

A carnation show consists of a number of divisions, each of which has a number of classes. Each class is in itself a competition, requiring the competitor to stage a fixed number of blooms of a given type or color. A class may require one vase, of say three blooms, scarlet self. Competitors place their vases of three scarlet blooms in the space on the show bench allocated for the class, together with a small card, on which they write the name or names of the cultivars in the vase, and a larger card that has their own name on one side and exhibitor's number on the other. The larger card is set down so that this number faces upwards and the exhibitor's name faces downwards. The other classes in the division may cover the various self-colored flowers in all the known carnation colors—white, pink, crimson, yellow, apricot, lavender, or purple—as well as classes for white fancies, red or pink fancies, yellow or apricot fancies, and picotees. Sometimes a class for clove-scented flowers is included. In this way like is judged against like, white selfs all in one class, yellow selfs all in another class, and so on. Seedlings and sports may be shown in competitive classes, whether named or not, but sports may not be shown in classes for new seedlings.

The judges select first, second, and third prize winners and mark the cards accordingly, and a steward turns the cards over and fixes the appropriate red, white, or blue sticker on the side with the exhibitor's name. Cards that do not have stickers attached are not normally turned over, therefore losers remain anonymous. Apart from the prize money the exhibits usually earn three points for first prize, two for second prize, and one point for third prize. The exhibitor having the highest total number of points in the division is awarded the trophy for that division, and a large handsome card giving details of trophy and name of winner is placed beside one of his or her successful exhibits. Similar handsome cards are given for best vase in the division and best bloom in the division and placed beside the successful exhibit. Where the best bloom in a division is in a vase of more than one bloom, a very small adhesive paper ribbon is fastened to its stem. You may have to look hard to see it. There are several divisions in a show, planned to bring the various grades of exhibitors together in competition. Some have classes of six blooms, some three, some two, and some one; occasionally there are classes for twelve blooms.

At most shows novices have their own division. Some shows declare a novice to be one who has never won a first prize for carnations, but I consider the wiser course that which states a novice can win a first prize in a novices' class and remain a novice, but ceases to be a novice when he wins the novices' division and its trophy. This saves a novice from being thrown to the lions at his first small success. The British National Carnation Society has another division that protects all beginners by barring exhibitors who have won the more prestigious trophies.

Some shows make a distinction between amateur and professional competitors. Professionals are those whose main source of income is obtained from horticultural activities, which I take to mean that amateurs may sell their wares or services provided most of their income is obtained from a non-gardening job. The old National Carnation and Picotee Society stipulated that amateurs could sell surplus plants of cultivars of their own raising, but anyone issuing a list of plants for sale would be deemed a trader and therefore not eligible to compete as an amateur. In those days there were amateur classes and open classes, but nowadays most carnation show classes are open to all. The magnificent trophies competed for are mostly those termed challenge trophies and are not for the winner to keep. Such trophies have to be returned to be competed for in the following year. Sometimes, although rarely, a trophy is offered for competition to be won outright, and then it becomes the property of the winner.

Visitors to carnation shows are enabled to compare cultivars, to learn which are the most successful and to study the cards with exhibitors' names and follow their progress through the classes. Since exhibitors' home towns or villages are named on the cards, visitors may also learn they have an interesting near-neighbor.

BORDER CARNATIONS

All dedicated exhibitors of border carnations grow their plants in pots in the greenhouse as young plants in their first year of flowering, mainly so as to obtain maximum size of bloom, and also, of course, for protection from the elements. Border carnations naturally produce flowers of desirable form; the standards required for exhibition are based on the natural flower, and therefore no secret tricks are necessary, nor any manipulation of the blooms themselves. In fact, there was a time when judges were instructed to pass over exhibits in which flowers had been "perceptibly dressed." It is acceptable, however, to rearrange a misplaced petal. Flowers must be fresh and clean and of a clear bright color or colors. The contour, or outline, should be as near circular as possible and the petal edges either smooth or very lightly but evenly fimbriated. The petals should lie flat, in regular tiers, and the outer, or guard, petals should overlap so that they have no gaps between them. The back of the flower is very important: the guard petals should form a flat surface at right angles to the calyx. Very often the back of the flower is the deciding factor in close competition. Any buds should be removed, as discussed in Chapter 8.

PINKS

Growing pinks for the show bench is different from growing show carnations in that good quality stems of pinks can be obtained from two-year-old (and sometimes older) plants grown in the open garden, although many dedicated pinks exhibitors nowadays grow plants in pots, protecting them from the elements and harsh weather. Most exhibitors, however, propagate their pinks every summer, usually immediately after the flowering, because, like strawberries *(Fragaria)*, pinks usually do best in their first year. Some exhibitors grow their pinks in pots, singly in 12- or 15-cm (5- or 6-in) pots or three in a 20-cm (8-in) pot, with compost, as described in Chapter 8. Watering and feeding of pinks are the same as for border carnations, but one does not disbud pinks because they must be exhibited with all buds, open and unopen, left on. Staking is not really necessary, but some keen growers use three thin split canes to a pot and make an encircling ring with garden twine. This prevents the stems from wandering, thereby making watering easier. When in bloom, lightly shade the plants from hot sunshine.

Pinks are staged and judged entirely differently from carnations. Pinks must be staged as a stem complete with all buds, although spent flowers may be removed. Since the stem includes its buds it follows that judges will show preference for stems containing a number of buds, and especially where some of those buds are fully or partly open. When staging, do remember to include a few shoots of *Dianthus* foliage to set off the exhibit. Foliage is compulsory in all shows sponsored by the British National Carnation Society and affiliated societies, and failure to comply invites disqualification of the exhibit; some small local shows may not have this requirement, so you may want to check with show authorities. Nevertheless, foliage always helps to improve the look of an exhibit.

Pinks are classified into various exhibition types. At specialist shows there are classes for single and double flowers. A single flower should contain five petals only; there are single pinks with six petals, but I have seen such pinks disqualified by the judges. Selfs are of one distinct color only, without markings. Bicolors have a distinct central zone, or eye, that contrasts with the ground color. Fancies have stripes or splashes that contrast with the ground color. Laced pinks, single and double, have a contrasting central eye and a continuous ribbon of the same or similar color extending from the eye all around the margin of every petal. The area enclosed by the marginal lacing should be of the ground color only and not marred by spots or splashes of the lacing color. For show purposes laced pinks are classified separately as those of white ground color and those of other than white ground color. Some laced pinks have so pale a ground color as to be almost white; when in doubt it is advisable to seek advice from the show superintendent. Some shows also have classes for older cultivars, including those that split their calyx, like 'Mrs. Sinkins' and 'Sam Barlow'. Classes may also be included for miniature pinks, and for those *Dianthus* called sweet william *(Dianthus barbatus)*. It is most important to study the show schedule very carefully and to seek advice from the show officials on any doubtful point. Standards of excellence for judging pinks are very similar to those for carnations, especially in regard to the form of the flower, which should be circular in outline with guard petals at right angles to the calyx. There should be no gaps between the guard petals of each open flower. Stems must be strong enough to support the flower so that they face upwards or forwards, but not downwards.

CALYX BANDS

With both carnations and pinks, judges pay special attention to the calyx, which should show no tendency to split. But there is a difference between a split calyx and a burst calyx. A burst calyx is the kind seen on the white garden pink 'Mrs. Sinkins', but I would say that a split that travels the whole length of the sepals is also to be regarded as a burst calyx, even when the petals do not hang out, as with 'Mrs. Sinkins'. Judges may differ about a split calyx, some regarding it as a very grave fault while others do not penalize a small split. Since the sepals of plants are not always exactly alike, it follows that some may have a slightly wider and longer opening space between sepals than some others, which some judges may regard as a split while others may not. However, the rules say that a burst calyx must invoke disqualification of the exhibit, but not a split calyx. The only exception would be in a class for old-fashioned pinks.

Calyx bands are useful for preventing split calyx on border carnations and perpetual-flowering carnations and can be left on the calyx right up to the last moment, but they must be removed before the flowers are judged. The rule states that calyx bands left on exhibits must disqualify them. As an exhibitor myself I know how easy it is to miss one little elastic band in a large vase of blooms. The most likely person to be caught out is the dedicated exhibitor who grows a large number of plants and enters numerous classes. He or she, with one or two others, makes the show by putting in so many fine blooms, but in the race against time to get all the exhibits perfectly staged and all entry cards filled in and checked over, the exhibitor misses one little elastic band out of a dozen in one exhibit. To disqualify this exhibitor, and so deprive him or her of the trophy he or she had worked a whole year to compete for, would be to bite the hand that feeds. In over thirty years of judging I have only once disqualified an exhibit for having a calyx band left on. It happened in the summer of 1989 and spoiled my record. It was at the Royal Botanical Gardens at Edgbaston on the occasion of the Birmingham Carnation Society's show in the city's centenary year. I must have snipped off scores of elastic bands in my time, but the one at Birmingham was just too much, a metal twist-tie that looked as though it might need strong pliers to remove it.

WIRING STEMS

Wiring of border carnations is prohibited in most classes at British National Carnation Society shows, the exception being a few classes that call for a large number of blooms to a vase. Most exhibitors now use foam blocks (Oasis), because this makes it so easy to place each stem in exactly the right position for pressing into the foam, where it then remains fixed. Some shows in the far north of England and in Scotland allow wired stems in all classes, even those with only one flower in a vase. One might assume that their flowers have weak stems and need wires to prop them up, but flowers grown in the cooler conditions of the north have stiffer stems than those grown in the south, so it seems absurd that they should need the stem supports denied to southern exhibitors. The growers from northern England and Scotland, however, argue that it is easier to stage wired flowers, since the top of the wire can be so manipulated that the flowers all face at the correct angle to be seen to their best advantage.

Packing and Set-Up

Having grown some fine flowers the next step is to get them to the show looking as good as they did on the plants. The most popular way to pack them is to put them into carnation boxes, which may be obtained from florists' shops. Strips of cardboard with slots in them to accommodate the calyces are fixed across the width of the box, while the stems go underneath the cardboard strips. The bloom collars should be left on to support the flowers and protect them from damage in transit. Wipe the stems dry before packing the blooms. Start off placing those with the longest stems in a row at the top end and work progressively down the box, with the shortest stems at the bottom end. When finished, tie the lid on with a loop of string at both ends. Some exhibitors make very elaborate, well-designed travelling boxes that have water-filled tubes to accommodate the stems while the blooms rest on the upper platform. These are very good for keeping flowers fresh on long journeys. I used tall flower-buckets with 2.5-cm (1-in) mesh wire netting in the bottom and across the top. A depth of water of 5 to 8 cm (2 to 3 in) was sufficient to keep the blooms fresh, and the stem bases were prevented from slipping about by the wire mesh. A sheet of greaseproof paper was placed across the top of the bucket over the wire netting and holes pushed in to accommodate the calyces so that the guard petals rested on clean white paper. Since they were to be transported some distance to the show by car, the flowers were covered with tissue paper to prevent sun-scorch. We came to learn to listen for undue splashings and to respect sharp bends in roads and especially humpback bridges.

Before leaving for the show, make sure you have all the necessary equipment for the job. You will need some carnation and/or pinks foliage because it is a rule that foliage must be used in every vase. You will be certain to need vase filling material apart from the foliage. I used reeds cut from the ditches and sometimes crumpled newspaper, but the modern method is best—the green Oasis foam block. I remember when I first saw this in a national carnation show. It was in a vase of 15 carnations exhibited by Sam Maxfield of Gravesend and it was white and called Florapak. Staging a 15-bloom vase is normally quite a task, but Sam put his up in a few minutes. Now almost every exhibitor uses the foam block, it is so easy to use. A useful tip when cutting the foam to fit the top of the vase is to cut out a small V-shaped wedge, which will allow for easier topping-up with water during a show of more than one day's duration.

Apart from the show schedule you will require scissors or a pen-knife and a pen to write your name cards. A towel is useful to keep your hands dry while handling the flowers. Almost all shows provide vases; the only exceptions I know of are for some classes for decorative effect, where exhibitors may use their own vase or bowl should they prefer. Consult the schedule carefully, and if in any doubt ask the show secretary's advice before staging.

Do allow plenty of time to get to the show and to stage your flowers without hurrying. Try to be there early; nothing is worse than arriving at the venue and finding it a hive of industry with little or no place to unpack your boxes of flowers and stage them with some degree of comfort. The first thing to do upon arrival is to locate the supply of vases and the water tap. Fill the vases you require plus a few larger ones. Take all your blooms out of their boxes and place them into the larger vases; then you can decide which classes to tackle first. Select your blooms for the first class, plus a spare bloom or two, and place these into their vase. Do the same for your next class and so on right through all your classes. Study your blooms in each vase carefully and place the rejects back into a larger vase.

You can then stage your blooms in earnest, first removing all paper collars, then almost filling your vase with water before fixing the foam firmly into the neck of the vase. With vases of three or more blooms, place the best bloom at the top. Just above a joint, cut the stem with a sloping cut and push it into the foam so that the first joint above the cut base rests on the surface. Some flowers have a knack of facing sideways, some to left and some to right, so let the flower decide which side of center it prefers and place it accordingly. Don't spread flowers out too much; I consider 2.5 cm (1 in) apart to be an effective spacing, except in vases of many blooms where they must almost touch in order to be able to get them all in presentably. About three strong healthy pieces of foliage should set the vase off nicely; I prefer the foam to be not too conspicuous. I dislike seeing one tiny miserable cutting stuck in a sea of foam; it shows lack of pride. Take your vase to its numbered place on the show bench and set it down without disturbing any exhibits already there. If your blooms face upwards then place your vase near the front; if facing forwards or inclined slightly downwards then place it at the back. Apart from this little touch there is no best place; the judges see all. Go through all your staging, setting down each vase as it is finished, thereby progressively giving yourself more space to work in.

When all vases are set down in their various class positions, write the names of the cultivars in each class on the cards provided and place them by their appropriate vases. Place the exhibitor's cards provided beside their appropriate vases, name side down, number side up. Then inspect each exhibit in turn, checking to make sure you have it in its correct class place together with its correct card. Check your blooms to make sure all calyx bands are removed and no calyx has burst, because both offenses warrant disqualification. Also check that your exhibits have no stray insect pests about them; judges abhor these. Then just lift each vase in turn; any that happen to be suspiciously light are probably without water. It happens at every show; beautiful blooms when staged but drooping a few hours later. When satisfied your exhibits are all in order, you could ask the show secretary or superintendent if there are any classes in which you may enter the best of your spare blooms. When the time allowed for staging has expired, all exhibitors leave the hall or tent and the judges and stewards start their work.

Judging

Judges usually work in pairs, although sometimes single-handed. Judges who are, or have been, exhibitors themselves appreciate the dedication, industry, and love for the flower of the exhibitors whose flowers they judge. They do not feel any sense of power or importance, but they do appreciate the faith in their ability shown by the show organizers and the trust that goes with it. Judges are not inspectors; they exist to choose the best of many fine flowers. They praise the good but do not denigrate the less good. Since all flowers cannot be perfect the judge must take account of the imperfections. Standards of excellence were agreed many, many years ago and still stand. It is important that exhibitors are aware of these standards as well as judges so that all know exactly where they stand. The most important attributes of a flower are form and freshness. The flower should be as near circular as possible and mature without being past its best. Self-colored cultivars should be of one clear color only, without trace of any other color. Flowers should be large, but not coarse. In vases of more than one flower the flowers should be evenly matched in size. An exhibit containing an infestation of pests or diseases is not considered at all. The British National Carnation Society standards define an infestation of pests as thrips, red spider mite, and aphids on foliage, calyx, and stems, *in quantity*. I take this to mean judges shouldn't go hunting for one or two. Flowers that have marks on them caused by insects, weather, transit damage, etc., stand little chance against perfectly clean flowers.

When judging, the first thing I do is to look over the whole division to take note of the general standard of the exhibits. The reason for this is that since the winner of the division and its trophy is to be the exhibitor with the highest total number of points, I must give first, second, and third places according to the standard in the whole division, not just that in its own class. Were I to judge each class entirely in isolation and give every class first, second, and third awards, then we could find the third-prize exhibit with only one point in one class to be of better quality than the first-prize exhibit with three points in the next class. I must therefore consider not only what is the best, second-best, and third-best in each class, but also how many points I should award it to be fair to all exhibitors in the division. This means that where I consider the best in a class to be worth only one point, I give that the third prize and award no first or second prizes in that class. So when visitors see this at a show it does not mean the judge is harsh but that he is doing his job properly and being fair to all exhibitors in the division. After all, most exhibitors enter the classes not just to win the prize money but to win the trophy.

My method when judging a class is to sort out the four or five possibles and delete the impossibles, those that stand no chance at all. I lose patience when co-judges point out faults in every exhibit in a class when some are obviously not in the running for a prize and should be eliminated right at the start. The less time wasted on no-hopers, the more time is allowed for judging the real contenders. In classes with a large number of blooms in a vase, most exhibits have a few flowers not quite as good as the rest. Sometimes the best blooms in each vase are so good, with so little to choose between vases, that the only way to judge is to count the number of good blooms and nearly good blooms and judge by numbers. There are times when competition is so close that classes are won on quality of stems and calyces, and sometimes on presentation, or good staging.

The British National Carnation Society

The British National Carnation Society holds three shows a year at Westminster—early summer, mid-summer, and autumn—and sponsors area shows in other parts of the country. There are many handsome trophies to be won, even for novices, for whom there are special classes. Members are allowed to show cultivars of their own raising in all classes, not just special classes, although there are divisions in which members show cultivars of their own raising to compete for a special trophy. There are special arrangements to allow distant members to exhibit; they may send their blooms by rail to a London station where they are carefully collected by an officer of the Society and staged by an experienced exhibitor. Floral art is well catered to with handsome trophies and cash prizes to match. The Society has always encouraged floral-art competitions, and its classes in all three London shows are open to all, even non-members. The only rule is that *Dianthus* material should predominate, which does not mean that carnations should overwhelm.

Although most members of the British National Carnation Society are content just to belong to the Society and remain in the background, those who would like to become judges should first make a point of becoming exhibitors. A judge who is, or has been, a successful exhibitor commands more respect than one who has no such experience. Aspiring judges usually act as stewards for judges and are thus enabled to learn how this exacting work is done. They do a little fetching and carrying for the judges and also put the red, white, and blue stickers on the exhibitors' cards. I often include the steward when conversing with a co-judge, and sometimes explain a particular point. The British National Carnation Society holds examinations to select new judges; knowledge gleaned from stewarding could just tip the scales in the applicant's favor.

Final Thoughts on Exhibiting

Nowadays at most shows there is less time than there used to be for staging flowers, especially for people who go to work all day. I remember when the Royal Horticultural Society hall at Westminster used to be kept open all night, and exhibitors from Scotland and the north of England would travel down to London on the night train after finishing work. If they booked after a certain hour at night they could obtain a day-return ticket at about half the cost of a period-return ticket. One Scottish gentleman would book a sleeping car but did not sleep on the bed; he placed his precious boxes of flowers on it. The northerners would stage their exhibits with plenty of time to do the job properly, then find chairs or boxes to sleep on in some quiet corner. Early next morning before the local exhibitors arrived, they would troop out for breakfast at a nearby café, and for a shave at the barber's shop right next door to the café.

I remember in 1950 the *News of the World* staged a National Gardens show at Olympia. The show did have a section for carnations, but the 10 August show date was a hopeless one as far as southern border carnation enthusiasts were concerned. There was an open class for a vase of fifty blooms of border carnations, unwired, with a prize of £20. I knew I stood little chance of competing, but I nevertheless grew a large number of plants outdoors, three to a 23-cm (9-in) pot, and disbudded them to leave three flowers per plant. By the end of July I was almost certain I would be able to cut about a hundred blooms or more by the time of the show, but fate dealt a cruel blow in the form of a heatwave. Blue skies and scorching sunshine every day for a whole week and not a breath of wind to stir the foliage, or the sheets of newspaper pushed over the tops of the canes to shade the flowers. I could only imagine what a mess a sudden storm could have caused—all that wet newspaper; I was more concerned with counting the diminishing band of possibles as their number dwindled by the hour. By the eve of the show, however, I had enough blooms, and a few spares, even though they were not up to my usual standard. I took heart from the fact that all the other carnation enthusiasts in the country had suffered the same impossible weather conditions and, having staged my blooms, without stem-wires, was reasonably pleased with my effort.

The £20 was as good as in my pocket, that is until a chap arrived from Ayrshire in full tartan regalia, kilt and sporran right down to the dirk in his woollen sock. I half expected to hear the sound of bagpipes. He was Robert Kennedy of the carnation nursery of Matthew Kennedy in Darvel, Scotland. I knew before he opened his box of blooms that I should be relegated to runner-up. He staged his flowers magnificently, not especially large blooms but beautifully fresh and with such clear bright colors. The show manager was delighted to see our exhibits in his top carnation class, and to show his appreciation he took us to the most sumptuously furnished lounge I had ever seen and regaled us with coffee, beer, and sandwiches. He then pulled together two pairs of the largest armchairs I had ever seen, which front to front made two beds. We both sank into oblivion until several hours later when awakened by a cheerful cockney lady office cleaner. A far superior sleeping facility to that of the RHS hall at Westminster.

Many enthusiasts would like to try their hand at showing, but just haven't the nerve to make their first effort. The really good thing about most border carnations and pinks is that their flowers grow naturally into what are called exhibition blooms—they need no grooming or titivating. Grow the plants with reasonable care, transport them carefully to the show venue, and you will not be disappointed. The difference between the winning exhibits and the also-rans is very small, so no one is going to disparage your efforts; in fact, you may well surprise yourself and find the judges have left some prize-cards beside your exhibits. You will most probably wonder why you held back for so long. I remember a time long ago when I had grown what I thought were some very fine dahlias and chrysanthemums and entered them in a big London show, where my exhibits were completely outclassed; this doesn't happen with carnations and pinks. One doesn't mind being beaten, but no one likes to be outclassed. Of course, when you enter the hall or marquee you will see exhibitors staging wonderful blooms, but remember that those exhibitors feel the same way about your blooms. From a distance your flowers look as good to them as theirs do to you. I have many times taken a quick glance at other exhibits in classes I have entered and thought I should be fortunate to win a third prize, yet when I looked really closely, after the judging, I could see all the little faults in the other exhibits that were not apparent at that first glance.

As with many gardening societies, the British National Carnation Society has a shortage of young active members to take over the reins in the future. In my earlier book on carnations published in 1966 I wrote that people are going to work shorter hours and have more leisure; I was right about that but was wrong with my guess that people would soon tire of television. People may have found less and less pleasure in motoring, but this has not prevented the great escalation in the numbers of motors and motorists on our overcrowded roads. My prediction that gardening and exhibiting would become more popular than ever is half-true; gardening certainly has, but exhibiting is not gaining popularity at quite the same pace.

Growing for exhibition does require dedication and takes up time. I think the increased popularity of taking holidays abroad and of motoring, which include visiting gardens open to the public, have both affected the numbers of exhibitors. Many people are just not very competitive; I have known a few gardeners who, when they could no longer run, jump, or hit sixes (a cricket term, for you Americans), turned to exhibiting at flower shows. I remember an occasion in the

Royal Horticultural Society hall when just such an exhibitor, a retired athlete, who had been trying for years to beat me on the show bench, upon finding the coveted red sticker on his card leapt several feet into the air and yelled out as though he had just scored the winning goal at a Football Association Cup Final.

Figure 14-2. My wife and I with our British National Carnation Society Open trophies, 1966.

Appendix I

Monthly Reminders

Border Carnations and Pinks

JANUARY

Refirm any young plants lifted by frost. Continue with final
potting.
Water pot plants carefully and only when really necessary.
Sow seeds of annual pinks and carnations under glass.

FEBRUARY

Weed and hoe outdoor plants shallowly.
Carefully remove any dead basal leaves from plants outdoors
and under glass.
Plants in pots require slightly more water now. Continue with
final potting.
Sow seeds of annual pinks and carnations under glass.

MARCH

Top-dress outdoor plants with a balanced fertilizer, hoed in.

Plant out pot-grown carnations and pinks when soil conditions permit.

Sow perennial border carnation and pinks seeds under glass.

Water pot-grown plants carefully. Ventilate greenhouse freely in good weather.

Spray against pests and diseases.

Remove stalks and winter buds on outdoor pinks; these rarely produce good flowers.

APRIL

Still time to plant out pot-grown pinks and carnations. Hoe shallowly.

Keep greenhouse plants supported by stakes with rings or ties.

Spray pots and paths with water on warm days to provide humidity and to keep the greenhouse cool. Plants require more water now.

Do *not* stop border carnations and old-fashioned pinks.

Spray against pests and diseases.

Still time to sow seeds of perennial carnations and pinks under glass.

End of month, feed pot plants with a balanced fertilizer.

MAY

Stake outdoor-grown carnation plants. Hoe shallowly.

Continue to support stems of greenhouse plants, and commence disbudding carnations.

Pot-grown plants require more water now and feeding with high-potash liquid fertilizer.

Spray pots and paths of greenhouse and ventilate freely.

Spray against pests and diseases, outdoors and under glass.

Transplant or pot up seedling plants.

Towards end of month, shade greenhouse.

JUNE

Keep outdoor plants hoed shallowly and fasten stems to stakes.

Give a high-potash liquid feed to mature plants outdoors.

Disbud two-year-old outdoor carnations moderately, and three-year-olds severely.

Spray pots and paths of greenhouse and ventilate freely.

Spray against pests and diseases, outdoors and under glass.

Continue disbudding greenhouse carnations. Feed plants in pots with a high-potash liquid fertilizer until buds show color.

Fit calyx bands on carnations (where required) when buds show color.

Pollinate pinks to produce your own seed.

Start taking cuttings of pinks.

JULY

Dead-head pinks to encourage repeat-flowering.

Pot on seedlings into 9-cm (3.5-in) pots.

Commence layering border carnations at middle to end of month.

Continue taking pinks cuttings.

Do not allow pot-grown plants to dry out.

Spray pots and paths of greenhouse and ventilate freely.

Spray against pests and diseases, outdoors and under glass.

Pollinate pinks and carnations to produce your own seeds.

Inspect seedlings in bloom every day; label and record promising flowers.

Pot early rooted pinks cuttings.

Prepare outdoor beds for planting seedling pinks and carnations.

Exhibit or visit flower shows to see how others grow them.

AUGUST

Finish layering by the end of the month. Keep layers moist, under glass and outdoors.

Spray pots and paths of greenhouse and ventilate freely.

Spray against pests and diseases, outdoors and under glass.
Continue to inspect flowering seedlings; label and record
promising blooms.
Plant out seedling plants.
Prepare outside beds and borders for planting rooted carnation
layers and potted pinks next month.
Sever earliest rooted layers from parent plants a week before
lifting.
Pot rooted cuttings of pinks.

SEPTEMBER

Sever rooted layers from parent plants a week before lifting.
Start potting earliest rooted layers and planting pinks and
carnations outdoors.
Remove shading from greenhouse.
Collect seedpods when tips start to turn brown and before they
crack open.
Watch out for seed-eating caterpillars in and around pods.
Dust against pests and diseases, outdoors and under glass.

OCTOBER

Plant out rooted layers and pinks in the open border.
Remove fallen leaves from around mature plants and sprinkle
slug bait under them.
Complete first potting of rooted layers.
Dust against pests and diseases, outdoors and under glass.
Water carefully in greenhouse, taking care to avoid splashing.

NOVEMBER

Clear away fallen leaves from around outdoor plants.
Final-pot plants as they become sufficiently rooted.
Water pots with care, avoid splashing.
Ventilate greenhouse freely on fine days.
Dust against pests and diseases. Clean glass with domestic bleach.

DECEMBER

Refirm any young plants lifted by frost.
Clear away fallen leaves from around outdoor plants.
Continue with final potting.
Water pots carefully and only when necessary.
Ventilate greenhouse freely on fine days.
Dust against pests and diseases.
Scarify surface of pots to remove moss.

Perpetual-Flowering Carnations

JANUARY

Remove old and decaying leaves from plants and scarify surface
   soil to remove moss.
Take cuttings.
Sow perpetual-flowering carnation seeds, and those of the
   Marguerite carnations to be grown for cut flowers. Soil
   temperature should be around 13°C (55°F).
Water only when absolutely necessary. Take care to avoid
   splashing.

FEBRUARY

Apply limestone dressing to older plants.
Remove dead and decaying leaves.
Pot rooted cuttings and continue taking cuttings.
Sow all kinds of carnation seeds, including Marguerite type and
   bedding plants. Soil temperature, 13°C (55°F).
Water carefully to avoid splashing, and only when absolutely
   necessary.
Spray against pests and diseases.

MARCH

Continue taking cuttings. Support plants using canes and wire hoops.

Repot autumn-rooted plants into 15-cm (6-in) pots and one-year-old plants into 20- or 23-cm (8- or 9-in) pots.

Stop young plants, leaving five or six pairs of leaves.

Transplant or pot seedlings and rooted cuttings.

Water plants carefully and ventilate freely in good weather.

Give older plants in final pots one high-nitrogen feed.

Spray against pests and diseases.

APRIL

Continue to stop young plants.

Plants need more water this month.

On warm days, spray pots and paths in the greenhouse, but not late in the day—foliage should be dry before nightfall.

Sunshine will cause temperatures to rise; ventilate freely to keep a cool atmosphere; maintain 7°C (45°F) at night.

Keep plants supported with canes and hoops.

Disbud as plants become ready.

Spray against pests and diseases.

MAY

Heating should now be discontinued, but be prepared to resume should frost threaten. Ventilate freely on warm days.

Repot young plants from 8-cm (3-in) to 15-cm (6-in) pots.

Spray pots and paths to maintain a cool greenhouse atmosphere.

Keep plants supported with canes and hoops.

Continue disbudding and stopping.

Stop young plants before they become too large.

Spray against pests and diseases.

JUNE

Shade greenhouse.
Continue to final-pot young plants.
Continue disbudding, supporting plants.
Spray pots and paths to keep greenhouse cool, and ventilate freely. Much watering needed now.
Stop young plants when growing freely.
Spray against pests and diseases.

JULY

Keep plants well supported and continue disbudding.
Stop young plants when they become ready.
Feed plants to keep them growing steadily without check.
Final-pot all plants still in small pots.
Spray pots and paths and ventilate freely.
Inspect plants regularly and do not allow them to dry out.
Spray against pests and diseases.

AUGUST

Keep plants well supported and continue disbudding.
Spray pots and paths and ventilate freely.
Repot strong healthy plants into 20- or 23-cm (8- or 9-in) pots to flower another season.
Feed established plants and do not allow plants to dry out.
Spray against pests and diseases; keep a close watch for signs of red spider mite.

SEPTEMBER

Continue disbudding.
Damp down less frequently; make sure foliage is dry by evening.
Ventilate freely when conditions allow.
Remove shading from glass.

Dust against pests and diseases.

Pick off dead leaves and flowers, but do not drop them where they may become infected with mildew or botrytis.

Feed established plants for steady growth.

OCTOBER

Commence heating greenhouse to maintain 7°C (45°F) minimum.

Water early in the day, taking care to avoid splashing.

Ventilate freely by day in good weather. Reduce ventilation in bad weather, but not completely.

Dust against pests and diseases.

Apply final feed to mature plants.

NOVEMBER

Ventilate freely on fine days, and reduce in bad weather, but not completely.

Water only when really necessary.

Start taking cuttings. Clean glass with domestic bleach.

Dust against pests and diseases.

DECEMBER

Take cuttings. Pot rooted cuttings into 8-cm (3-in) pots.

Scarify surface of established plants to remove moss.

Keep plants clean by picking off dead leaves.

Ventilate judiciously in spells of pleasant weather.

Water carefully to avoid splashing.

Treat pests and diseases by dusting or fumigating.

Appendix II

Societies and Suppliers

Specialist Societies

Many keen gardeners join specialist societies; I used to belong to several at one time but am now content with two: the Royal Horticultural Society and the British National Carnation Society. At one time it was quite easy to meet and talk to professional growers and breeders, but I believe there are fewer such experts in societies nowadays, and amateur growers in increasing numbers are taking up raising new cultivars of their favorite flowers. Most societies have regular meetings throughout the year, which encourages socializing, and shows at which their particular flower can be seen exhibited, grown to perfection.

The professed aim of the British National Carnation Society—formed in 1949 from the amalgamation of the existing border carnation and perpetual-flowering carnation societies—is to expand and improve the cultivation of carnations, which includes garden and greenhouse carnations and garden pinks. The benefits of membership include free advice from the Society's experts, free admittance to and participation in the Society's competitions at the Royal Horticultural Society hall at Westminster, interesting newsletters and an annual *Year*

Book containing lively articles on growing and showing, and socializing in general, including the annual general meeting held in London. A discount scheme is also operated entitling members to discounts on orders placed with participating carnation-specialist nurseries. Members are mostly very friendly and free and easy. An outstanding feature of the BNCS is that all the officers of the Society work voluntarily and are unpaid.

The Marchioness of Salisbury, Patroness of the Society since 1979, is a most knowledgeable horticulturist and a keen gardener, very interested in carnations and pinks and particularly in conserving old cultivars. Lady Salisbury attends almost every carnation show and studies all the exhibits with the greatest interest.

Many other local carnation societies have been established in Great Britain, most of them affiliated to the British National Carnation Society, and they hold their own carnation shows; other affiliated societies have carnation classes in their schedules. Dates of the various societies' shows and their addresses are contained in the British National Carnation Society *Year Book*. For further information write to the Hon. Secretary, British National Carnation Society, 23 Chiltern Road, St. Albans, Hertfordshire AL4 9SW, U.K.

The old American Carnation Society, based in Philadelphia and later in Denver, was dissolved on 1 May 1981, but ten years later, in 1991, the American Dianthus Society was founded by Rand B. Lee. Its members are interested in carnations and pinks of all kinds. A very comprehensive newsletter called *The Gilliflower Times* is published quarterly by the American Dianthus Society. In addition to informative articles, it also contain details, with addresses, of plant sources throughout the United States, and offers a seed distribution scheme to its members. The address is given below.

Carnations are also popular in Western Australia, around Perth, and in South Australia in the Adelaide district, where shows are held by several horticultural societies. New Zealand has the Auckland Carnation, Gerbera and Geranium Society, which holds regular meetings and shows, and publishes informative news bulletins.

OVERSEAS SOCIETIES

North America

American Dianthus Society
c/o Rand B. Lee
P.O. Box 22232
Santa Fe, New Mexico 87502-2232, U.S.A.

North American Rock Garden Society
P.O. Box 67
Millwood, New York 10546, U.S.A.

New Zealand

Auckland Carnation, Gerbera and Geranium Society
Auckland Horticultural Headquarters
990 Great North Road
Point Chevalier
Auckland, New Zealand

Carnation and Dianthus Circle of the Canterbury Horticultural
   Society
Canterbury Horticultural Society
P.O. Box 369
Christchurch, New Zealand

Specialist Growers of Carnations and Pinks (U.K.)

Allwood Bros.
Mill Nursery, London Road
Hassocks, West Sussex BN6 9NB
(01273) 844229
Border, perpetual-flowering, and spray carnations and pinks.
   Visitors welcome; phone for appointment.

R. Bowers
Hillside, Town Lane
Charlesworth
Hyde, Cheshire SK14 6HA
(01457) 863926
Picotee border carnations only. Visitors welcome; phone for
appointment.

Doug Cottam
Chesswood, Skipton Old Road
Colne, Lancashire BB8 7AD
(01282) 863527
Pinks and border and perpetual-flowering carnations

Craven's Nursery
1 Foulds Terrace
Bingley, West Yorkshire BD16 4LZ
(01274) 561412
Old-fashioned, rock garden, and modern pinks

W. J. Dunn
4 Avon Crescent, Glassford
nr. Strathaven, Lanarkshire ML10 6TP
(01357) 520398
Border carnations only

R. and T. Gillies
22 Chetwyn Avenue, Bromley Cross
Bolton, Lancashire BL7 9BN
(01204) 306273
Perpetual-flowering carnations and pinks; Tri-port stakes and
support rings.

Greenacre Nursery
Gorsey Lane
Banks, Southport PR9 8ED
(01704) 26791
Border, perpetual-flowering and spray carnations and pinks

Greenslacks Nurseries
Ocot Lane, Scammonden
Huddersfield, Yorkshire HD3 3FR
(01484) 842584
Dianthus species and alpines. Exporters

Hayward's Carnations
The Chace Gardens
Stakes Road, Purbrook
Waterlooville, Hampshire PO7 5PL
(01705) 263047
Border and perpetual-flowering carnations and pinks. Visitors
welcome; phone for appointment.

Holden Clough Nursery
Holden, Bolton-by-Bowland
Clitheroe, Lancashire BB7 4PF
(01200) 447615
Dianthus (pinks), species and cultivars. Exporters. Visitors welcome;
phone for appointment.

Marshall's Malmaison
4 The Damsells
Tetbury, Gloucestershire GL8 8JA
(01666) 502589
Malmaison carnations only

Mills' Farm Plants and Gardens
Norwich Road
Mendlesham, Suffolk IP14 5NQ
(01449) 766425
Old-fashioned, modern, and rock garden pinks. Visitors welcome.

P. Russell
Little Acre, Spinfield Lane
Marlow-on-Thames, Buckinghamshire SL7 2JN
(01628) 484630
Border carnations

Southview Nurseries
Chequers Lane, Eversley Cross
Basingstoke, Hampshire RG27 0NT
(01734) 732206
Old-fashioned, Allwoods, and modern pinks. Visitors welcome;
 phone for appointment.

Steven Bailey
Silver Street, Sway
Lymington, Hampshire SO41 6ZA
(01590) 682227
Border, perpetual-flowering, and spray carnations and pinks.
 Visitors welcome; see catalogue for times.

Three Counties Nurseries
Marshwood
Bridport, Dorset DT6 5QJ
(01297) 678257
Pinks and dianthus

Timpany Nurseries
77 Magheratimpany Road, Ballynahinch
Co. Down, N. Ireland BT24 8PA
(01238) 562812
Dianthus species and alpines. Exporters

Woodfield Bros.
Wood End, Clifford Chambers
Stratford-on-Avon, Warwickshire CV37 8HR
(01789) 205618
Perpetual-flowering and Malmaison carnations. Visitors welcome
 by appointment at weekends.

TRADE SUPPLIER OF PINKS

H. R. Whetman and Son
Houndspool
Dawlish, Devon EX7 0QP
(01626) 863328

North American Suppliers of Pinks and Dianthus Species

Arrowhead Alpines
P.O. Box 857
Fowlerville, Michigan 48836, U.S.A.
(517) 223-3581
Dianthus (pinks) species and species cultivars

Busse Gardens
5873 Oliver Avenue S.W.
Cokato, Minnesota 55321-4229, U.S.A.
(612) 286-2654
Dianthus (pinks) species and species cultivars

Canyon Creek Nursery
3527 Dry Creek Road
Oroville, California 95965, U.S.A.
(916) 533-2166
Dianthus (pinks), including old cultivars

Carroll Gardens
444 East Main Street
P.O. Box 310
Westminster, Maryland 21158, U.S.A.
(301) 848-5422
Dianthus (pinks), including old cultivars and species cultivars

Flowerplace Plant Farm
P.O. Box 4865
Meridian, Mississippi 39304, U.S.A.
(601) 482-5686
Dianthus

The Fragrant Path
P.O. Box 328
Fort Calhoun, Nebraska 68023, U.S.A.
Seeds

Hortico Inc.
723 Robson Road, RR #1
Waterdown, Ontario L0R 2H1, Canada
(905) 689-6984
Dianthus (pinks) species and species cultivars

Jackson and Perkins Co.
P.O. Box 1028
Medford, Oregon 97501, U.S.A.
(541) 776-2000
Dianthus (pinks) and border carnations

Joy Creek Nursery
20300 N.W. Watson Road
Scappoose, Oregon 97056, U.S.A.
(503) 543-7474
Dianthus (pinks), old cultivars and species cultivars

Logee's Greenhouses
141 North Street
Danielson, Connecticut 06239, U.S.A.
(203) 774-8038
Dianthus (pinks), including old cultivars and Malmaison carnations

Porterhowse Farms
41370 S.E. Thomas Road
Sandy, Oregon 97055, U.S.A.
(503) 668-5834
Dianthus (pinks) species and species cultivars

Powell's Gardens
9468 U.S. Hwy. 70 East
Princeton, North Carolina 27569, U.S.A.
(919) 936-4421
Dianthus

Sandy Mush Herb Nursery
Route 2, Surrett Cove Road
Leicester, North Carolina 28748, U.S.A.
(704) 683-2014
Dianthus (pinks) species and species cultivars

Siskiyou Rare Plant Nursery
2825 Cummings Road
Medford, Oregon 97501, U.S.A.
(541) 772-6846
Dianthus (pinks), old cultivars and species

Tiedemann Nursery
4835 Cherry Vale Avenue
P.O. Box 926
Soquel, California 95073, U.S.A.

White Flower Farm
Route 63
Litchfield, Connecticut 06759-0050, U.S.A.
(203) 496-9600
Dianthus (pinks) and species cultivars

Wrenwood of Berkeley Springs
Route 4, Box 361
Berkeley Springs, West Virginia 25411, U.S.A.
(304) 258-3071
Dianthus

Overseas Trade Suppliers of Perpetual-Flowering Carnations

P. Kooij and Zonen B.V.
Hornweg 132, P.O. Box 341
1430 AH Aalsmeer, Holland
U.K. Agent: Trevor Turner Marketing, Fursdon Hill Farm,
   Sherford, Kingsbridge, South Devon TQ7 2BD, U.K., (01548)
   531281

M. Lek and Zonen B.V.
Nieuwveens Jaagpad 47
2441 EH Nieuwveen, Holland

Van Staaveren B.V.
P.O. Box 265
1430 AG Aalsmeer, Holland
U.K. Agent: Peter J. Smith, Chanctonbury Nurseries, Ashington,
    Pulborough, West Sussex RH20 3AS, U.K., (01903) 892870
U.S. Agent: Fred C. Gloeckner and Co., 15 East 26th Street,
    Madison Square, New York, New York 10010, U.S.A.
    (including 'Gipsy' plants)
Canadian Agent: Yoder Canada, P.O. Box 370, Leamington,
    Ontario NHH 3W3, Canada, (519) 326-6121

California Florida Plant Co., L.P.
P.O. Box 5310
Salinas, California 93915, U.S.A.
(408) 754-2767
Including Adorable series dwarf pot plants

Other Sources

Additional information on plant sources may be found in the current edition of the following books:

North America
The Andersen Horticultural Library's Source List of Plants and Seeds. Minnesota Arboretum, Chanhassen.
Gardening by Mail and Taylor's Guide to Specialty Nurseries, by Barbara J. Barton. Hougton Mifflin, New York.

British Isles
The Plant Finder. Royal Horticultural Society, London.

France
Guide des Meilleures Adresses pour Trouver Vos Plantes. Hachette, Paris.

Germany
Pflanzen-Einkaufsführer. Ulmer, Stuttgart.

U.S. Department of Agriculture Hardiness Zones

Range of Average Minimum Temperature for Each Climatic Zone

ZONE	°F	°C
1	< −50	< −45.5
2	−50 to −40	−45.5 to −40.1
3	−40 to −30	−40.0 to −34.5
4	−30 to −20	−34.4 to −28.9
5	−20 to −10	−28.8 to −23.4
6	−10 to 0	−23.3 to −17.8
7	0 to +10	−17.7 to −12.3
8	+10 to +20	−12.2 to −6.7
9	+20 to +30	−6.6 to −1.2
10	+30 to +40	−1.1 to +4.4
11	> +40	> +4.4

Bibliography

Allwood, M. C. 1912. *The Perpetual-flowering Carnation*. Cable.

Allwood, M. C. 1947. *Carnations and All Dianthus*. 3rd ed. Allwood Bros.

Allwood, M. C. 1962. *Carnations for Everyman*. Allwood Bros.

Bailey, L. H. 1938. *The Garden of Pinks*. MacMillan.

Bailey, S. 1951. *Growing Perpetual-flowering Carnations*. Ernest Benn.

Bailey, S. 1982. *Carnations*. Blandford Press.

Bird, R. 1994. *Border Pinks*. Timber Press/Batsford.

British National Carnation Society. 1972. *New Register of Dianthus*. British National Carnation Society.

Brotherston, R. P. 1904. *The Book of the Carnation*. Bodley Head.

Cook, E. T. 1905. *Carnations, Picotees, Wild and Garden Pinks*. Geo. Newnes.

Cook, T. H., J. Douglas, and J. F. McLeod. c.1910. *Carnations and Pinks*. Jack.

Dick, J. H. 1915. *Commercial Carnation Culture*. A. T. De La Mare.

Dodwell, E. S. 1885. *The Carnation and Picotee*. N.p.

Douglas, J. 1946. *Border Carnations and Cloves*. 3rd ed. J. Douglas.

Duthie, R. 1988. *Florists Flowers and Societies*. Shire Publications.

Fenn, P. A. 1956. *Carnations*. W. G. Foyle.

Galbally, E. L. 1955. *Register of Hardy Border Carnations*. J. and E. Galbally.

Galbally, J. H. W. 1957. *Border Carnations, Picotees and Pinks*. Collingridge.

Galbally, J. H. W. 1966. *The Complete Guide to Border Carnations*. Collingridge.

Genders, R. 1955. *Carnations and Pinks for Pleasure and Profit*. Littlebury.

Genders, R. 1962. *Garden Pinks*. John Gifford.

Gerard, J. 1597. *The Herball*.

Gibson, J. L. 1949. *Carnations for Amateurs*. Collingridge.

Hessayon, D. G. 1990. *The BioFriendly Gardening Guide*. pbi Publications.

Hogg, T. 1820. *Treatise on the Carnation, etc*. Cox and Baylis.

Holley, W. D., and R. Baker. 1963. *Carnation Production*. William C. Brown.

Hollingsworth, B. 1958. *Flower Chronicles*. Rutgers University Press.

Hughes, S. 1991. *Carnations and Pinks*. Crowood Press.

Ingwersen, W. 1949. *The Dianthus*. HarperCollins.

Jarratt, J. 1988. *Growing Carnations*. Kangaroo Press.

Lamborn, L. L. 1901. *American Carnation Culture*. Alliance.

Lawrence, W. J. C., and J. Newell. 1939. *Seed and Potting Composts*. Allen and Unwin.

Maddox, J. 1810. *The Florist's Directory*. Harding and Wright.

Mansfield, T. C. 1951. *Carnations in Colour and Cultivation*. Colling.

McQuown, F. R. 1953. *Pinks Register*. British National Carnation Society.

McQuown, F. R. 1955. *Pinks, Cultivation and Selection*. MacGibbon and Kee.

McQuown, F. R. 1965. *Carnations and Pinks*. Collingridge.

Ministry of Agriculture, Fisheries and Food. 1954. *Manual of Carnation Production*. H. M. Stationery Office.

Moreton, C. O. 1955. *Old Carnations and Pinks*. Geo. Rainbird.

Morton, R. J. 1953. *Perpetual-flowering Carnations*. Collingridge.

National Carnation and Picotee Society. 1892. *Carnation Manual*. Cassell.

Rodale. *Organic Gardening Encyclopedia*. Rodale Press.

Royal Horticultural Society. 1983. *International Dianthus Register*, second edition. Royal Horticultural Society.

Sanders, T. W. 1911. *Carnations, Picotees and Pinks*. Collingridge.

Shewell-Cooper, W. E. 1960. *Carnations and Pinks*. A. B. C. Gardening Series. English University Press.

Shewell-Cooper, W. E. 1977. *Basic Book of Carnations and Pinks*. Barrie and Jenkins.

Sitch, P. 1975. *Carnations for Garden and Greenhouse*. John Gifford.

Smith, F. 1989. *Plantsman's Guide to Carnations and Pinks*. Ward Lock.

Thomas, H. H. 1916. *The Carnation Book*. Funk and Wagnalls.

Ward, C. W. 1903. *The American Carnation*. A. T. De La Mare.

Weguelin, H. W. 1905. *Carnations, Picotees and Pinks*. Collingridge.

Whitehead, S. B. 1956. *Carnations Today*. John Gifford.

Williams, F. N. 1889. *Notes on Pinks of Western Europe*. West, Newman.

Williams, F. N. 1890. *The Pinks of Central Europe*. West, Newman.

Wright, W. P. 1906. *Pictorial Practical Carnation Growing*. Cassell.

Yepsen, R. B. 1976. *Organic Plant Protection*. Rodale Press.

Subject Index

Index of Cultivars